Malevolent Nurture

MALEVOLENT NURTURE

WITCH-HUNTING
AND MATERNAL POWER
IN EARLY MODERN ENGLAND

DEBORAH WILLIS

CORNELL UNIVERSITY PRESS

ITHACA AND LONDON

First published 1995 by Cornell University Press.

Printed in the United States of America

☉ The paper in this book meets the minimum requirements of the American National Standard for Information Sciences–Permanence of Paper for Printed Library Materials, ANSI Z39.48–1984.

Library of Congress Cataloging-in-Publication Data

Willis, Deborah, 1952–
    Malevolent nurture : witch-hunting and maternal power in early modern England / Deborah Willis.
        p.   cm.
    Includes bibliographical references and index.
    ISBN 0-8014-3004-6 (cloth : alk. paper).—ISBN 0-8014-8194-5 (paper : alk. paper)
    1. Witchcraft—England—History.   2. Witches—England—History.
3. Mothers—England—Social conditions.   4. Persecution—England—History.   5. Shakespeare, William, 1564–1616—Knowledge—Occultism.
6. Witchcraft in literature.   I. Title.
BF1581.W55   1995
133.4'3'0942—dc20   95-16429

CONTENTS

LIST OF
ILLUSTRATIONS

PREFACE

When I first began work on a book about witch-hunting and gender in early modern England, I did not know that it was also going to be about mothers. But as I began to look more closely at relevant documents, it became evident that the crime of witchcraft was often described in terms of the maternal. Witches were—or were believed to be—mothers "gone bad," women past childbearing years who used their mothering powers against neighbors who had enraged them. To acquire their magic, women fed and cared for demonic imps as if they were children. In exchange, imps would bring sickness and death to other households—often the households of younger mothers.

Although most features of these beliefs have been known to scholars for some time, few have explored the implications of the witch as mother. That is in essence what I do here, in the hope of contributing to a better understanding of cultural practices that sent many innocent people to their deaths. I have concentrated on the period 1563–1611, examining a variety of nonliterary texts—state papers, trial records, pamphlets, religious tracts—as well as selected plays by William Shakespeare. In England, the establishment of a flourishing professional theater and the rise of secular prosecutions against the crime of witchcraft roughly coincided: statutes passed in 1563 led to a steady series of trials beginning in the 1570s, and the first playhouse was built just outside London in 1574. It is during these years that basic features of witch-hunting were established and that witchcraft emerged as a distinctively female crime—a crime often punished, on stage and in trial courts, as a perverse use of maternal power.

I am deeply grateful to the many teachers, students, friends, and family who have helped me bring this project to completion. I thank first and foremost my teachers at the University of California, Berkeley, Janet Adelman and Stephen Greenblatt, who unwittingly nurtured the beginnings of this project in a dissertation about Shakespeare. Their suggestions and support since then have been invaluable and their areas of disagreement inspiring. I am further indebted to the larger community of scholars at Berkeley in the 1970s and 1980s who made Renaissance studies seem a rich and welcoming field; in this regard, I remember Stephen Booth with special fondness.

Colleagues and students in the English Department at the University of California, Riverside, have also contributed generously and insightfully to the completion of this book. I thank especially John Ganim and Ralph Hanna, who read early versions of the manuscript and made many helpful suggestions, and Steven Axelrod, whose general encouragement was crucial. I am grateful also to the larger community of colleagues and friends who have made Riverside an intellectually stimulating place to live and work—to Rise Axelrod, Joe Childers, Geoff Cohen, Kim Devlin, Carole Fabricant, George Haggerty, Katherine Kinney, Parama Roy, Carole-Anne Tyler, and Alice Wexler, among many others; and to Greg Bredbeck, John Briggs, Milton Miller, Stan Stewart, and Margi Waller, who have helped to keep multiple Renaissances alive and well at UCR. Colleagues from the History Department helped to make this book genuinely interdisciplinary; I thank Sharon Salinger, Arch Getty, and especially Richard Godbeer for their insights and advice. So also did UCR's Center for Ideas and Society. A resident fellowship from the Center greatly aided the completion of this book.

Among students I thank Jeanie Moore, Leslie Bennett, René Breier, and Scott Crider for many valuable insights; I thank also Kathy Patterson and Donovan Cocas for their perceptive work on witchcraft and Shakespeare. Andrew Rempt wrote an undergraduate paper on Lady Macbeth that still seems to me better than most published work; he and Michael Heumann will be long remembered for their astonishing performance of scenes from *Macbeth* using puppets. Marcie Heid was a reliable, efficent, and accurate research assistant in the final stages.

Earlier versions of sections of Chapters 1 and 2 have appeared in Deborah Willis, "Shakespeare and the English Witch-Hunts: Enclosing the Maternal Body," included in *Enclosure Acts: Sexuality, Property, and Culture in Early Modern England*, edited by Richard Burt and John

Michael Archer (Ithaca: Cornell University Press, 1994). Copyright ©
1994 by Cornell University. I thank Cornell University Press for permission to use that material here. Portions of various chapters have also been
presented as papers at meetings of the Modern Language Association, the
Rocky Mountain MLA, the Renaissance Conference of Southern California, and the Shakespeare Association of America. I am indebted to the
conveners of several SAA seminars for arranging fruitful scholarly encounters—in particular, to Frances Dolan and Gillian Kendall. Thanks
are also due to many colleagues in the field who have provided helpful
comments or general good cheer, Lynda Boose, Richard Burt, Judith
Haber, Jeff Knapp, Barbara Bono, Michael Schoenfeldt, Linda Woodbridge, and various unknown readers of the manuscript among them. In
addition, I am grateful to the staff of the Huntington Library and the
Tomás Rivera Library at UC Riverside for their valuable assistance.

Finally, I thank family and friends for keeping my faith in a future
"after the book" alive. Nancy Rettig was an important support in dark-
est hours. Kathy Teller, Stephen Phillips, Deborah Raphael, Gary Whit-
mer, Mona Simpson, and Ben and Margo Watson reminded me that there
was a world elsewhere. Most especially, I thank Joseph Millard for his patience, self-reliance, and general encouragement during the years of work
that went into little else but this book.

DEBORAH WILLIS

Riverside, California

Malevolent Nurture

CHAPTER ONE

INTRODUCTION

According to two documents among the state papers of 1590, an unnamed London informer told the sheriff's office that a Mrs. Dewse had engaged the services of Robert Birche, by reputation a conjurer.[1] She sought through his magic art to revenge herself upon her enemies, the "theeves" and "villaynes" she believed were responsible for driving her husband, keeper of Newgate Prison, from office—an expulsion "which would bee both her and her childrens undoinges." The first document names several men; among them, "Mr Younge," "Sir Rowland Heyward," and "Sye." Mrs. Dewse asked Birche to make of these men wax images and then to "pricke" them "to the harte" to cause the men's death. Failing that, he was to use his art to make them perish "in a damp"—that is, of typhus—as had happened in Oxford at the Black Assize of 1577, when a number of judges, jurymen, and lawyers had abruptly died of that disease. In that incident, the "damp" was widely attributed to the sorcery of a bookseller, on trial for selling banned Catholic books.[2]

Birche was reluctant to accommodate Mrs. Dewse. He was "lame," he said, and therefore unable to make the images. According to the second document, he even piously lectured her: "She were beste to take good

---

1. *Calendar of State Papers Domestic—Elizabeth* 2 (1581–1590): 644, reprinted in W. H. Hart, "Observations on Some Documents relating to Magic in the Reign of Queen Elizabeth," *Archaeologia; or, Miscellaneous Tracts relating to Antiquity* 40 (1866): 395–96.
2. A brief account and list of documents associated with this case can be found in George Lyman Kittredge, *Witchcraft in Old and New England* (Cambridge: Harvard University Press, 1929), pp. 89, 419–20 n. 90.

heede how she dealte and whom she trusted in such matters. . . . The best meanes was to pray to God that hee would turne her enemies hartes." But the angry wife was determined to make the images herself if only Birche would stand by and correct her mistakes. After several visits from Birche, Mrs. Dewse completed three pictures under his guidance. She made "one for Mr Younge & put a pynne into his harte, another for Sir Rowland Heyward & putt a pynne to his harte & another under his ribbes, & the third picture for Sye & put two pynnes into his eyes." Mrs. Dewse was apparently satisfied by the results: "She thanked God that some of her pictures did work well." Birche was paid a sum of money, sent a sugar loaf and lemons, and asked to come again "divers times."

As it happened, Mrs. Dewse had indeed placed her trust in the wrong man. Birche himself, after his very first visit, reported on their dealings to her enemy, Mr. Young—Justice Young, that is, as he is termed in the second document. Birche's subsequent visits could be considered something of a "sting" operation, as, under Young's direction, he cleverly but deviously gathered more information about Mrs. Dewse's intentions while leading her to commit the acts of sorcery on her own. The first document closes with an account of the sheriff's search of her home, during which he found two pictures hidden in "a secret place" of her cupboard, "with pynnes sticked in them" just as the informant had said.

The second document is a statement taken from Birche himself after the sheriff's visit. Far from being discouraged, Mrs. Dewse now planned her revenge to extend up the social ladder to the Privy Council: she would add the sheriff, the recorder, the lord chamberlain, and even the lord chancellor to her list of intended victims. This ambition was apparently enough to prompt the sheriff to further action. She was apprehended that very day.

What happened to Mrs. Dewse? Was she charged and tried under the 1563 Act against witchcraft, which criminalized the use or practice of "anye Sorcery Enchantment Charme or Witchcrafte, to thintent . . . to hurte or destroye any person in his or her Body, Member or Goodes"?[3] If so—assuming none of her victims actually fell ill or died—she would have been subject to a year's imprisonment, during which she would also be

3. C. L'Estrange Ewen, *Witch Hunting and Witch Trials* (London: Kegan Paul, Trench, Trubner, 1929), p. 17. The first anti-witchcraft statute was passed in 1542, at the end of Henry VIII's reign, then repealed in 1547 under Edward VI. According to Ewen, only one case (which resulted in a pardon) has survived from this period. See Ewen, pp. 11, 13–18, for the texts of the 1542 and 1563 statutes.

placed in a pillory on four market days to "openly confesse" her error and offense. If her sorcery was successful, of course, she would have been subject to the death penalty, joining the many hundreds of others—almost all of them women—executed for witchcraft in England between 1563 and 1736, when the law was finally repealed.

Her name is missing from the exhaustive lists historians have compiled of persons tried under the witchcraft statutes in this period, but other documents allow us to piece together more of Mrs. Dewse's story.[4] In the period preceding her involvement with sorcery, one Humphrey Gunston had charged her husband, William Dewse, with "sundry abuses and misdemeanours . . . concerninge her Majestie." Dewse, in response, had filed actions against Gunston for slander. But Gunston prevailed: the keeper of Newgate Prison was about to be charged and bound over for trial for "treason, murder, or felony" around the time Mrs. Dewse contacted the conjurer Birche. Among Gunston's supporters were the three men targeted by Mrs. Dewse: Justice Young, a justice of the peace who frequently served as examiner and torturer in cases involving allegedly seditious Catholics; Sir Roland Heyward, also a justice of the peace and twice mayor of London; and Nicholas Sye, probably an underkeeper at Newgate Prison. These men had petitioned the lord chamberlain and other officials on Gunston's behalf.

Mrs. Dewse herself named Gunston as one of her husband's enemies, though the informant does not include him as one of the targets of her image magic. It appears, then, that at the time she was under investigation, her husband was on the verge of being forced out of the office of keeper by the collaboration of two influential justices of the peace and a prison underkeeper, who supported Gunston's charges and blocked Dewse's suits to the high officials who were formerly his patrons. That, at any rate, is what Mrs. Dewse believed: the "knaves" Heyward, Young, and Sye had "made the lord Chamberleyne that hee would not reade her husbandes peticions, and the Lord Chauncelor who was ever her husbandes frend would do nothing for her, & Mr Recorder whom she thought would not have bene her enemie, he likewise did now (as shee heard) take his parte that should have her husbandes office."

Was Gunston angling for Dewse's office, as Mrs. Dewse seems to have believed? Or were these men simply trying to remove from office a man

---

4. John R. Dasent, ed., *Acts of the Privy Council*, new series, 25 vols. (London: Eyre and Spottiswoode, 1897), 16:388, 17:47–48, 19:111–12. In the documents, William Dewse's name is spelled a variety of ways, among them Dews, Dyos, Dios, Devyes, and Devies.

they considered corrupt? Heyward and Young could have opposed Dewse because they suspected him or his wife of Catholic sympathies— undesirable especially in a prison keeper at Newgate, where many suspected Catholic conspirators were held. Mrs. Dewse reportedly told Birche that by helping her to achieve her revenge he would "greatly please God, for one of them was that thiefe Younge who lived by robbing papists." God, apparently, would be pleased because they had punished an enemy of the Catholic church, despite their ungodly methods. Moreover, her fallback plan, to make these men die "as they did at the assises at Oxford" was modeled on the sorcery of a seditious Catholic bookseller.

Or were the charges against the keeper and Mrs. Dewse entirely made up? Perhaps Young and Heyward wanted their man in Dewse's office for personal advantage, not for religious reasons at all; perhaps Young and Heyward cynically concocted a tale of attempted witchcraft in order further to discredit Dewse through his wife. As is true of most cases of witchcraft, we have only the accusers' statements to go on; the accused witch can no longer speak for herself.

We may use these fragmentary documents to invent many "stories" about Mrs. Dewse. What is clear enough, however, is that the charge of witchcraft is embedded in a larger drama of intrigue, rivalry, and revenge, of power struggle over office and retaliation for its loss. Mrs. Dewse's case, though it involves relatively minor players, resembles a type of politically motivated charge of witchcraft which seems to have especially interested William Shakespeare. Typically in such cases, a charge of witchcraft is made against someone believed to have designs against the monarch or some highly placed official. The charge is frequently combined with accusations of treason or conspiracy against the state. In fact, the charge—and perhaps also the actual practice of witchcraft—may emerge from factional struggle, may be part of one aristocratic group's attempt to displace its rivals and remove them from power. Shakespeare's first tetralogy—written around the time of Mrs. Dewse's arrest—centers on a number of such politically embedded accusations: Joan of Arc, burned at the stake for her treasonous witchcraft against England; Eleanor, Duchess of Gloucester, who consulted with the witch Margery Jourdain and a male conjurer in a plot to advance her husband at the expense of King Henry VI's life; Jane Shore and Queen Elizabeth, widow of Edward IV, accused of witchcraft by Richard III in an attempt to destroy his political enemies. Shakespeare, of course, most famously considers the intersection of witchcraft, treason, and ambition later in his career, in *Macbeth*.

The case of Mrs. Dewse and the cultural practices that helped to produce it provide an important context for Shakespeare's construction of witchcraft and treason; but Shakespeare's plays in their turn, I believe, also provide a context for "reading" the historical phenomenon of witch-hunting. Shakespeare is particularly suggestive on one issue. Why were the victims of the hunt overwhelmingly female? Why, for example, is Mrs. Dewse the object of this particular investigation and not the male conjurer whom she engaged?[5] Why Mrs. Dewse and not the husband who paid for and apparently endorsed, however fearfully, her involvement with sorcery?

The documents concerning Mrs. Dewse do make it clear that she was caught in the cross fire of a power struggle between males over which she had little control. Assuming the charges against her to be at least partly true, she probably turned to sorcery as a last resort, when her husband's own attempts to defend his position had faltered. In so doing, she stepped out of place as a woman, in a sense usurping her husband's role, appropriating for herself an agency usually restricted to males. Yet, on the surface at least, it seems unlikely that the motives behind her arrest had much to do with her sex or with the perception that her behavior had violated gender norms. Such also appears to be the case more generally. According to the major historians of English witchcraft, witch-hunting was not a thinly disguised method of woman-hunting, nor were the hunts merely an excuse to wipe out midwives, female healers, widows with property, or women suspected of sexual transgression.[6]

5. If Birche turned informer for the authorities, he probably had been offered immunity from prosecution in exchange for his services: thus there may be a simple explanation for why he, and not Mrs. Dewse, escaped punishment. Yet so it went for most other male practitioners of magic: the conjurer, the sorcerer, the cunning man, the magus—for one reason or another, few ended up in court for the crime of witchcraft, fewer still were executed. Such male witches may have existed in great numbers, yet it appears that they were seldom suspected of practicing harmful magic, seldom truly feared as dangerous by their neighbors or by the authorities.

6. Barbara Ehrenreich and Deirdre English, in *Witches, Midwives, and Nurses: A History of Women Healers* (New York: Feminist Press, 1973), first advanced the claim that witches were midwives or female healers persecuted because they threatened an emergent male medical establishment. They have been criticized by many for a partial reading of the evidence. See Geoffrey Scarre, *Witchcraft and Magic in 16th and 17th Century Europe* (Atlantic Highlands, N.J.: Humanities Press International, 1987), p. 36; Leland Estes, "The Medical Origins of the European Witch Craze: A Hypothesis," *Journal of Social History* (Winter 1983): 271–84; G. R. Quaife, *Godly Zeal and Furious Rage: The Witch in Early Modern Europe* (London: Croom Helm, 1987), pp. 92–93; and especially David Harley, "Historians as Demonologists: The Myth of the Midwife-Witch," *Social History of Medi-*

Yet in Shakespeare's plays witchcraft is clearly intertwined not only with treason but also with gender transgression. Shakespeare's witches and the women associated with them, often endowed with masculine traits, regularly step out of place and become usurpers of the male role. Paradoxically, because they act like men, they also become associated with mothers: they recall that period of life when women dominate the lives of their male children, when the gender hierarchy of the adult world is inverted. Joan la Pucelle, the armed maid with a male warrior's strength, for example, is seemingly empowered by "God's mother" and turns English males from fierce dogs into "whelps" who run crying away (*1 Henry VI* 1.5.25–26). For Shakespeare, typically, the witch or witch-like woman is one who can make the adult male feel he has been turned back into a child again, vulnerable to a mother's malevolent power.

Witches were women, I believe, because women are mothers: witchcraft beliefs encode fantasies of maternal persecution. To readers of Shakespeare criticism or psychoanalytic commentary, this will not seem a surprising or particularly original claim.[7] Nonetheless, in historians' analyses of the witch-hunts, the witch's relation to the maternal has seldom been explored. Though in the last twenty years historians have asked with increasing urgency why women formed the vast majority of

---

cine 3 (1990): 1–26. In England the midwife or village healer may have been somewhat more vulnerable to a charge of witchcraft than the average female, but many of the accused are neither; many, perhaps most, local healers were male; and there is little or no evidence that links the impetus for prosecution with male physicians. Quaife's suggestion that the clergy were more likely to feel a rivalry with local healers is borne out in the attacks on "white" magic in many religious tracts.

Widows in some countries, including England, were represented among the accused in numbers above their proportion of the general population; see Scarre, *Witchcraft*, p. 26; and Alan Macfarlane, *Witchcraft in Tudor and Stuart England: A Regional and Comparative Study* (New York: Harper and Row, 1970), p. 64. Most of the accused were poor, however, and had little property to pass on; English officials did not have a financial incentive to prosecute as they did in some countries. See Keith Thomas, *Religion and the Decline of Magic* (New York: Scribner's, 1971), pp. 456–57.

Occasionally, but by no means regularly, the witch had a history of sexual transgression. See Macfarlane, *Witchcraft*, p. 160; and Thomas, *Religion*, p. 568.

7. See especially Janet Adelman, "'Born of Woman': Fantasies of Maternal Power in *Macbeth*," in *Cannibals, Witches, and Divorce: Estranging the Renaissance*, ed. Marjorie Garber (Baltimore: Johns Hopkins University Press, 1987), pp. 90–121, now reprinted with revisions in Adelman's book *Suffocating Mothers: Fantasies of Maternal Origin in Shakespeare's Plays, "Hamlet" to "The Tempest"* (New York: Routledge, 1992); my argument is indebted to Adelman's work at many points. Most psychoanalytically informed essays on *Macbeth* make a connection between the witches and maternal fantasy, and a number of them are cited in my chapter on that play.

those prosecuted under England's witchcraft statutes, they have not, by and large, focused on women's roles as mothers or caretakers of small children, or considered the psychological fallout of Renaissance mothering.[8] The mother is absent from the most influential studies of English and Scottish witchcraft, those by Alan Macfarlane, Keith Thomas, and Christina Larner.[9] With some exceptions, the same is true of studies of witchcraft in Europe and the American colonies.[10] Mrs. Dewse was a

8. Essays that explicitly take up the "woman question" include Alan Anderson and Raymond Gordon, "Witchcraft and the Status of Women—the Case of England," *British Journal of Sociology* 29 (June 1978): 171–84; and Clarke Garrett, "Women and Witches: Patterns of Analysis," *Signs* 3 (Winter 1977): 461–70. Both essays provoked subsequent commentary. See J. K. Swales and Hugh V. McClachlan, "Witchcraft and the Status of Women: a Comment," *British Journal of Sociology* 30 (September 1979): 349–57; and Alan Anderson and Raymond Gordon, "The Uniqueness of English Witchcraft: A Matter of Numbers?" *British Journal of Sociology* 30 (September 1979): 359–61; "Comments on Garrett's 'Women and Witches'" by Judith H. Balfe in *Signs* 4 (Autumn 1978): 201–2, and by Claudia Honegger, Nelly Moia, and Clarke Garrett in *Signs* 4 (1979): 792–98, 798–802, 802–4. Several books on European witch-hunting contain substantial treatments of the role of gender and appraisals of current research: among them, see Brian P. Levack, *The Witch-Hunt in Early Modern Europe* (London: Longman, 1987); Quaife, *Godly Zeal*; and especially Merry E. Wiesner, *Women and Gender in Early Modern Europe* (Cambridge: Cambridge University Press, 1993), pp. 218–38. Many "local studies" of English witchcraft also address the issue at least in passing; they are cited in Chapter 2.

9. Macfarlane, *Witchcraft in Tudor and Stuart England*; Thomas, *Religion and the Decline of Magic*, pp. 437–583; Christina Larner, *Enemies of God: The Witch-Hunt in Scotland* (London: Chatto and Windus, 1981) and *Witchcraft and Religion: The Politics of Popular Belief* (Oxford: Basil Blackwell, 1984). After this book was substantially completed, I came across two essays by J. A. Sharpe that relate witches and mothers in ways that support aspects of my argument. See *Witchcraft in Seventeenth-Century Yorkshire: Accusations and Counter-Measures*, Borthwick Paper No. 81 (York: University of York, 1992), pp. 18–19, and especially "Witchcraft and Women in Seventeenth–Century England: Some Northern Evidence," *Continuity and Change* 6 (1991): 179–99. They stand as an important exception to my generalizations about the omission of mothers from historical studies of English witchcraft.

10. John Demos, in the context of a much larger, multidimensional study, discusses the witch as nurse and offers a psychoanalytic interpretation of aspects of accusers' responses to the witch, relating them to infantile fantasies about mothers; see *Entertaining Satan: Witchcraft and the Culture of Early New England* (Oxford: Oxford University Press, 1983), pp. 172–210. Although Demos's psychoanalytic assumptions are somewhat different from mine, his argument has similarities to the one I offer in Chapter 2; I am indebted to his analysis. In *The Devil in the Shape of a Woman: Witchcraft in Colonial New England* (New York: Norton, 1987), Carol F. Karlsen discusses motherhood in a more restricted sense; her major focus is on women and patterns of inheritance. It is perhaps significant that both of these exceptions come from studies of colonial American witchcraft, which has close affinities with English witchcraft; at the same time, because fuller records survive for many American cases, the relationships and family histories of participants can be reconstructed in greater detail than in English cases. It may also be true that the role of mother is not as relevant in continental Europe, where witch-hunting was a far more virulent affair, and the

mother, and she apparently turned to sorcery in part *as* a mother: her husband's loss of office threatened to be the "undoing" of her children as well as herself. As mother and wife, dependent on her husband for economic security and social position, Mrs. Dewse had interests that intersected with his; her magical acts, designed to help and avenge him, implicate her in his treasonous activities. Those acts eerily encode a nightmare version of her maternal role; the doll-like wax images to be pierced by pins suggest children over whom a controlling but monstrous mother holds the power of life and death. In Shakespeare's first tetralogy and *Macbeth*, witches, wives, and mothers are endowed with similar nightmare powers; by both magical and nonmagical means, they manipulate men and make them feel as if they are dependent and powerless children. Like Mrs. Dewse, these women also use their powers to aid and abet "traitors" who threaten what other characters see as legitimate political authority. But whereas Mrs. Dewse's maternal role is glimpsed only briefly in the documents connected to her case, Shakespeare's plays foreground the links between the witch and the mother, making a malevolent, persecutory power associated with the mother's body, voice, or nurturant role a central feature of her ability to threaten order. In doing so, Shakespeare's texts invite us to think again about the significance of gender in the English witch-hunts. The maternal plays only a minor role in the case of Mrs. Dewse, but in other witchcraft cases of that day in England the connection between the figures of the witch and the mother is, I hope to show, undeniable.

Reading the English Witch-Hunts

Whereas historians have only recently begun to give sustained attention to gender in their analyses of the English witch-hunts, literary critics have been almost too ready to assume that gender is the only significant factor: for some writers, witch-hunting is, at its heart, woman-hunting. In many studies of early modern literature, witches—"real" as well as fictive—are routinely considered to be gender transgressors, punished primarily for their defiance of patriarchal norms. For Cather-

---

legal system, social practices, and psychological dynamics were significantly different from those in England; accordingly, the profile of the typical witch may also have been quite different. Among other things, continental witch stereotypes emphasized the sexual deviance of the witch.

ine Belsey, for example, the English witch-hunts involved "the demonization of women who were seen as voluble, unwomanly and possessed of an unauthorized power," and "witches were . . . women who failed to conform to the patriarchal ideal of femininity." For Karen Newman, "Witches threatened hegemonic patriarchal structures . . . as cultural producers, as spectacle, as *representatives* of an oppositional 'femininity.' "[11] Such generalizations contain a partial truth; representations of the witch in early modern literary and dramatic texts often did register male anxieties about female unruliness or sexual power, and the language of witchcraft could be used to denigrate or otherwise discourage a variety of female behaviors. Thus in *The Winter's Tale*, Leontes castigates Paulina as a "mankind witch" when she defies his commands, and Polixenes later accusingly comments on Perdita's "excellent witchcraft" when he is dismayed by the power her beauty exerts over his son (2.3.67, 4.4.424).[12] Yet when we turn to look at specific cases in which women were accused of witchcraft, these generalizations do not seem to tell us very much about what convinced a community that a particular woman was a witch or what made her the object of legal prosecution. The woman accused as a witch may have implicitly violated patriarchal norms by her angry speech or assertive behavior, but so had many other women never associated with witchcraft. The gender implications of her actions seldom appear to have been her accusers' major concern. Nor were accused women regularly associated with erotic power or sexual offenses in England. On the rare occasions when

11. Catherine Belsey, *The Subject of Tragedy: Identity and Difference in Renaissance Drama* (London: Methuen, 1985), pp. 185–86; Newman, *Fashioning Femininity and English Renaissance Drama* (Chicago: University of Chicago Press, 1991), p. 69. Some critics perceive failure to conform to political norms as well as patriarchal ones. For Peter Stallybrass, "Witchcraft beliefs are one way of asserting distinctions . . . including definitions of political and familial roles. They can be used, for instance, to account for the 'unnatural' ambition of a rival or for the 'unnatural' power of a woman"; Lady Macbeth, he goes on to suggest, "implicitly subverts patriarchal authority in a manner typically connected with witchcraft" ("*Macbeth* and Witchcraft," in *Focus on "Macbeth,"* ed. John Russell Brown [London: Routledge and Kegan Paul, 1982], pp. 190, 197). According to Sarah Beckwith, "Witches then are those women who are fantasized as the simultaneous subverters of the family and the state" ("The Power of Devils and the Hearts of Men: Notes towards a Drama of Witchcraft," in *Shakespeare in the Changing Curriculum*, ed. Lesley Aers and Nigel Wheale [London: Routledge, 1991], p. 151). My point here is not that these critics are entirely wrong; as will become clear in the course of the book, I agree with several of these statements when their context is more carefully specified.

12. William Shakespeare, *The Winter's Tale*, ed. J. H. P. Pafford (Arden Edition; London: Methuen, 1973).

an accused woman was alleged to have caused male impotence, it was a side issue having little bearing on the case.[13]

Those literary critics who have associated the witch with fantasies about the mother, I believe, come closer to a central feature of actual witchcraft cases. Janet Adelman has written evocatively about Shakespeare's *Macbeth* and the imagery of maternal danger at the heart of constructions of the witch; Gail Paster has discerned the witch-hunter's fear of maternal power in "the almost obsessive attention that English authorities paid" to the witch's teat.[14] Yet it remains to be demonstrated that fantasies about the mother played a significant role in witch-hunting outside of these limited contexts, nor have historians or literary critics shown how such fantasies may have informed the prosecution of specific cases. That is, in essence, what I try to do in this book. And in so doing, I try to clarify the relation of literary constructions of the witch to the very specific beliefs, attitudes, and social practices that made particular individuals subject not only to "the violence of representation" but also to physical violence and death at the hands of the state and of local communities. I have focused, therefore, on those textual practices that most immediately pertain to the legal prosecution of women and men for the crime of witchcraft as well as on selected literary texts.

The witch-hunts were, of course, a highly complex, multidetermined affair, involving the poor and the very poor at the village level as well as a "prosecuting class" made up of gentry-level and aristocratic judges, justices of the peace, clerics, magistrates, and kings. Peasant and elite, low, middle, and high, male and female—persons from diverse social backgrounds had different yet overlapping reasons to fear and loathe the witch. The historians Alan Macfarlane and Keith Thomas have offered the most powerful analysis of witchcraft at the village level; despite their relative lack of attention to gender issues, their detailed studies of individual witchcraft cases in the context of social and economic tensions and complex networks of popular magical belief are the starting point for any serious understanding of witch-hunting in England. Christina Larner, exploring the Scottish witch-hunts, has integrated their approach with a closer examination of the role of the state apparatus and the ruling elites.

13. On male impotence, see Thomas, *Religion*, pp. 437, 538.
14. Adelman, *Suffocating Mothers*, pp. 130–47; Gail Kern Paster, *The Body Embarrassed: Drama and the Disciplines of Shame in Early Modern England* (Ithaca: Cornell University Press, 1993), p. 247.

"Peasants left to themselves," she notes, "will identify individuals as witches and will resort to a variety of anti-witchcraft measures in self-defence; they cannot pursue these measures to the punishment, banishment, or official execution of even one witch, let alone a multiplicity of witches, without the administrative machinery and encouragement of their rulers."[15]

Although these historians have nothing to say about the relation of witches to mothers, they all take up the "woman question" at least briefly. For Keith Thomas, the preponderance of women among those accused of witchcraft is most plausibly explained "by economic and social considerations, for it was the women who were the most dependent members of the community, and thus the most vulnerable to accusation." For Alan Macfarlane, it was not women's dependence but a conservatism implicit in their social position that made them vulnerable; they were the "co-ordinating element" in village society, and "if witchcraft . . . reflected tensions between an ideal of neighborliness and the necessities of economic and social change, women were commonly thought of as witches because they were more resistant to such change." Thomas and Macfarlane agree that, as Thomas says, the "idea that witch-prosecutions reflected a war between the sexes must be discounted," chiefly because village-level accusers and victims were as likely to be female as male, if not more so.[16] Considering that both conducted their research in the late 1960s, it is not surprising that neither employs gender or patriarchy as a category of analysis, and their discussions of witches as women takes up no more than a few pages.

Christina Larner, while stressing the political and religious factors involved in the hunts, has explored the "woman question" in somewhat more detail and found that the witch-hunts were "sex-related," though not "sex-specific." For elites and peasantry alike, the women who became targets of the hunts had clearly violated norms regarding appropriate behavior for women: they were angry and demanding, not meek, mild, and compliant. Larner does not believe that a "war between the sexes" can be discounted as an element in the hunts merely because a majority of accusers were women themselves, as Thomas and Macfarlane suggest. Patriarchal beliefs and practices often have the effect of dividing women against each other, Larner argues; because of their dependence on men,

15. Macfarlane, *Witchcraft in Tudor and Stuart England*; Thomas, *Religion*; Larner, *Enemies of God*, p. 2.
16. Thomas, *Religion*, p. 568; Macfarlane, *Witchcraft*, pp. 161, 160.

"most women will not only conform, but also attack women who by their nonconformity threaten the security of conformist women."[17]

Versions of Larner's argument have surfaced not only in literary criticism but also in a wide range of feminist accounts of the witch-hunts, the more polemical of which are likely to portray the witch as a heroic protofeminist resisting patriarchal oppression and a wholly innocent victim of a male-authored reign of terror designed to keep women in their place.[18] If it is acknowledged at all that women also hunted witches, such women are represented as lackeys of patriarchy, conservative defenders of male-defined notions of women's roles, mere cogs in the phallocentric wheel. As Larner's own argument attests, even in more historically sensitive accounts, feminists have typically considered women who accused other women of witchcraft to be doing little more than mouthing a male script. Thus for one feminist historian, "the patriarchal system . . . explains why many women accused other females: if a woman displeased or threatened the men of her community, she would also be seen as dangerous by the women who depended on or identified with those men." These

17. Larner, *Witchcraft and Religion*, p. 86.
18. Some examples include Mary Daly, *Gyn/Ecology: The Meta-ethics of Radical Feminism* (Boston: Beacon Press, 1978); Andrea Dworkin, *Woman Hating* (New York: E. P. Dutton, 1974), pp. 118–50; Robin Morgan, "The Network of the Imaginary Mother," in *Lady of the Beasts: Poems* (New York: Random House, 1970). WITCH was the acronym of a late 1960s women's liberation group, and the witch has continued to be a powerful symbol invoked by a wide range of feminist groups. See also Silvia Bovenschen, "The Contemporary Witch, the Historical Witch, and the Witch Myth: The Witch, Subject of the Appropriation of Nature and Object of the Domination of Nature," in *New German Critique* 15 (Fall 1978): 83–119. Bovenschen describes uses of the witch in European demonstrations by feminists; she celebrates the "anarchic" energies of the mythic impulse behind such uses while ridiculing the "rearguard" interest in the witch of "ivory tower" scholars, with their delusions of autonomy and their foot-dragging emphasis on historical accuracy. Her discussion, engaging as it is in its "bad girl" iconoclasm, reinscribes the notion of an autonomous "ivory tower," sealed off from politics, and masks the new feminist possibilities that careful attention to historical texts can open up. But Bovenschen's point about the "rearguard" nature of scholars' work on witchcraft is well taken. The feminist texts I have mentioned are all products of the 1970s; although scholarly witchcraft studies have a long history, for the most part, not until the 1980s did historians give sustained attention to the question of gender in the witch-hunts. Larner's essay first appeared in 1981. These feminist essays, moreover, do not concern themselves specifically with England, but generalize about the European hunts as a whole. In those countries where true "witch panics" took place, where torture was used and hundreds, even thousands, were killed at one time, it makes more sense to represent such practices as products of a misogynist "sado-torture" machine, as Mary Daly does. Nevertheless, it is disturbing to note the uncanny resemblence of Daly's rhetoric to that of Heinrich Kramer and Jacob Sprenger in the *Malleus Maleficarum* (Cologne, 1486) she so deplores; her text puts a demonized male enemy in the place of the witch.

women, she goes on to suggest, may have been trying "to outdo their op-
pressors in scorning persons perceived as outsiders, in hope of being accepted, or tolerated, themselves."[19]

Like other feminists, I am interested in understanding the relation of
the witch-hunts to early modern gender constructions and to systems of
male dominance. But such formulations, useful as they may be in some
contexts, misleadingly represent the hunts as an all-male, univocally
misogynist, top-down phenomenon, ascribing a monologic unity of self
to the participants in the hunts which elides tensions and discontinuities
in women's relations with other women and in early modern culture more
generally.[20] Instead, I attempt in this book to distinguish between different types of discourse about the witch and to demonstrate that repre-
sentational strategies tended to vary according to the class and gender
positions of their authors. In considering village-level constructions of the
witch (crucial in determining the witch's gender), I take issue especially
with the widely held feminist view that assigns the woman accused of
witchcraft to the role of rebellious protofeminist and the female accuser
to that of patriarchal conformist. Village-level quarrels that led to witchcraft accusations often grew out of struggles to control household boundaries, feeding, child care, and other matters typically assigned to women's
sphere. In such quarrels, the woman accused of witchcraft was as likely
to be the one urging conformity to a patriarchal standard. Her curses and
insults were experienced not as violations of proper feminine conduct but
as verbal assaults on the other woman's reputation for "neighborly nurture," assaults that might also cause harm to loved ones under her care.
The accuser, in turn, defamed the witch as a perverse and destructive
mother. Engaged in a complex struggle for survival and empowerment

19. Anne Llewellyn Barstow, "On Studying Witchcraft as Women's History: A Historiography of the European Witch Persecutions," *Journal of Feminist Studies in Religion* 4
(1988): 17–18. Another study midway between history and polemic is Marianne Hester,
Lewd Women and Wicked Witches: A Study of the Dynamics of Male Domination (London: Routledge, 1992). Hester, though she engages with Macfarlane's and Thomas's work
and examines some primary sources, unconvincingly concludes that "overall, the witch-
hunts were an instance of male sexual violence against women . . . [and] a part of the 'dynamics of domination' whereby men at the time maintained dominance over women" (p.
199). Like Barstow, she views female accusers as motivated by the need to avoid being stigmatized themselves: "The fact that many women incriminated each other must also be seen
. . . as an indication of the pressures they felt to avoid being accused of witchcraft, or to attempt to lessen the accusation against them" (p. 201); such accusations may also reflect internalization of the pervasive misogyny of their society, she adds.

20. For some similar criticisms, see Sharpe, "Witchcraft and Women," pp. 179–82.

within a patriarchal culture, both women stood in an uneasy relation to definitions of female identity which privileged nurturing behavior and well-governed speech.

In the chapters that follow I examine witch-hunting in early modern England as a social, legal, and theatrical practice, building on and to some extent rewriting the formulations of Macfarlane, Thomas, and Larner by focusing on the figure of the mother. Mothers appear in this book in several different senses. They are, first of all, cultural products: "mother" is a historically specific set of identities and practices delineated in a variety of early modern discourses—domestic, religious, legal, economic—and "written" also in oral tradition. Second, mothers are actual persons: a woman is not born a mother but becomes one when she assumes one of the maternal identities her culture makes available to her. Thus I am concerned not only with the mother in discourse but also with "real" mothers caught up in witchcraft trials. Third, mothers are sites of infantile fantasy: as representations shaped especially by a child's internal needs and desires, fantasies about the mother may be internalized and projected onto others, then reimagined in successive stages on into adulthood. Such fantasies are also shaped by the child's particular experiences of mothering and by the cultural discourses in and through which maternal identities are constructed. Finally, "mother" carries a variety of figurative meanings: the maternal could be incorporated into a variety of other early modern female identities—nurse, healer, domestic manager, "mother" of one's community or country. Many aspects of "women's work" involved some form of care giving or nurture, for adults if not for children; women frequently performed a maternal or quasi-maternal function for husbands, kin, grown children, servants, neighbors, and livestock.

The witch herself was one of these figurative mothers—a perverse one who used her powers of nurture malevolently against neighbors. The witch's maternal features are most evident in village-level discourse, but elite texts of the period also engage with the witch as mother, though often in strikingly different ways. In order to bring the class- and gender-specific aspects of discourse about the witch into relief, I examine individual cases and witch-hunting texts at four different social sites. Chapter 2 offers an extended look at the village-level witchcraft quarrels. Although men as well as women accused women of witchcraft, witch-hunting at the village level, I suggest, may largely have been a form of women's work. Quarrels that led to accusations of witchcraft often began between older and younger women, though husbands then came forward to make formal accusations to authorities. Their quarrels typically found expression in a language of insult infused with references to the maternal function. As a quarrel escalated, the younger woman conferred upon the older one the attributes of an invasive and malevolent mother, who used her powers to suckle, feed, and nurture childlike demonic "imps" in order to bring sickness and death to the households of other mothers. The witch was feared for her ability to retaliate and to harm others through magic—a magic acquired through her maternal power.

In gentry-level and aristocratic texts, however, a different profile emerges. The witch loses some but not all associations with the malevolent mother; she is featured, rather, as an enemy of God and a rebel against the state, and her crime is betrayal rather than magical harm. In the process she is also demoted; whereas in village-level discourse the witch is almost always a dominating mother who controls childlike demonic imps, in elite discourse—influenced by Calvinist doctrine and continental theories of the demonic pact—she is subordinated to a diabolic male "master," becoming the servant or "drudge" of a devil now represented not as a child but as an adult male endowed with frightening powers, a rival of God and the godly fathers who rule in his name. The image of the envied maternal breast is replaced with that of the female body "open" to diabolic influence; Satan rules both the witch and her "imps." Imagined in terms of the mother-child dyad at the village level, the witch in elite discourse is often reconfigured in terms of a perverse but patriarchal family.

In Chapter 3 I focus especially on two gentry-level religious tracts by the Protestant clergyman George Gifford, which rewrite the village-level witch in the terms I have sketched. I then compare them briefly with writings by William Perkins, a contemporary who shared many of Gifford's theological assumptions. Gifford tried to shift the emphasis of witch-hunting away from the legal prosecution of witches toward a biblically based critique of popular belief in many types of magical causation. In so doing, he engaged directly with village-level beliefs about the witch: reconfiguring the witch by divesting her of her malevolent maternal power is part of his explicit strategy. Perkins saw the witch as a clear and present danger and promoted prosecutions; his discourse elides almost all traces of the malevolent mother, replacing her with the figure of the betraying servant of Satan. Both texts share what appears to be a patriarchal agenda. Gentry-level discourse worked to undo the village-level associa-

tion of the witch with maternal *power*, to reassert her subordinate position by making her dependent on a male devil.

In Chapter 4 I turn to aristocratic witch-hunting, first examining the
events surrounding the passage of the 1563 Act against witchcraft at the
beginning of Elizabeth's reign, at a time when the new queen was attempting to distinguish herself from her Catholic predecessor, Mary I, and was
engaged in a growing rivalry with Mary Queen of Scots; both relationships
eerily repeat aspects of village women's quarrels. The bulk of this chapter,
however, is devoted to James VI and I's extensive involvement in and pro-
motion of the first large-scale witchcraft trials in Scotland, in 1590–1591.
The witches involved had allegedly practiced their magical arts against the
king as well as against local enemies; some charged that they were also as-
sisting the rebellious plots of the fifth earl of Bothwell, nephew and heir of
the man who murdered James's father and eloped with his mother, Mary
Queen of Scots, when James was a young child. James's involvement, I
hope to show, was significantly shaped by his difficult relationship with his
two powerful "mothers," Mary and Elizabeth I, who frequently "betrayed" him in his confrontations with an unruly Scottish aristocracy. Dependent on these political mothers in some obvious and unavoidable ways,
James could play out his resentments and reassert patriarchal dominance
over the maternal through witch-hunting. At the same time, his actions
also registered the ways that Mary and Elizabeth's powers were intertwined with those of a male aristocracy; in the documents and state papers
connected with the North Berwick trials we can again glimpse the transformation of the village-level witch, a "mother" to familiars with more or
less autonomous powers, into the betraying servant of diabolic male "masters"—human as well as supernatural—who had as their chief aim rebellion against the state.

In the last section of the book, Chapters 5 and 6, I turn to the discourse
of a "middling sort," William Shakespeare. Like other playwrights of his
time, Shakespeare constructs the witch as a complex hybrid, made up of
elements drawn from both village-level and elite discourse, as well as from
a wide array of literary and intellectual traditions. I examine in detail
Shakespeare's witchcraft plays, *Henry VI, Parts 1, 2, and 3, Richard III,*
and *Macbeth,* which place the witch in a larger context of political intrigue, rebellion, and civil war. For Shakespeare, witches have maternal
features and mothers have witch-like powers. At the same time, such characters typically betray established authority by their alliances with diabolic male rivals. In a manner reminiscent of the elite texts discussed in

this book, these plays call attention to the underlying weakness of the witch and the threat posed by mothers and wives who step out of subordinate roles. Yet they examine the element of displacement in witchcraft accusation, placing the persecutory dynamic in a larger context of disrupted father-son relations and family and political structures under pressure from patrilineality.

Despite their many differences, the texts examined in this book all demonstrate that in early modern culture the figure of the witch was closely intertwined with that of the mother. Witch-hunting, it further appears, emerged in a context of increasing anxieties about mothers and the maternal role. A growing body of research suggests that in sixteenth-century England ambivalence about mothers, maternal power, and the maternal function was intense and becoming more so as the century wore on. Ambivalence was structured into a variety of economic, social, and ideological formations that were changing in response to the Reformation and the expansion of the nation-state, among other factors. Especially among elite families, conflict could be a regular feature of relations between mothers and sons when husbands provided for wives in ways that disadvantaged their male heirs.[21] Studies of the wills of elite and "middling" families show that mothers made decisions about wealth and property; such exercises of power could arouse resentment as well as inspire gratitude among their children. By the end of the century, moreover, married women along with widows had gained the significant right to file suits on their own behalf in Chancery court—suits that often brought them into conflict with their children.[22]

The sixteenth century also saw changes in ideological constructions of the "ideal" mother. By the latter half of the century, in conduct literature and in Protestant handbooks for Christian households, a new emphasis was placed on the wife's role as nurturer and caretaker of small children, at the expense of her other duties as household manager or producer of domestic goods.[23] At the same time, the health and well-being of the child

---

21. See Barbara J. Harris, "Property, Power, and Personal Relations: Elite Mothers and Sons in Yorkist and Early Tudor England," *Signs* 15 (Spring 1990): 606–32; and "Women and Politics in Early Tudor England," *Historical Journal* 33 (1990): 259–81.

22. On women's wills, see Susan Dwyer Amussen, *An Ordered Society: Gender and Class in Early Modern England* (Oxford: Basil Blackwell, 1988), pp. 78, 91–93. On women's suits in Chancery, see Mary L. Cioni, *Women and Law in Elizabethan England with Particular Reference to the Court of Chancery* (New York: Garland, 1985).

23. See especially Susan Cahn, *Industry of Devotion: The Transformation of Women's Work in England, 1500–1660* (New York: Columbia University Press, 1987), pp. 96–108.

came to be viewed as more dependent on the quality of her care. Motherhood, for these authors, was no longer simply one of the many important tasks in a domestic economy but a woman's "special vocation," drawing upon her "natural" virtues of compassion and pity and her biological capacity to breast-feed. In particular, the long-standing practice in aristocratic and gentry-level households of employing wet nurses to feed and care for young children became a matter of heated debate, even as many families continued to employ such nurses throughout the period.

Partly because theory often outran practice, along with this new ideal came a new sense of women's potential for what I am calling malevolent nurture. Wet nurses—regularly drawn from the lower classes—could be dangerous, for their milk might be "contaminated" by their low social origins, might pass vice and coarseness as well as disease along to infants. Aristocratic and gentry-level women were increasingly construed as negligent or "unnatural" if they refused to breast-feed and preferred other household tasks or activities that took them outside the home. Even when women confined themselves to their "special vocation" as nurturing mothers, they could be found wanting. Mothers might "spoil" their children with too much love; they might deform the child in the womb if they gave way to anger or strange imaginings. Some, considering women intellectually deficient and given to excessive passions, believed they were dangerous as teachers of all except very young children; sons especially should be handed over to male tutors as soon as possible.

A variety of other practices associated with the maternal function became the object of anxiety and suspicion in the later sixteenth century. New constructions of motherhood as a valued "special vocation," it seems clear, went hand in hand with new anxiety about women's capacity for malevolent nurture; maternal power, however generative, could also be used to maim, deform, or destroy children and others under women's care. These changes in the social construction of mothering, which exacerbated ambivalence about maternal power, closely corresponded to the period of witchcraft prosecutions in England. In the pages that follow, I suggest that fearful, hostile fantasies about mothers and others associated with the maternal role (fantasies that for a variety of reasons could not be more directly acknowledged or expressed) may have found an outlet by being displaced onto women who resembled but were also in important ways distinguished from them—that is, onto the needy, demanding older women who typically were accused of witchcraft. Witch-hunting, moreover, began at a time when an unusual number of women had inherited or were claimants to highly visible—and hotly contested—positions of power. Queens such as Elizabeth and Mary I provide the most obvious examples, but female rule could take many forms: sixteenth-century women exercised power over others as patrons, marriage brokers, and household managers, among other roles. Such women, often at the center of religious and political controversy and the subject of debates about the propriety of female rule, generated anger and rage as well as loyal support. My working assumption has been that women "on top" inevitably carried associations with mothers, who, even in the most patriarchal cultures, exercise power over children. For those dependent on women rulers, feelings of anger or hostility toward them could be as dangerous and as internally threatening as feelings about actual mothers—with which they were, in any case, intertwined. Hostility toward these figurative mothers might also be displaced onto the witch.

Like the witch on stage, this book is a hybrid: part historical reconstruction, part literary/cultural analysis, it draws on the methods of social historians and new historicist literary critics.[24] Viewed from within early modern literary studies, it is a hybrid in another sense, the product of feminist-psychoanalytic approaches as well as new historicist ones. To some readers these approaches will seem incompatible: whereas feminists have noted the relative absence of women's voices in much new historicist work,[25] new historicists have often found psychoanalytic methods, femi-

24. Relations between these two groups have not always been harmonious: historians have criticized literary new historicists—often with justification—for "anecdotalism," over-reliance on literary evidence, and totalizing notions of "power" or of culture, among other things. See David Cressy, "Foucault, Stone, Shakespeare, and Social History," *English Literary Review* 21 (Spring 1991): pp. 121–33; Stephen L. Collins, "Where's the History in the New Literary Historicism? The Case of the English Renaissance," *Annals of Scholarship* 6 (1989): 231–47. Similar criticisms have been made by those based in literary studies as well. See Brook Thomas, *The New Historicism and Other Old-Fashioned Topics* (Princeton: Princeton University Press, 1991); H. Aram Veeser, ed., *The New Historicism* (New York: Routledge, 1989); and Carolyn Porter, "Are We Being Historical Yet?" *South Atlantic Quarterly* 87 (Fall 1988): 743–86. For new historicist responses, see Stephen Greenblatt, "Resonance and Wonder," in *Literary Theory Today*, ed. Peter Collier and Helga Geyer-Ryan (Ithaca: Cornell University Press, 1990), pp. 74–90; and essays by Greenblatt and Louis Montrose in Veeser, *The New Historicism*. Although I have attempted to avoid some of the more obvious problems associated with the new historicism, I am persuaded that literary scholars have a contribution of their own to make to the interdisciplinary study of the past, growing out of the "reading practices" special to their field.

25. Feminists in the 1980s were often critical of the omission of women or issues of gender and sexuality in much new historicist work, though otherwise sympathetic to the project of integrating literary analysis and history. For some representative critiques, see Judith Newman, "History as Usual? Feminism and the 'New Historicism,'" *Cultural Critique* 9

nist or otherwise, to be at odds with the impulse to "estrange" the past. They have been suspicious of the essentializing transhistoricism that can result from the uncritical application of psychoanalysis to earlier periods. In this, they have echoed even more strident objections of historians to its use.[26] I have tried to remain sensitive to the strangeness of early modern modes of subject construction and to the social institutions in which they

---

(Spring 1988): 87–121; and Carol Thomas Neely, "Constructing the Subject: Feminist Practice and the New Renaissance Discourses," *English Literary Renaissance* 18 (Winter 1988): 5–18. Much of the synthesizing of feminist and new historicist work, however, has come from materialist feminists rather than psychoanalytically oriented ones. See, for example, Karen Newman, *Fashioning Femininity*; and the essays collected in *The Matter of Difference: Materialist Feminist Criticism of Shakespeare*, ed. Valerie Wayne (Ithaca: Cornell University Press, 1991). An exception is Valerie Traub, *Desire and Anxiety: Circulations of Sexuality in Shakespearean Drama* (London: Routledge, 1992); Traub explicitly situates her critical approach at the intersection of feminist, psychoanalytic, and new historicist practices (pp. 3–18); in addition, some critics, such as Lynda Boose and Carol Neely, have incorporated psychoanalytic insights into their work along with social history.

26. Stephen Greenblatt sets forth a new historicist critique of psychoanalysis in "Psychoanalysis and Renaissance Culture," in *Literary Theory/Renaissance Texts*, ed. Patricia Parker and David Quint (Baltimore: Johns Hopkins University Press, 1986). Juliana Schiesari responds to this essay (from a Lacanian perspective) in *The Gendering of Melancholia: Feminism, Psychoanalysis, and the Symbolics of Loss in Renaissance Literature* (Ithaca: Cornell University Press, 1992), pp. 23–25. See also Valerie Traub's Introduction to *Desire and Anxiety*, pp. 13–18. (For a response by a historian to historians' criticisms of psychohistory, see Thomas A. Kohut, "Psychohistory as History," *American Historical Review* 91 [1986]: 336–54.) Schiesari points out that Greenblatt's insistence on early modern subjectivity as institutional product is not inconsistent with the (Lacanian) understanding of a subject as formed in and through the "discourse of the Other," that is, through the "social institution of patriarchy, which organizes, through a determined set of injunctions and prescriptions (the 'symbolic order'), the very nomenclature of family relations." While I agree that psychoanalytic theory can be integrated with an understanding of the subject as socially constructed, Schiesari seems to reproduce the new historicist tendency toward a "totalizing" notion of culture. Even assuming her notion of patriarchy to be historically inflected, we end up with a "structural unconscious" formed by what seems to be a single, internally cohesive metadiscourse. Traub points out another problem in Greenblatt's essay, the idea that identities are always produced in conformity with "norms," which, she says, elides the diversity of early modern identities and the possibility of resistance, reducing difference "to a transitory moment in an overdetermined teleology." Along with Traub, I aim toward a historically nuanced use of psychoanalysis which acknowledges that subjects are formed not in and through a single cultural discourse but through multiple, often inconsistent or contested ones; moreover, individual subjects internalize such discourses in the context of very specific, socially differentiated experiences of family relations and cultural institutions.

For the most part, however, I have simply taken it on faith that the friction between psychoanalysis and new historicism can be enabling. In so doing, I emulate Greenblatt's own practice as he describes it elsewhere: "My own work has always been done with a sense of just having to go about and do it, without establishing first exactly what my theoretical position is" ("Toward a Poetics of Culture," in Veeser, *The New Historicism*, p. 1).

were embedded. Yet even a use of psychoanalytic theory attentive to historical nuance will remain to some extent tainted by anachronism and blind to aspects of early modern "difference." Integrating psychoanalytic theory—theories, one should say—with the inevitably fragmentary knowledge we have about early modern subject formation is a complex project, likely to be only partially successful.

Nevertheless, a history that treats subjects as if they have no unconscious, no childhood, no life haunted by a past of intrapsychic conflict, strikes me as inadequate and misleading. In the case of the witch-hunts, what needs to be explained is an emotional response as well as a set of cultural formations: the witch arouses fear, anxiety, and anger in her neighbors. Thus, especially in Chapter 2, I draw on psychoanalytic theory primarily to come to a better understanding of the phenomenon known as bewitchment and of the persecutory anxieties related to it, which lie at the heart of many witchcraft cases. Bewitchment makes itself known by a variety of mental and physiological events that resemble neurotic symptoms; the historian can hardly avoid offering some sort of psychological interpretation of them. Macfarlane and Thomas, though drawing primarily on social and anthropological theory, themselves include guilt, a psychological component, in their analysis of the motivations for witch-hunting.

Psychoanalysis, moreover, may impart a strangeness of its own, drawing attention to disturbing or unusual aspects of past beliefs and practices which might otherwise remain hidden. Because persecutory anxiety has seemed to me a central feature in witchcraft accusations, I have drawn especially on the work of Melanie Klein, whose chief preoccupations—with fantasies about mothers and maternal "part-objects," with infantile thought processes, envy, aggression, and retaliatory fears—have a special relevance to many issues involved in witch-hunting, particularly at the village level. Early modern child-rearing practices, economic pressures, and changing religious doctrines, I suggest, contributed to a cultural matrix in which persecutory anxieties of the sort Klein analyzed were especially likely to arise. My approach is not consistently Kleinian throughout the book, however. Klein's work has seemed to me most useful in understanding village-level beliefs about the witch. Other theorists have been more influential in my account of elite male subjectivity. I have been especially influenced by other object-relations theorists, as disseminated in feminist Shakespeare criticism, as will be evident in later sections of the book. There are problems with any theoretical apparatus, and I hope that my use of psychoanalytic theory will not be taken as a wholesale endorsement of everything about it.[27] My interpretations are in any case provisional, and critics affiliated with other tendencies within psychoanalysis will undoubtedly read the evidence in different ways.[28]

Like many witchcraft studies, mine focuses on the mental world of the accusers more than on the identity of the witch. Because the surviving documents about the witch-hunts largely comprise statements by the prosecuting classes and "confessions" produced by coercive means, some scholars have proceeded under the assumption that we can make credible statements about the beliefs only of accusers: the effect of this assumption (if not the intention) is to imply that witchcraft accusations were a matter of pure projection and that those accused were totally innocent scapegoats.[29] Other scholars have maintained that there were "guilty" witches

27. Among other things, I am sympathetic to critiques of psychoanalysis that have questioned the "normalizing" implications of theoretical models that unproblematically assume a universal subject. In addition, Klein's work has been persuasively criticized for the "biologism" of her assumptions about aggression and gender identity; for postulating that infants from the time of birth have the cognitive capacity for fantasy; for treating infantile fantasy as a realm seemingly untouched by the social or cultural; for employing a terminology that pathologizes the mental states of infants and young children (e.g., "paranoid-schizoid position"); and for minimizing the effects of the "real" behavior of mothers upon the child's mental representations of maternal objects. The last item mentioned, however, has also brought Klein praise from some feminists, who have cited her views as a partial exception to the general tendency of psychoanalysis toward "mother-blaming." See especially Janice Doane and Devon Hodges, *From Klein to Kristeva: Psychoanalytic Feminism and the Search for the "Good Enough" Mother* (Ann Arbor: University of Michigan Press, 1992). While these feminist critics have an important point, in my view they oversimplify psychoanalytic views of the mother's role; they take metaphors of origin too literally and too readily assume fixed attitudes to what is more generally understood to be a complex and in many ways unresolved issue. For what it's worth, I am more inclined to agree with Klein's critics than her defenders on this point.

28. Indeed, other readings have already been attempted. See Robert A. LeVine, *Culture, Behavior, and Personality* (Chicago: Aldine, 1973), pp. 249–81; Norman Cohn, *Europe's Inner Demons: An Enquiry Inspired by the Great Witch-Hunt* (New York: Basic Books, 1975); and especially Demos, *Entertaining Satan*, pp. 153–210. Though Demos's argument takes the work of Erik Erikson as its starting point, it has some Kleinian features and overlaps with mine in some important areas (pp. 160–63, 172–81, 197–205). See also Newman, *Fashioning Femininity*, pp. 58–60. Newman finds in Klein's revision of Freud a "remarkably compelling narrative through which to read the discourses of English witchcraft" but (writing primarily as a new historicist) doesn't pursue such a reading because of its "naturalizing" and "ahistorical" implications.

29. Few recent writers seize the rationalist high ground in the manner of R. H. Robbins (*The Encyclopedia of Witchcraft and Demonology* [New York: Crown, 1959]) or H. R. Trevor-Roper (*The European Witch-Craze of the Sixteenth and Seventeenth Centuries* [New York: Harper, 1969]), who dismissed two hundred years of witchcraft belief as virtual delirium. But most give much greater emphasis to the mechanism of accusation and persecution than to the possible beliefs and practices of the accused. Although Thomas, Macfarlane, and Larner do think many accused women fell into the "difficult neighbor" category and that a

as well as persecutory fantasies about them. Though I discuss many witch-craft beliefs in terms of fantasy, I recognize that those fantasies were some-times constructed around a partial truth or, once in place, were (partly) confirmed by actual behavior. Some women undoubtedly were innocent scapegoats or, at worst, difficult and quarrelsome neighbors. Others may have self-consciously practiced a transgressive but primarily "white" magic. Still others may have genuinely intended to harm or kill neighbors or authorities by magical means: Mrs. Dewse was probably one of them.

Chapters 2 and 4 include some discussion of "real" witches. For the most part, however, I focus on accusers' constructions of the witch and motiva-tions for witch-hunting, attempting also to distinguish class- and gender-related differences among them. But how can we disentangle peasant voices from elite, accused from accuser? As Carlo Ginzburg has written of the Eu-ropean witch-hunts, "On witchcraft . . . we possess only hostile testimonies. . . . The voices of the accused reach us strangled, altered, distorted." The same could be said for their peasant accusers. Ginzburg's method has been to take the "anomalies" and "cracks" that undermine the coherence of witch-hunters' documents as his starting point. Similarly, Clive Holmes, in his study of specifically English witchcraft, has shown that though peasant and elite beliefs cannot be fully disentangled and each, over time, influenced the other, it is still possible to detect "dissonances" between them and to discern patterns and themes that recur in widely separate cases.[30] My pro-cedures are loosely modeled on theirs.

---

few may have intentionally practiced maleficium, they often treat the actions or beliefs of the accused as more or less irrelevant to the construction of the witch stereotype or to the mech-anism of witch-hunting. Thus in "James VI and I and Witchcraft," *Witchcraft and Religion*, pp. 3–22, Larner represents James as defining the witch for Scotland in the light of his en-counter with continental demonology, quite unaffected by his nine months' face-to-face in-vestigation of the North Berwick witches. Similarly, in Stuart Clark, "Inversion, Misrule, and the Meaning of Witchcraft," *Past and Present* 87 (May 1980): 98–127, discourse about the witch seems to become a self-enclosed language game, following out the logic of antithetical thinking, without reference to the "actual activities of real agents." Carlo Ginzburg, *Ec-stasies: Deciphering the Witches' Sabbath* (New York: Pantheon, 1991), criticizes this ten-dency to restrict the field of inquiry to the history of persecution (p. 11), in the course of mounting an argument that the witches' sabbath is not merely the construct of authorities but a "cultural compromise formation," a hybrid product of a conflict between elite and folk be-liefs, the latter with roots in a shamanistic pagan tradition associated with the cult of Diana.

30. Ginzburg, *Ecstasies*, p. 10; Clive Holmes, "Popular Culture? Witches, Magistrates, and Divines in Early Modern England," in *Understanding Popular Culture: Europe from the Middle Ages to the 19th Century*, ed. Steven L. Kaplan (Berlin: Mouton, 1984), pp. 86–111. Both Ginzburg and Holmes respond to Richard Kieckhefer's discussion of method in *European Witch Trials: Their Foundation in Popular and Learned Culture* (Berkeley: University of California Press, 1976). See also Kieckhefer, *Magic in the Middle Ages* (Cam-bridge: Cambridge University Press, 1990).

Intertwined with the problem of distinguishing peasant voices from elite is that of differentiating "magic" from "religion." Keith Thomas maintains in *Religion and the Decline of Magic* that magical practices were best understood as specific, fragmentary, "primarily oriented toward practical solutions to immediate problems," and not part of a larger system of belief or "world view." Hildred Geertz, among others, challenged Thomas's approach. By making magic a less privileged category, Thomas was uncritically adopting the ideological categories of sixteenth-century Protestant reformers who were redrawing the boundaries of "true religion."[31] My own reading of the evidence tends to support Thomas's view that popular as well as elite voices constructed magic as a set of specific techniques, practical in their aims, often overlapping with "religion" yet also distinguishable from it. Magical practices may be readily integrated into a larger system of beliefs, an organized cult, a world view, but they also have a life of their own, surviving apart from such systems or shifting easily from one to another. Thus today the magical practices of modern feminist and New Age witches closely resemble those of early modern cunning folk; divination, techniques for finding lost treasure, love potions, herbal remedies, amulets, healing rituals—these are the stock in trade of both groups. The occult bookstore and mail order catalog have replaced the local village healer operating out of her own home, making a little extra money from her neighbors. Yet the gender ideology, assumptions about nature, and highly psychologized system of beliefs which inform the discourse of present-day feminist or New Age witches would be quite alien to the sixteenth-century cunning woman, whose magical beliefs coexisted comfortably with her Christian ones.

In any case, both magic and religion were gendered phenomena, and villagers who accepted magic and reformers who opposed it found a common enemy in the witch. The question remains: why were the individuals prosecuted for witchcraft almost always women? I have no "complete" answer, but I do believe a better understanding of the significance of gender in the witch-hunts can be gained by exam-

31. Hildred Geertz's criticisms appear in "An Anthropology of Religion and Magic I" and Keith Thomas's response in "An Anthropology of Religion and Magic II," both in *Journal of Interdisciplinary History* 6 (Summer 1975): 71–109. See also Richard Godbeer's thoughtful comments in *The Devil's Dominion: Magic and Religion in Early New England* (Cambridge: Cambridge University Press, 1992), pp. 9–13. Ginzburg and Holmes also discuss the Geertz-Thomas exchange.

ining the varying ways the figures of the witch and mother are intertwined in early modern English culture. That is what I attempt in the following pages, pursuing a trajectory opened up by the Shakespearean text.

CHAPTER TWO
(UN)NEIGHBORLY NURTURE

In consulting a conjurer, Mrs. Dewse was not doing anything particularly unusual. The documents about her case, however, do not make it very clear what sort of conjurer Robert Birche was. He "advises" a prisoner at Newgate named Atkinson, we are told—as an astrologer or diviner, perhaps. The relatively lowly status of his clientele would suggest he was not a magician of the learned elite like John Dee, but the anonymous informant also mentions a courtly connection: Birche "was knowen and well thoughte of by Sir Edward Hobby." If his reluctance to accede to Mrs. Dewse's wish to harm her enemies is indicative of his customary practice, he is probably an urban and relatively sophisticated counterpart of the "white witch" or "cunning man" of the English countryside. Such magical practitioners might employ a wide range of techniques, chiefly for benign ends, and they were normally contrasted with the witch who practiced *maleficium*—that is, magic used for harmful ends, to cause sickness or to kill. The charms, amulets, divinatory techniques, herbal remedies, and incantations of the white witch were used to cure sickness, help people find lost or stolen items, divine future events, and protect against harm or other misfortunes, among other things; in return for their work, such practitioners received social prestige and sometimes small sums of money.[1] They were common throughout medieval and early modern England, as the work of such historians as Alan Macfarlane and Keith Thomas has made clear, and though some more puritan members of the clergy condemned their magic as vigorously

---

1. See Macfarlane, *Witchcraft*, p. 126.

as they did witchcraft, in the formative years of the witch-hunts the "cunning folk" were widely tolerated by church, state, and general populace. Shakespeare and other Renaissance playwrights refer to them frequently in benign terms.

The cunning folk included both male and female practitioners, in what exact proportions is unclear. It is also difficult to tell to what extent such practices were gendered. At the elite level, astrologers, alchemists, and learned magicians were almost always male, but at the village level most types of magical practitioners could be either male or female. Macfarlane's study of Essex cunning folk called in before the ecclesiastical courts for petty offenses suggests that specialization may sometimes have followed gender lines: males may have predominated in the finding of lost and stolen goods; females to have been preferred for counterwitchcraft measures. Thomas's more inclusive work suggests, however, that both men and women regularly engaged in healing, divination, and most other magical subspecialties.[2]

Given a mixed community of male and female magical practitioners, why were women viewed as the primary agents of a specifically malevolent magic? In literary contexts, in religious polemic, and in a few actual trials (usually political cases involving elite victims) the male magician was often represented in sinister terms. Presumed to have access to forbidden knowledge, he was kept under surveillance by both state and ecclesiastical authorities. Yet the male magician was rarely feared by his neighbors as a source of harmful magic, rarely made the object of accusation. In the relatively few cases in which men were actually indicted, they often escaped conviction and execution.[3] Women, not men, had a virtual monopoly on maleficium; women, not men, were believed most likely to bring sickness and death to their neighbors' households.

In what follows, I explore the foundations of this belief, in popular constructions of the witch as a malevolent mother and in the quarrels—often between women—that typically led to accusations of witchcraft. Ultimately, I relate the accusatory process to the psychological fallout of the

---

2. Ibid., p. 127; Thomas, *Religion*, pp. 177–252.

3. Father Rosimund, for example, supposedly the ringleader of the four Windsor witches executed in 1579, appears to have escaped conviction. See Barbara Rosen, ed., *Witchcraft in England, 1558–1618* (Amherst: University of Massachusetts Press, 1991), pp. 83–90. Another example is the case of Cicely Celles and her husband, which I discuss later in this chapter.

child's experiences of anger, dependence, and fear in its earliest relationships. Put baldly, early modern women and men were most likely to fear a specifically *magical* danger when they got angry at someone who resembled their mother or nurse.

The Witch as Malevolent Mother

If, as Christina Larner has maintained, the impetus for prosecuting witchcraft as a crime ultimately came "from above," it was nevertheless primarily villagers who identified particular individuals as witches. Moreover, by providing "informations" and testifying against them, villagers played a crucial role in determining the outcome of trials. When anti-witchcraft legislation was passed in 1563, magistrates and other members of the learned elites intervened in and to some extent transformed a pre-existing body of popular beliefs about witches and a set of informal witch-hunting practices; they did not create them. Thus, to understand why those accused of witchcraft were almost always women, it is helpful to begin by looking closely at the beliefs of those most directly involved in making witchcraft accusations.

We have no direct access to those beliefs, of course. Sources for the study of popular beliefs about the witch are fragmentary and present a variety of problems for the interpreter, not least of which is the fact that popular views were almost always filtered through those of the elite magistrates, doctors, or clergymen who recorded them. Nor is it possible to speak of a *single* view of the witch, even at the village level. In the process of distinguishing popular views from elite, historians have also begun to delineate regional differences and changes across time.[4] Yet the profile of the witch put forward by Alan Macfarlane and Keith Thomas in their pioneering works still remains an important guide to key features of popular belief and of the role villagers played in bringing particular women to trial. The profile I offer here relies heavily on their findings, supplemented and at times modified by the work of other historians and by my own reading of pamphlets and other documents related to specific witchcraft cases in the period 1563–1611 (for the title page of one such pamphlet,

---

4. See Clive Holmes, "Popular Culture?" and "Women: Witnesses and Witches," *Past and Present* 140 (August 1993): 45–78; also Annabel Gregory, "Witchcraft, Politics, and 'Good Neighborhood' in Early Seventeenth-Century Rye," *Past and Present* 133 (November 1991): 31–66.

see figure 1).[5] Because four of the pamphlets relate cases from Essex County, as does Macfarlane's book, my profile is skewed toward that county. Some pamphlet authors, moreover, do more than reprint or summarize informants' statements and may be biased according to ideological agendas not evident to the modern reader. My profile, in addition, is based on a relatively limited number of examples, chosen because they offer the most detailed accounts (outside the archives) of the quarrels leading up to the accusations for the early period of the witch-hunts. My generalizations must be evaluated with these limitations in mind. Nevertheless, although my emphases differ, the profile I set out is, for the most part, consistent with those of historians who have done in-depth archival work.[6]

The "typical" witchcraft case began when an older woman had a falling out with a neighbor—often another woman, usually a younger one. The older woman tended to be poorer, and frequently the falling out occurred after she had gone to her neighbor with a request for food or some domestic item or for access to land, and the neighbor refused her request. The woman went away, cursing her neighbor openly or muttering

5. Aside from the accounts of Macfarlane, Thomas, and other historians, my profile of the witch is derived from the abstracts of trial records contained in C. L'Estrange Ewen, *Witchcraft and Demonianism: A Concise Account Derived from Sworn Depositions and Confessions Obtained in the Courts of England and Wales* (London: Heath Cranton, 1933); and from pamphlets about witchcraft trials from the period 1563–1611, most of which incorporate informants' statements from the trials into their text. The following pamphlets have been especially important to my discussion: *The examination and confession of certaine Wytches at Chensforde in the Countie of Essex* (London, 1566); *A detection of damnable drifts, practized by three Witches arraigned at Chelmisforde in Essex* (London, 1579); *A Rehearsall both straung and true, of hainous and horrible actes committed by Elizabeth Stile, Alias Rockingham, Mother Dutten, Mother Devell, Mother Margaret, Fower notorious Witches, apprehended at winsore in the Countie of Barks* (London, 1579); W. W., *A true and iust Recorde, of the Information, Examination and Confession of all the Witches, taken at S. Oses in the countie of Essex: whereof some were executed, and other some entreated according to the determination of Lawe* (London, 1582); *The Apprehension and confession of three notorious Witches, Arreigned and by Justice condemned and executed at Chelms-forde* (London, 1589); and *The Witches of Northamptonshire . . . Who were all executed at Northampton* (London, 1612). These pamphlets are reprinted (some abridged, all with modernized spelling) in Rosen, *Witchcraft in England*. The pamphlet by W. W. about the St. Osyth witches is also available in a facsimile edition edited by Anthony Harris (Delmar, N.Y.: Scholars' Facsimiles and Reprints, 1981). In this chapter, when I quote material from these pamphlets I cite the Rosen anthology, except in the case of lengthy quotations from the pamphlet by W. W., which I quote from the facsimile edition.

6. Themes with which this chapter is especially concerned—of the witch's malevolent mothering and of women accusers preoccupied with issues related to the maternal role—are evident in Holmes, "Popular Culture?" Holmes, "Women"; and Gregory, "Witchcraft, Politics, and 'Good Neighborhood' "; and especially in Sharpe, *Witchcraft in Seventeenth-Century Yorkshire* and "Witchcraft and Women."

A Detection
of damnable driftes, practi-
zed by three VVitches arraigned at
Chelmissforde in Essex, at the
laste Assises there holden, whiche
were executed in Apꝛill.
1 5 7 9.

Set foꝛthe to discouer the Ambushementes of
Sathan, whereby he would surpꝛise vs
lulled in securitie, and hardened
with contempte of Gods
vengeance thꝛeatened
foꝛ our offences.

Imprinted at London for Edward White,
at the little North-dore of Paules.

Figure 1.   Title page from *A Detection of damnable driftes* (1579), STC 5115,
by permission of The British Library.

under her breath. Later, some misfortune happened to the neighbor or her family. A child fell sick, a wife or husband died, cattle or sheep died, a freak storm destroyed the crops, the milk went sour, the butter would not turn. The neighbor recalled the cursing of the old woman and suspected the misfortune was the product of her witchcraft.

What happened next? There were several possibilities. The neighbor might appeal to one of the local "cunning folk" to confirm the diagnosis of witchcraft, identify the witch, and procure some form of countermagic to "undo" the witch's maleficium. The neighbor might turn to the church or to prayer. She might also try to appease the witch in some way. Or she might try any combination of these. Such were the major remedies available to villagers throughout the Middle Ages and into the Renaissance. But after the passage of anti-witchcraft laws, the neighbor might also appeal to the local justice of the peace—that is, she might inform against the suspected witch. The justice might then open an inquiry and interview other informants. A grand jury would determine whether indictments should be handed down and a trial held. If so, the accused witch was on her way to imprisonment, execution, or if she was lucky, acquittal. The trial itself functioned as a kind of countermagic, with judges and jury taking over some aspects of the role of the cunning folk: the witch's exposure and forced confession also dissolved her magical powers.

What did it take to convict and sentence to death someone accused of witchcraft? It was not usually possible to catch the witch in the act of practicing her art; instead, the gathering weight of circumstantial evidence determined the fate of the accused. Reports of her curses and angry words, followed in a timely fashion by misfortunes, were key items of circumstantial evidence leading to indictment. But other factors provided valuable support, such as sightings of small animals (cats, weasels, ferrets, dogs, frogs, toads, "imps") around her home or in her vicinity, accounts of visions or dreams in which the accused appeared to the victim or the victim's relatives, and deathbed identifications of the witch. By the time a woman was brought to trial, she had already developed a reputation for troublesome behavior and hostility toward her neighbors, and she was suspected of having practiced maleficium for many years. Indictment was most likely when she was "notoriously defamed" by her neighbors and a number of "the better sort" came forward to testify against her.[7] The

---

7. *The Work of William Perkins*, ed. Ian Breward (Appleford, England: Sutton Courtney Press, 1970), p. 602.

death penalty would typically be applied when she was convicted of using her magic to cause a human death. Once an investigation was under way, the accused woman's body would be examined for the devil's mark or "teat." Any unusual fleshy protuberance, especially one in a "private place," would be taken as further confirmation of the charge of witchcraft. Finally, a confession (extracted under duress but seldom torture) would help to seal the witch's fate.

It is possible that the behavior that focused suspicion on a particular individual was more likely to be exhibited by a woman than by a man. Was it the woman's role in sixteenth-century village communities to go to neighbors with requests for food or other items? Were they more likely to become dependent on resentful neighbors as they aged? Were they more likely to indulge in verbal abuse or to resort to harmful magic when they became involved in a quarrel? Men had alternatives not available to women: they could take up the sword or go to court with their grievances. Even approximate statistics for such matters are not easy to come by, but anecdotal evidence suggests that men also asked to borrow items from neighbors; they too could be poor and downwardly mobile; they too uttered curses and practiced many types of magic. That women might be more likely to fall into at least some of these categories is probable; yet such factors, taken by themselves, seem insufficient to explain women's near monopoly on the witch's role.

Another approach to explaining the witch's gender is suggested by the witch stereotype itself, which associates the practice of harmful magic with misdirected nurture. Although popular beliefs do not assume the witch must be biologically female, they do represent the witch in terms of the maternal. The mark or teat that confirms her as a witch is also the means by which she acquires her demonic power; it is in effect a third nipple by which she feeds her familiars, or "imps"—the demonic spirits who inhabit the bodies of small animals and help her to carry out her magic. The witch, moreover, is older, usually postmenopausal; her body—already a source of anxiety—in effect encodes maternal rejection of the human child.[8] Her womb no longer fertile, her breasts no longer

8. Even a critic of witchcraft beliefs such as Reginald Scot is willing to lend some credence to the notion of the "evil" or "witching eye," relating it to the bodily state of postmenopausal women. He describes the views of a number of authorities who believed the eyes can send a tangible power or "vapor" to infect others with the diseases or corruption of their own blood. "Old women," he says, "in whome the ordinarie course of nature faileth in the office of purging their naturall monethlie humors, shew also some proofe hereof. For . . . they leave in a looking glasse a certeine froth, by meanes of the grosse vapors

capable of producing milk, she nevertheless can feed and care for a counterfamily of demonic imps. Her witchcraft is frequently directed against the children of her neighbors and almost always against domestic activities associated with feeding, nurture, or birth. When animals rather than people are targets of the witch's magic, cattle and the milk they produce are especially likely to be affected.

Village-level witchcraft beliefs encode a fantasy of the witch as a mother with two aspects. She is a nurturing mother to her brood of demonic imps but a malevolent antimother to her neighbors and their children. Over and over again in the trial records, the accused women are addressed as "Mother"—Mother Grevell, Mother Turner, Mother Dutten, Mother Devell, Mother Stile—following everyday village convention.[9] These women continue to be associated with the social role of mother even after they have aged and their own children are grown. And if we read the "confessions" of women accused of witchcraft as to some degree revealing beliefs they, or others, may have actually held and enacted, it is possible that these women find in their supernatural children—who are fed blood of the witch's body as well as human food, wrapped in wool and tucked into pots to sleep for the night, fussed over and called pet names—substitutes who fill the gaps left by the earthly children they no longer have to care for. At the same time, however, the witch is a monstrous mother to her neighbors. She uses her maternal powers perversely, to enlist the aid of the demonic in bringing sickness and death to the households of other mothers, in defiance of her neighborly obligations.

To a large extent, the witch's symmetrical opposite in the village community can be thought of as the "gossip"—a word derived from godpar-

---

proceeding out of their eies. Which commeth so to passe, bicause those vapors or spirits, which so abundantlie come from their eies, cannot pearse and enter into the glasse, which is hard, and without pores, and therefore resisteth: but the beames which are carried . . . from the eies of one bodie to another, doo pearse to the inward parts, and there breed infection, whilest they search and seek for their proper region. And as these beames & vapors doo proceed from the hart of the one, so are they turned into bloud about the hart of the other: which bloud disagreeing with the nature of the bewitched partie, infeebleth the rest of his bodie, and maketh him sicke" (*The Discoverie of Witchcraft*, ed. Hugh Ross Williamson [1584; Carbondale: Southern Illinois University Press, 1964], p. 399). The old woman's body is a site of contagion because it is presumed to be the site of too much unpurged bloud. Scot is quoting classical authorities, it should be added, not popular belief; the "evil eye" does not seem to be a factor in English trials. But his willingness to entertain such views suggests that even an educated, skeptical Englishman could be prone to a profound suspicion of the postmenopausal female body.

9. Ewen, *Witchcraft and Demonianism*, pp. 154, 158, 159.

ent and still related to that more specialized role.[10] The gossip was the female neighbor called in to assist at childbirth and during the "lying in" period, a "nurturing neighbor" who acted as midwife and helped to care for her neighbor's children, who participated in an informal village network in which women offered each other aid and advice about child care, sickness, and other areas of domestic management. These women were mothers in several senses: they "mothered" each other, they mirrored each other as mothers, and they acted as substitute mothers for each other's children. The aid and advice they offered each other could involve magic—midwifery, for example, included a range of magical techniques for helping ensure the safety of mother and child during the difficult time of childbirth. But midwives could use their magic to cause miscarriage or injury to mother and child, just as other gossips might seek to harm instead of help. The witch was in a sense the gossip "gone bad," a woman who brought envy, anger, and hatred into a community's informal networks of female neighbors.[11] She used her mothering powers to betray other mothers.

Such beliefs seem driven in part by women's anxieties about situations in which they or their children were especially vulnerable and over which they had little control. It is clear, at any rate, that women were actively involved in making witchcraft accusations against their female neighbors. Macfarlane finds that as many women as men informed against witches

10. Fairy tales in which the witch is set against the fairy godmother have an obvious relevance here.

11. Michael Macdonald's study of the seventeenth-century physician Richard Napier, whose patients included over a hundred who suspected they had been bewitched, provides some suggestive evidence. Macdonald's exploration of these cases led him to criticize Macfarlane's emphasis on the failure to give alms as a source of witchcraft quarrels. "The [witchcraft] allegations Napier's clients made were occasioned by a wider range of social and personal obligations than almsgiving," he notes. "The most interesting of these concerned the custom of inviting village women to assist at a childbirth. . . . When birth was at hand, village women were invited to attend. The importance contemporaries attached to these displays of feminine solidarity is plain. The law prevented midwives from delivering babies without other women present; women whose travails had been marred by strife were said to have consequently gone mad. Mary Aussoppe became anxious and utterly depressed after a disgruntled neighbor cursed her during her labor. The woman burst into the house, fell to her knees and 'prayed unto God that Mary Aussoppe might never have herself [i.e., be at peace]. . . . The plague of God light upon her, and all the plagues in hell light upon her.' Five of Napier's clients thought that women whom they had not invited to their deliveries had bewitched them: Participation in this feminine rite was an essential duty and privilege of village women, and omitted neighbors had reason to be angry" (*Mystical Bedlam: Madness, Anxiety, and Healing in Seventeenth-Century England* [Cambridge: Cambridge University Press, 1981], pp. 108–9).

in the 291 Essex cases he studied; about 55 percent of those who believed they had been bewitched were female.[12] The number of witchcraft quarrels that began between women may actually have been higher; in some cases, it appears that the husband as "head of household" came forward to make statements on behalf of his wife, although the central quarrel had taken place between her and another woman. In the 1581 St. Osyth trials, for example, in which indictments were handed down against at least twelve witches, two-thirds of the quarrels described involved women.[13] Husbands were the named informants for wives' quarrels in about six cases. It may, then, be misleading to equate "informants" with "accusers": the person who gave a statement to authorities was not necessarily the person directly quarreling with the witch. Other studies support a figure in the range of 60 percent. In Peter Rushton's examination of slander cases in the Durham church courts, women took action against other women who had labeled them witches in 61 percent of the cases. Ronald Sawyer's study of the medical practice of Richard Napier shows that, among those patients who thought themselves bewitched, 59.3 percent were women. J. A. Sharpe also notes the prevalence of women as accusers in seventeenth-century Yorkshire cases, concluding that "on a village level witchcraft seems to have been something peculiarly enmeshed in women's quarrels."[14] To a considerable extent, then, village-level witch-hunting was women's work.

Given the fragmentary nature of the trial records, it is difficult to reconstruct the series of events that brought a woman to accuse her neighbor. It is clear, however, not only that many quarrels involved women but also that female networks of shared mothering involved competition and conflict as well as mutual support. For example, take the case of Cicely Celles. In one informant's statement she is seen "chiding and railing" at another woman who has been engaged to replace Cicely as a wet nurse

---

12. Macfarlane, *Witchcraft*, pp. 160–61.

13. According to my reading of the statements, sixteen quarrels took place between women; five between a woman and an accusing male-female couple; nine between a woman and an accusing man. See W. W., *A true and iust Recorde*.

14. See Peter Rushton, "Women, Witchcraft, and Slander in Early Modern England: Cases from the Church Courts of Durham, 1560–1675," *Northern History* 18 (1982): 116–32; Ronald C. Sawyer, " 'Strangely Handled in All Her Lyms': Witchcraft and Healing in Jacobean England," *Journal of Social History* 22 (Spring 1989): 461–85; Sharpe, *Witchcraft in Seventeenth-Century Yorkshire*, p. 18. Sharpe develops this point more fully in his article "Witchcraft and Women." Macfarlane's findings also suggest that most witch-finders were women. *Witchcraft*, p. 127.

for a neighbor's child. "Thou shalt loose more by the having of it, than thou shalt have for the keeping of it," Cicely predicted ominously; within a month, the neighbor's own four-year-old daughter was dead.[15] In another statement, Cicely was involved in an incident with a young mother who was preparing to go to church with her new baby. Several women, including Cicely, gathered around. After the other "gossips" cooed over the baby and complimented it, Cicely uttered a dark prediction: the child would die soon, and the mother would never bear another. And indeed, a short time later, the child died.[16] The mother, however, refused to accuse Cicely of witchcraft, instead praying God to forgive Cicely if she had "dealt in any such sort." But the husband of the woman who replaced Cicely as wet nurse was not so forbearing. He came forward to accuse Cicely of causing the death of his young daughter, and it was for this death that she was indicted, along with her husband, for witchcraft. Her husband was acquitted, but Cicely, though eventually reprieved, was convicted and sentenced to death.

As these examples suggest, the witch had much in common with the shrew and the scold. Such village "types," objects of informal social control as well as legal regulation, indicate the high anxieties aroused by women's tongues, especially when exercised in anger and directed against husbands.[17] The ideal wife, in the male view, was "silent but for the Word" or had a voice that was "ever soft and low." But the witch directed her angry words especially at other women, and the level of verbal violence could reach alarming proportions when one woman vilified another for her neighborly failings. One vivid example of an accused woman's verbal violence was recorded by Sir Thomas Smith, a judge who presided over several early witch trials, including that of Anne Vicars in 1570:

Another woman of Stapleford Abbots said, that about three years past she was coming from Rumford market with this Anne Vicars, and suddenly the said Anne cast up her nose into the air and smelt; which the other marvelled at, and

15. W. W., *A true and iust Recorde*, sig. D8v. For abstracts of the documents connected to this case, see Ewen, *Witchcraft and Demonianism*, pp. 155, 162–63.

16. W. W., *A true and iust Recorde*, sig. D3. The incident recalls the christening scene in "Sleeping Beauty."

17. For attitudes toward shrews and scolds, see especially Lynda E. Boose, "Scolding Brides and Bridling Scolds: Taming the Woman's Unruly Member," *Shakespeare Quarterly* 42 (Summer 1991): 179–213; and D. E. Underdown, "The Taming of the Scold: the Enforcement of Patriarchal Authority in Early Modern England," in *Order and Disorder in Early Modern England*, ed. Anthony Fletcher and John Stevenson (Cambridge: Cambridge University Press, 1985), pp. 116–36.

asked her if she saw any thing, or if there were any carrion there? And she said, she smelt either a whore or a thief. At last she espied the wife of one Ingarsole, going a great way before them: whereat the said Vicars cried out with an oath, "I told you, I smelt either a whore or a thief;" and making great haste to overtake her, when she came at her, she cast her apron upon the side of her face next unto her; and then went backwards a great way, with her face towards the said Ingarsole's wife, casting her apron over it, and making many crosses, saying, as it were, certain prayers; but what, this examinant could not tell; but marvelled much at her behaviour, and said she was to blame to slander her that was an honest woman, and so known among her neighbours for twenty years. But upon this, Ingarsole's wife fell extremely sick, and lost one of her eyes with a stroke, as she thought, that came unto her, she could not tell how, in the plain field, where neither was bush nor tree, or other creature.[18]

It is impossible to tell if Anne was in fact casting a spell upon Ingarsole's wife. Did the wife have a guilty conscience about some past indiscretion which manifested itself as a psychosomatic "stroke" in response to Anne's "slander"? The incident suggests, among other things, how easy it might be to confuse verbal violence with the casting of a spell, and clearly such bitter personal attacks were capable of generating intense emotional reactions whether or not magic was suspected.

In "chiding and railing" at her female neighbor, Cicely Celles was not directly violating gender hierarchy. Nor was the accuser playing a primarily "male-identified" role, compliantly enforcing a patriarchal model of feminine behavior, as Christina Larner, Catherine Belsey, and others have suggested.[19] The witch, in fact, was as likely to be the one urging

18. John Strype, *The Life of Sir Thomas Smith* (Oxford: Clarendon Press, 1820), p. 99. For some other examples of the witch's verbal (and even physical) violence, see Rosen, *Witchcraft*, pp. 144, 155.

19. Belsey explains women's frequent appearance as accusers by paraphrasing Larner: "Witches were, as their appearance tended to demonstrate, 'unwomanly.' . . . As Larner points out, other women were as readily offended as men, because women who conformed to the requirements of patriarchy felt threatened by its repudiation" (*The Subject of Tragedy*, p. 187). The example from *The Witches of Northamptonshire* used by Belsey in illustration rests on what appears to be the pamphlet writer's interpretation, and even he puts things in more equivocal terms: the series of events that led to Mistress Belcher's witchcraft accusation against Joan Vaughn began when Joan "whether of purpose to give occasion of anger to the said Mistress Belcher, or but to continue her vile and ordinary custom of behavior, committed something either in speech or gesture so unfitting and unseeming the nature of womanhood that it displeased the most that were there present" (Rosen, *Witchcraft*, p. 345). Belsey quotes only the last half of the passage. It is not clear from the pamphlet if Joan and Mistress Belcher had a history of friction, but it does seem clear that Joan insulted Mistress Belcher as well as violated standards of proper feminine behavior.

conformity to a patriarchal standard: her angry words might call into question her neighbor's credentials as a nurturer or stress some other failure of female identity. The accuser might in turn become as angry and sharp-tongued as the witch herself, defaming her as a perverse and destructive mother. Patriarchy helped to shape the terms of these quarrels: in a culture where women's value was crucially determined by their ability to bear children and nurture others, women readily perceived their own prestige and access to power as dependent on their performance as mothers and domestic workers.[20] Women's conflicts circulated in and through narcissitically charged objects closely associated with the maternal function—children, hens, butter, cows, milk, and so forth—and women competed with other women in a world where priorities were set largely by men. But these quarrels also enacted women's strategies for empowerment within patriarchal culture. Moreover, quarrels were used to negotiate what women wanted and needed *from one another*, not merely what men wanted from them. As quarrels played themselves out, village women tested and redefined the limits of acceptable female anger, sanctioning some forms of expression and punishing others, distinguishing excessive demands from reasonable requests.

Through reciprocal acts of defamation, women participated in a larger rhythm of early modern life: the English village could be a highly fractious place.[21] While neighborly cooperation made mutual survival possi-

20. On the centrality of maternity to early modern women's identity, see, among others, Cahn, *Industry of Devotion*, pp. 94–108, 178–81: "Maternity, of course, was important for all social classes, not just the aristocracy. The aspect of maternity that all classes most valued was fertility—the ability to conceive live infants" (p. 94); also Patricia Crawford, "The Construction and Experience of Maternity in Seventeenth-Century England," in *Women as Mothers in Pre-industrial England: Essays in Memory of Dorothy McLaren*, ed. Valerie Fildes (London: Routledge, 1990), p. 19: "When a couple was childless, this was usually considered to be the wife's 'fault.' A childless woman was labelled a barren woman. . . . Barren wives lacked social status and respect, and the higher their social position, the unhappier was their lot." Moreover, as housewife and domestic manager, a woman was expected to nurture adults as well as children. "Both men and women regarded the care of children, the preparation of meals, and the nursing of the ill as exclusively the woman's duty," according to Katherine Usher Henderson and Barbara F. McManus, *Half Humankind: Contexts and Texts of the Controversy about Women in England, 1540–1640* (Urbana: University of Illinois Press, 1985), p. 63. Women's agricultural work also tended to link them to the maternal function: milking cows, caring for hens, attending to the birth of livestock.

21. Amussen, *An Ordered Society*, pp. 134–79; Anthony Fletcher, "Honour, Reputation, and Local Officeholding in Elizabethan and Stuart England," in *Order and Disorder in Early Modern England*, ed. Anthony Fletcher and John Stevenson (Cambridge: Cambridge University Press, 1985), pp. 92–115; Martin Ingram, *Church Courts, Sex, and Mar-*

ble, neighborly disagreements of many sorts and competition over everything from local officeholding to seating in church regularly provoked insults, quarrels, brawls, lawsuits, hurt feelings. Informing much of this competitiveness was an intense concern with social position: to maintain or—better yet—to improve one's standing in the community required constant exertion. In theory one was "born" to a particular station in life, but in fact, one's situation was far more precarious. Social identity was determined by factors such as wealth, conduct, and accomplishment, as well as "birth" and kin relations, and no real consensus existed on the relative importance of different factors.[22] As a result one's position was often in flux and open to contestation, as one's wealth and "reputation" ebbed and flowed.

What was true of villages, moreover, was replicated at higher social levels. The honor quarrels of aristocrats, duels, blood feuds, "faction" at court, and treason trials offer further testimony of the fractiousness of early modern English society as well as the overriding importance of "reputation." All classes had a long tradition of using aggression as a means of resolving disputes over status and position. A slight to one's reputation had to be met with some form of action to repair it. At the same time, forces were at work to keep that aggression from turning into open violence. In the sixteenth century, state and religious authorities took steps to curb brawling and dueling and to discourage blood feuds.[23] Litigation offered an attractive alternative. Slander suits, common already at the beginning of the century, increased considerably after 1560, as people took to both secular and ecclesiastical courts to clear their good names.

---

riage in England, 1570–1640 (Cambridge: Cambridge University Press, 1987), pp. 29–34, 304–19; J. A. Sharpe, *Defamation and Sexual Slander in Early Modern England: The Church Courts at York*, Borthwick Papers No. 58 (York: University of York, 1980); Keith Wrightson, "Two Concepts of Order: Justices, Constables, and Jurymen in Seventeenth-Century England," in *An Ungovernable People: The English and Their Law in the Seventeenth and Eighteenth Centuries*, ed. John Brewer and John Styles (London: Hutchinson, 1980).

22. On the complexity of rank and status and the ambiguity of social identity, see Amussen, *An Ordered Society*, pp. 137–51; Ruth Kelso, *The Doctrine of the English Gentleman in the Sixteenth Century* (Gloucester, Mass.: Peter Smith, 1964); Keith Wrightson, *English Society, 1580–1680* (New Brunswick, N.J.: Rutgers University Press, 1982), pp. 17–38; Joyce Youings, *Sixteenth-Century England* (Harmondsworth: Penguin, 1984), pp. 110–29.

23. For references regarding the honor quarrels of the upper classes and the measures taken by the central government to curb them, see Chapter 5, notes 24 and 25.

Among these suits, those brought by women against other women made up a large percentage of the total—evidence, again, of the conflictual aspects of women's relationships.[24] Both witchcraft trials and slander suits show that women shared in the culture-wide obsession with reputation, displaying much the same sensitivity to slights as men. Both originated in quarrels and reciprocal defamation, which played out complex struggles to control the signifying practices that determined social identity and power. At the same time, there were important differences. Slander cases regularly focused on women's sexual behavior: the defendant in a slander suit had called another woman dishonest, a base quean, an arrant whore. Witchcraft cases focused on what I am calling neighborly nurture.[25] The witch's words generally involved a threat as well as an insult. The female defendant convicted in a slander suit was required to perform public penance or pay money damages. The convicted witch was imprisoned or executed.

Most important, witchcraft quarrels produced not only insults and anger but also anxiety, visions, "fits," fears of magical harm. More than a contest over social categories was involved. Thomas and Macfarlane contend that the anxieties generated in the course of a witchcraft quarrel arose from the conflict between "neighborliness" and "individualism." As they see it, an accusation of witchcraft was fueled by the guilt a neighbor experienced and simultaneously resisted after denying another neighbor's request for help. This denial constituted an "individualistic" transgression of traditional codes of communal sharing.[26] Guilt manifested itself in the

24. For women's slander suits against other women, see especially Amussen, *An Ordered Society*, pp. 101–4; Ingram, *Church Courts*, pp. 302–3; and Laura Gowing, "Gender and the Language of Insult in Early Modern London," *History Workshop* 35 (Spring 1993): 1–21. Gowing's essay focuses on gender differences in the language of insult but, in the process, also makes it clear that, like the female accuser of a witch, the woman who called another woman "whore" was not merely mouthing patriarchal injunctions against improper female conduct but might be involved in a complex battle to control her own environment. Defaming someone for "loose" behavior was one of the only ways a wife could take action against another woman's adulterous relationship with her husband, and the "whore" might threaten not only to alienate a husband's affections but also to drain money from the household and disrupt family life.

25. To be sure, there is an area of overlap here. Sometimes women used slander suits to defend themselves against charges of witchcraft, and in the course of a witchcraft quarrel, either party might call the other a whore. For slander suits involving a charge of witchcraft, see Ingram, *Church Courts*, pp. 298, 300; Rushton, "Women, Witchcraft, and Slander"; Sharpe, *Witchcraft in Seventeenth-Century Yorkshire*. For cases in which the accused witch was called a whore or loose woman, see Rosen, *Witchcraft*, pp. 115, 150, 185.

26. Macfarlane, *Witchcraft*, pp. 192–98; Thomas, *Religion*, pp.552–69.

apparently psychosomatic illnesses that sometimes befell victims and in the dreams and visions sometimes experienced by the accusers or their families. It manifested itself especially in the accusers' habitual interpretation of subsequent misfortunes as retaliation for the injury to the refused neighbor.

Thomas and Macfarlane cast the accusing neighbor in the role of "individualist" and the witch as the defender of older norms of "neighborliness" in place before the Protestant Reformation and the sixteenth-century poor laws. But in the quarrels involving Cicely Celles, for example, it is difficult to see what norm of neighborliness her opponents would feel they were violating. Quarrels could begin when the accused refused to pay a debt, when she wanted to buy goods at too low a price, when she trespassed on a neighbor's land.[27] Moreover, one could be unneighborly by asking for too much as well as by giving too little; in several cases, in fact, informants drew attention to the excessive expectations of the accused.[28] Neighborliness required courtesy and a certain balance in exchanges, not just one-way giving. Accusers did sometimes retrospectively come to view their actions as lacking in charity, but in many quarrels the situation was far more ambiguous.[29]

27. The accused witches Agnes Herd and Joan Robinson both owed money to their accusers. See Rosen, *Witchcraft*, pp. 147–49, 156. On another occasion, Agnes Herd refused to return a dish she had borrowed (p. 147). Cicely Celles wouldn't meet Richard Ross's price for malt (p. 132) and the Celleses' cattle trespassed on the Rosses' grounds (p. 132). In such situations, the witch seems arguably as "unneighborly" as her neighbor, if not more so.

28. Macfarlane mentions a few cases in which informants suggested that they might have been too stingy with the witch. Others, however, suggested a history of generous giving which informants felt the witch had not sufficiently appreciated. According to an ostler's testimony, Mother Stile, "using to come to his master's house, had oftentimes relief given her by him. And on a time not long since she coming to his master's house when there was little left to be given her, for that she came somewhat late, yet he giving her also somewhat at that time, she therewith not contented went her ways in some anger and, as it seemed, offended with the said ostler for that she had no better alms" (Rosen, *Witchcraft*, p. 89). Mother Staunton "came often to the house of one John Hopwood of Walden, and had continually her requests. At the last, being denied of a leathern thong, she went her way offended" (p. 98). Joan Pechey became angry when the collector for the poor gave her bread that "was too hard baked for her" (p. 110).

29. Some cases, I should also add, do suggest the accuser's abuse of the woman accused. My point here is not that accusers never experienced "real" guilt for their actions. Anxiety symptoms can look the same whether "real" guilt or unconscious fantasy or—most likely— some combination of the two is causing them. But historians and critics should avoid routinely reading such symptoms as the product of guilt for actual wrongdoing, especially when many cases suggest that in the original quarrel, the accused is at least as out of line as the accuser. And feminists should avoid automatically reading accusers' responses as knee-jerk

Such cases suggest a more complex dynamic was at work than Thomas and Macfarlane's formulation allows for. Neighborliness involved more than an obligation to give alms, and violating its codes was unlikely to be the sole cause of guilt.[30] Conflicts over neighborliness could become intertwined with gender issues; both the witch and her female accuser stood in an uneasy relation not only to ideals of neighborly conduct but also to definitions of female identity which privileged nurturing behavior and well-governed speech. But witchcraft quarrels undoubtedly had an intrapsychic dimension as well as an interpersonal one: the social factors offer only a partial insight into the fears, anxieties, and resentments that shaped particular experiences of bewitchment and motivated accusations. Psychoanalytic theory can supplement social history and cultural analysis, enabling us to better understand the emotional dynamics of accusers' illnesses, visions, and interpretations of misfortune.

The accuser felt anxiety and feared retaliation after a quarrel with her neighbor, I believe, not so much because she had violated the code of neighborliness as because she had injured a body unconsciously associated with the mother of childhood. The accuser confronted in her neighbor a woman of her own or her mother's generation whom she addressed as "Mother" and who was associated with the quasi-maternal "gossips" to whom she turned for help and advice. But instead of offering support, the older woman required it for herself. Generally, her age and social circumstances were making her more dependent on her neighbors and less able to participate in the reciprocal exchanges that made for good relations between them. At the same time, her requests for help were often expressed as demands and she became angry and difficult when refused, murmuring against her neighbor if not cursing her outright. She was needy but also anger-provoking. Many in her community may have been content to put up with her: whether

---

conformity to patriarchal constraints upon "woman's tongue." We need to acknowledge the emotional complexities of women's quarrels with one another (and the complexities of their power relations). Thomas and Macfarlane do, in fact, recognize that the "typical" witch is a woman with a difficult temper (as do Larner, Demos, and many other historians); what they don't do is take bad temper into account in their formulations about "neighborliness."

Judgments about individual quarrels will remain open to interpretation, especially since the evidence is so fragmentary. Some cases do suggest verbal violence is coming more from the accuser than the accused. See Rosen, *Witchcraft*, pp. 117, 131, also 122. My overall impression is that in most of the cases in this period "blame" was mixed, that is, the accuser was both justifiably and unjustifiably angry with the witch and (I suspect) had trouble distinguishing the two; hence the ambivalence encoded in subsequent responses.

30. On the ambiguity of "neighborliness," see especially Wrightson, *English Society*, pp. 51–57.

refusing or extending help, they afterward thought no more about it; she was a scold or a nuisance but not a witch capable of magical harm. But other neighbors felt increasingly threatened by her sinister presence and suspected her of causing their misfortunes. Such neighbors—the old woman's future accusers—may have unconsciously experienced their own anger as a form of magical attack, giving them reason to fear magical retaliation.

The selection of a particular woman as a witch thus depended not only on behavior of the accused and its social meanings but, even more decisively, on the type of intrapsychic conflict the quarrel aroused in the accuser. Many, if not most, "difficult" older women were not thought of as witches: magical endangerment was at least partly in the mind of the beholder. The work of Melanie Klein and those who have built on it seems especially suggestive with regard to the accuser's experience of magical persecution in the course of a witchcraft quarrel.[31]

31. For Klein's collected work, see *The Writings of Melanie Klein*, ed. Roger Money-Kyrle et al., 4 vols. (London: Hogarth Press, 1975). For an introduction to her work, see Phyllis Grosskurth, *Melanie Klein: Her World and Her Work* (New York: Knopf, 1986); Hanna Segal, *Introduction to the Work of Melanie Klein* (London: Hogarth Press, 1973); and R. D. Hinshelwood, A *Dictionary of Kleinian Thought* (London: Free Association Books, 1991). For a selection of significant writings, see *The Selected Melanie Klein*, ed. Juliet Mitchell (New York: Free Press, 1987). For one attempt to adapt Klein's thought for social theory, see C. Fred Alford, *Melanie Klein and Critical Social Theory* (New Haven: Yale University Press, 1989).

Klein's work has been influential in the American and British psychoanalytic communities, though not without criticism and revision. Grosskurth's biography traces Klein's conflicts with Freud, Anna Freud, and others during her lifetime. For a guide to more recent controversies, see Phyllis Tyson and Robert L. Tyson, *Psychoanalytic Theories of Development: An Integration* (New Haven: Yale University Press, 1990), pp. 71–74. D. W. Winnicott, Otto Kernberg, and Margaret Mahler, among others, have been important revisers of her work. The continuing dialogue between Kleinian and other psychoanalytic theorists is evident in such articles as Howard B. Levine, "Freudian and Kleinian Theory: A Dialogue of Comparative Perspectives," *Journal of the American Psychoanalytic Association* 40 (1992): 801–26; and Joseph Sandler, "On Internal Object Relations," *Journal of the American Psychoanalytic Association* 39 (1991): 859–79. Feminists have increasingly engaged with her work. See Juliet Mitchell's Introduction to *The Selected Melanie Klein*; Nancy Chodorow, *Feminism and Psychoanalytic Theory* (New Haven: Yale University Press, 1989), pp. 199–218; Doane and Hodges, *From Klein to Kristeva*; Claire Kahane, "Questioning the Maternal Voice," *Genders* 3 (Fall 1988): 82–91; Susan Rubin Suleiman, "On Maternal Splitting: A Propos of Mary Gordon's *Men and Angels*," *Signs* 14 (Autumn 1988): 25–42; Ann Scott, "Melanie Klein and the Questions of Feminism," *Woman: A Cultural Review* 1 (November 1990): 127–34; this issue was entirely devoted to appraisals of Klein's work. "Womanliness as a Masquerade," an essay that has significantly influenced feminist film criticism, is by Joan Riviere, a Kleinian analyst (reprinted in *Formations of Fantasy*, ed. Victor Burgin et al. [London: Methuen, 1986], pp. 35–61). An important earlier feminist text influenced by Klein is Dorothy Dinnerstein, *The Mermaid and the Minotaur* (New York: Harper and Row, 1976), esp. pp. 91–114.

Her theoretical formulations and clinical findings often focus on the persecutory fantasies of infants and young children, fantasies that reappeared also in the analyses of some adults, taking forms that eerily parallel many witchcraft beliefs. While it is risky to apply theories derived from clinical work with twentieth-century subjects to the early modern period, the parallels seem striking enough to warrant further exploration.

For Klein, persecutory anxiety has origins in infancy and early childhood, when the growing child experiences inevitable frustrations and must learn to cope with feelings of anger and aggression toward the mother (or other caretakers). At this early stage of development, the child is still dominated by primary-process modes of thinking and conflates angry wishes with destructive acts; at the same time, the mother is experienced as having extraordinary, seemingly omnipotent powers. Also referred to as "magical thinking," primary-process modes of cognition should not automatically be equated with the magical beliefs of the early modern or premodern periods. Such culturally legitimated magical beliefs organize and in various ways revise childhood perceptions, bringing them into line with "adult" cognitive processes. The young child, for example, at first equates almost any wish with an act, only slowly learning to separate internal from external reality. For the early modern magical practitioner, however, wishes only became acts under certain conditions or after following special procedures—rituals, incantations, manipulations of image or word.

Nevertheless, such beliefs could allow anxieties about hostile feelings toward one's caretakers to persist into adulthood, tacitly confirming the child's notion that angry thoughts can cause damage to loved ones or bring on other misfortunes. Klein's clinical work led her to conclude that the fear of magically damaging the mother was a crucial factor in the formation of persecutory anxiety. When a child experiences its hostile fantasies about the mother as actually injuring or destroying her, the child often comes to fear that the mother will retaliate in kind.

Among little girls in particular, Klein found, the "leading female anxiety situation" occurs when "the mother is felt to be the primary persecutor who, as an external and internalized object, attacks the child's body and takes from it her imaginary children. These anxieties arise from the girl's phantasied attacks on the mother's body, which aim at robbing her of its contents . . . and result in the fear of retaliation by similar attacks."[32] At first the child copes with its hostile feelings by splitting mental representations of the mother into "good" and "bad," one to be loved, the other to be hated with impunity. But sooner or later, the growing child recognizes that the "good" and "bad" mothers are really aspects of the same person; angry feelings then endanger the mother who is loved and depended on. Under "good enough" conditions, the child learns to tolerate ambivalence about the mother, to view her on a more human scale and make reparation for the injuries (real and imagined) done to her, and to integrate the internalized "good" and "bad" representations of her which form the basis for the adult superego. But for some this integration may be only partly successful; a variety of factors may mean that even as adults they will have difficulty tolerating ambivalence about the women they place in the position of mother and will be vulnerable to inner persecution from an aspect of the superego which embodies an "attacked and therefore frightening mother."[33] When provoked into anger and unconscious destructive fantasy by those associated with the mother, the vulnerable adult may again resort to splitting in an attempt to protect the internalized mother from damage, projecting her "bad" aspects onto "other" women, who resemble the mother but need not be protected. The woman who comes to represent this split-off "bad" mother will be experienced as a persecutor, poised to retaliate in response to the initial attack.

Klein links the child's hostile feelings and fantasies about the mother to envy. Envy is experienced as the child becomes increasingly aware of its

32. "The Psycho-analytic Play Technique: Its History and Significance," in *The Selected Melanie Klein*, p. 48. Note the flexible boundaries of the maternal body in the child's imagination: it may include not only what an adult understands to be "in" that body—breasts, breast milk, womb, etc.—but also things outside that body the mother is associated with or assumed to control, such as children.

33. Ibid., p. 49. For Kleinian and non-Kleinian psychoanalysis, the superego is to be considered not a unitary mental structure but the result of an ongoing series of internalizations at different developmental stages: what is referred to as a single entity may have both "primitive" (i.e., infantile) and "adult" features, and the rules, values, and prohibitions one internalizes will almost inevitably have some inconsistent or contradictory features. "Integration" is a relative term here (Tyson and Tyson, *Psychoanalytic Theories of Development*, pp. 207–27). It is also important to stress that for Kleinians the "mother" the child internalizes is not an accurate representation of the mother's actual behavior; rather, this representation will be affected ("distorted") by the child's level of cognitive and psychic development and the severity of the mother's imagined retaliation will be a function of the intensity of the child's rage. Nor is rage at the mother to be assumed to be the result of "bad mothering." To what extent and in what ways the mother's actual behavior participates in producing persecutory anxiety or a harsh superego is a complex question, the subject of debate within the psychoanalytic community.

dependence on a figure separate from itself; it is "a spoiling hostility at the realization that the source of life and goodness lies outside," leading the child to seek to appropriate the attributes of the mother it especially needs and desires and to fantasize about stealing and incorporating parts of her body.[34] Both boys and girls at first envy the breast, and envious, hostile fantasies about the mother along with the persecutory fears to which they give rise may become especially intense at the time of weaning.[35] Narcissistic wounds later in life may reactivate the sense of powerlessness and dependence associated with infantile envy in adults who have not securely established "narcissistic equilibrium."[36] Sensitive to external criticism, they may end up in what Kleinians identify as the "paranoid vicious circle." Prompted to angry fantasy and projection, the vulnerable adult becomes anxious about further attack by a persecutory figure, in what becomes an ever-escalating cycle of hostility and fear.[37]

Witchcraft quarrels resemble such vicious circles of escalating hostility and fear, and neighbors frequently seem to have been responding in the light of persecutory fantasy to the women they came to call witches. In the early stages of a quarrel, the accuser already saw the older woman as troublesome and intrusive. By gestures or speech—or perhaps merely by her neediness—the older woman implied criticism of her neighbor and

34. Hanna Segal, quoted in Hinshelwood, *A Dictionary of Kleinian Thought*, p. 357.

35. See Klein, "Weaning," in *Writings of Melanie Klein*, vol. 1. Early modern families may have intensified the child's experience of envy in a number of ways: the lack of alternatives to breast-feeding would have heightened the importance of the mother's breast; weaning, as Janet Adelman and Gail Paster have described it, could be an especially harrowing experience; and hierarchies within the family unit based on birth order and gender may have intensified sibling rivalry and competition for the mother. If Adelman (*Suffocating Mothers*, pp. 4–5) is right that early modern child-care practices tended to prolong infantile dependence in circumstances that heightened the child's experience of maternal deprivation, the child's envy of what the mother (or wet nurse) had and might take away would similarly have been heightened.

36. Not a Kleinian phrase; see Tyson and Tyson, *Psychoanalytic Theories of Development*, p. 111. My use of it perhaps indicates a non-Kleinian element in my argument; my emphasis on the narcissistic vulnerabilities of the participants in a witchcraft quarrel—so evident in the early modern sensitivity to slights—may be at odds with the Kleinian tendency to downplay "external reality." It may not be irrelevant that analysts of other theoretical orientations have criticized Kleinians for their insensitivity to the narcissistic vulnerability of patients. See Sidney Fine and Esther Fine, "Four Psychoanalytic Perspectives: A Study of Differences in Interpretive Interventions," *Journal of the American Psychoanalytic Association* 38 (1990): 1017–41.

37. Hinshelwood, *A Dictionary of Kleinian Thought*, p. 377. The paranoid vicious circle, though especially associated with the deep disturbances of psychotic adults, is also to be observed in milder, less pathological forms in children at a certain stage of development, neurotics, and the bereaved.

could easily be resented for setting an excessively high standard of neighborly nurture. The accuser's sensitivity to criticism would have been culturally reinforced by the great stress placed on "reputation" at all social levels. But for those especially vulnerable, the quarrel could set in motion a darker complex of feeling, reviving in the unconscious hostile fantasies about the envied, omnipotent mother and mobilizing fears of her magical retaliation. Such fantasies, I suggest, are what gave these fears their specifically magical character, producing the phenomena contemporaries grouped under the term *bewitchment*.

When the accuser refused the old woman who came to her for food or help, she also replayed a hostile attack on the figure who gave her life, food, and support in childhood and who provided her with a basis for her own identity. The misfortunes construed as punishments for such refusals regularly involved the loss of things a child envies about the mother's body and believes she controls: milk, milk products, food, domestic items, birth, babies, children, husbands. Having injured the old woman, the accuser came to fear that her own extended maternal body was threatened by a mother far more powerful than herself.

The old woman's curse externalized those inner fears and put them into words. Refusals of help frequently prompted a threat to "get even" or an appeal to the vengeance of God.[38] The curse was itself an act of "notorious defamation," sometimes publicly humiliating to the accuser, who was wounded with words even before she was convinced of their magical power. Age, if not social position, gave the older woman who spoke those words some authority. Though not family or kin, she was nevertheless a potential member of the accuser's "extended family" of neighbors and friends. Because the older woman was neither inside nor fully outside the ambit of the accuser's affiliative networks, her angry words could be neither readily accepted nor wholly dismissed: they dramatized the ambiguity of neighborly obligation. It was the misfortune that followed the curse which turned the old woman into a witch, confirming the accuser's inner

38. Threats to "get even" or words to that effect were, for example, made by the accused witches Elizabeth Bennett, Anne Kerke, and Alice Trevisard; See Rosen, *Witchcraft*, p. 122; Ewen, *Witchcraft and Demonianism*, pp. 189, 194–95, 199. The wish that the "vengeance of God" be visited upon someone also seems to have been a fairly common expression. In George Gifford, *Dialogue concerning Witches and Witchcraftes* (London, 1593), one suspected witch is described as "wishing the vengeance of God to fall upon" her neighbor (p. E). Thomas Cooper, in his tract *The Mystery of Witchcraft* (1617), described the typical witch as "invocating on her bare knees (for so the manner is) the vengeance of God" upon her enemies. Quoted in Thomas, *Religion*, p. 512.

expectation of attack and calling into question her psychic and bodily boundaries—and those of her household as well. Once a curse seemed to "light," when it accurately predicted misfortune, it would be clear that the old woman had "forspoken" her neighbor—the supernatural equivalent of putting out a contract on one's gangland enemy. Imputed to her curse was the uncanny compelling power the child first imputes to its own anger and to its mother's words of reproof.

Before the curse took effect, the accuser might consciously feel the older woman was a "bad" mother who deserved to be rejected; unconsciously, however, she might also feel that she herself had injured the "good" mother of childhood. Ultimately, the accuser sensed the two were the same; to preserve her attachment to the "good" mother, she must accede to the "bad" mother's request or be overwhelmed by anxiety. Many of the physical ailments interpreted by accusers as bewitchment may have been anxiety related. The wife of Robert Cornell watched Mother Staunton draw a circle with a knife outside her door after being denied milk; the next day when Mrs. Cornell passed through that door, she was "taken sick, and began to swell from time to time as if she had been with child."[39] Mistress Belcher, after striking Joan Vaughn for publicly insulting her, at home that night was "suddenly taken with . . . a griping and gnawing in her body"; servants could scarcely hold her and get her into bed. Her face "was many times so disfigured by being drawn awry that it bred both fear and astonishment to all the beholders," and she continually cried out, "Here comes Joan Vaughan! Away with Joan Vaughan!"[40]

---

39. Rosen, *Witchcraft*, p. 97. A preoccupation with swelling is a theme in a number of cases; here it is explicitly linked with pregnancy. In other cases as well, swelling affecting both adults and children perhaps become attributed to witchcraft partly because of associations in children's fantasies with the mother's pregnant body. Strange swellings attributed to witchcraft also occurred in the course of food production, as when Edmund Osborne's wife, making beer after requesting that Agnes Herd pay a debt of three pence, found her mash "wrought up . . . a handbreadth above the vat and then sinked again; then she did heat an iron red hot and put the same into it and it rose up no more. And then she let go, and then she did seethe [boil] the wort [unfermented beer], and when it was sodden it stank in such sort as that they were compelled to put the same in the swill tub" (p. 150).

40. Rosen, *Witchcraft*, p. 346, and see 95, 150. One might add many more examples, including the possible epileptic fit of a young girl, brought on by Anne Kerke, in Ewen, *Witchcraft and Demonianism*, p. 189. Men also exhibit seemingly "hysterical" symptoms. Robert Sannever, for example, used "threatening words" to a servant of his (the daughter of a suspected witch), and found "his mouth drawn awry, well near up to the upper part of his cheek" (p. 130). A male servant of one Thomas Spicer offended Mother Nokes by taking the gloves of her daughter, "which he protesteth to have done in jest." When Mother Nokes asked him to return the gloves, he laughed and walked off to fetch home certain cattle.

Occasionally, ailments seem to encode attempts to "undo" the injury done to the witch; digestive disorders, for example, could be read as symbolic attempts to return food to the mother whom the child has deprived. After a quarrel, John Chandler "never ate any meat that digested in him, but ever it came up again as soon as it was down." The quarrel had been with his stepdaughter over some money she had received from her mother, a convicted witch (as well as his wife). His digestive ailment, perhaps, was the symbolic "undoing" of his attempt to deprive his stepdaughter of her mother's "food."[41]

But the largest number of witchcraft accusations were responses to misfortunes that must have had only a coincidental relation to the quarrel. Those misfortunes likely to be interpreted as the product of witchcraft affected those types of things over which the young child believes the

---

Mother Nokes then reportedly said to her daughter, "Let him alone, I will bounce him well enough," at which point the servant lost the use of his limbs and had to be sent home by his master in a wheelbarrow, where he lay in bed "with his legs across" at least eight days (pp. 98–99). Rosen comments that this is "a classic position of certain kinds of hysteria."

This particular story raises some interesting questions. Is the servant flirting with the daughter? If so, does the daughter welcome these attentions or resent them? Is the daughter testifying against her mother or is she being quoted by another source, perhaps the servant's master? The mother may be intervening to protect her daughter, or to control her; in either case, the servant has "injured" the mother by a sexual advance upon the daughter and is accordingly (self-)punished by his strange paralysis. John Demos's analysis of New England cases may be relevant here: he notes that males in young adulthood were especially vulnerable to bewitchment, and he relates this vulnerability to the conflicts over autonomy men often experienced at this stage of their lives. *Entertaining Satan*, pp. 156–57.

The most spectacular instances of apparently hysterical symptoms, however, are associated with cases of possession. In these, the witch's "victims" are usually (pre)adolescent girls. The Throckmorton children were one of several such cases in the 1590s to gain widespread public attention; they provided material for several pamphlets, among them *The most strange and admirable discoverie of the three Witches of Warboys, arraigned, convicted, and executed at the last Assizes at Huntington, for the bewitching of the five daughters of Robert Throckmorton Esquire, and divers other persons* (London, 1593), a substantial portion of which is included (along with related materials) in Rosen, *Witchcraft*, pp. 227–97. In this case the children eventually persuaded the adults that the source of their affliction was Mother Samuel, a seventy-six-year-old neighbor. The course of their possession resembles that of the young girls who precipitated the Salem trials and enacted mother-daughter conflicts even more transparently than usual.

In some later cases, "fits" brought on by witchcraft were rediagnosed by doctors as cases of "the Mother," that is, *hysterica passio*, the wandering womb; see the cases of Mary Glover and Joan Harvey in Ewen, *Witchcraft and Demonianism*, pp. 196–99, 191–93. Cases of possession were also notoriously open to fraud, as in those staged by John Darrel. See Rosen, *Witchcraft*, pp. 298–302.

41. Rosen, *Witchcraft*, p. 94. Here money is equated with food. For another case involving a digestive ailment, see Ewen, *Witchcraft and Demonianism*, p. 199.

mother to have "omnipotent" control. Women in particular blamed the
witch for disruptions of the birthing process and for the sickness and
death of young children. Shortly after refusing to sell Joan Robinson a pig
(and angry to be criticized for not doing so?), Alice Walter blamed her because the Walters' "sow would not let her pigs suck, but did bite and fly
at them as though she had been mad." Two years later, when she again refused Joan a pig, another sow gave birth, and "all the farrow of pigs,
being ten, came out . . . and stood one before another in a tracked place
like horses in a team, being all dead to the number of nine, and the tenth
was drowned by the pond side."[42] Alice perhaps saw in the pig the retaliatory mother whom she had unconsciously attacked and projected the
image onto Joan; the first sow in particular enacted a fantasy of maternal
retaliation quite explicitly.[43] In many other cases, mothers (sometimes
along with the children themselves) attributed the "strange" sicknesses of
children to the witch. Richard Saunder's wife, after refusing Mother
Staunton yeast, found her "young child in the cradle . . . taken vehemently sick, in a marvelous strange manner, whereupon the mother of the
child took it up in her arms to comfort it; which being done, the cradle
rocked of itself six or seven times."[44] Agnes Leatherdale attributed her
child's illness to the witch Ursula Kemp when the child was "taken . . .
with a great swelling in the bottom of the belly and other privy parts."
Many more examples could be offered. Not uncommonly, quarrels between children became quarrels between their mothers. The daughter of
Ellen Smith "did fall out and fight" with the daughter of one Widow
Webb, for unexplained reasons. The next day, Ellen Smith crossed paths
with Widow Webb's daughter and gave her "a blow on the face." As soon
as the child arrived home she "sickened and, languishing two days, cried
continually 'Away with the witch! Away with the witch!' and so died.
And in the morning immediately after the death of that same child, the
said Goodwife Webb espied, as she thought, a thing like to a black dog go
out at her door, and presently at the sight thereof she fell distraught of her
wits."[45] Here, both daughter and mother blamed a mother who had

---

42. Rosen, *Witchcraft*, p. 155.

43. These examples recall one of the ingredients the witches use in the cauldron scene of
Macbeth: "Pour in sow's blood, that hath eaten / Her nine farrow," commands the first
witch (4.1.78–79).

44. Rosen, *Witchcraft*, p. 96. At least two other mothers blamed Staunton for their children's sickness.

45. Ibid., pp. 109, 95.

taken punitive action against the daughter. The fantasy of magical retaliation merely repeats and extends an actual deed.

Women also frequently blamed a witch when things went wrong with their butter making, their milking of cows, their bees' production of honey, their hens' laying of eggs.[46] Not only do these things relate to the mother's role in feeding, they also suggestively parallel the transformative powers of the mother's body—that is, the power of her body to produce life within it and to transform (as early modern belief would have it) blood into mother's milk. Hens that refused to lay or cows that gave blood instead of milk suggested the disruption and diabolical reversal of this process.

Just how the witch performed her magic could be ambiguous, but most often the witch's curse was believed to be carried out by her familiars or demonic imps (see figure 2). Such beliefs bring into relief the centrality of the maternal breast in village constructions of the witch, for the witch characteristically acquired her power over the demonic through her power to feed. Imps would do her will in exchange, often enough, for human food; informants' statements offer many instances of witches who fed their imps milk from a bowl, beer, bread, small pieces of meat, and so forth (see figure 3). But the imps were hungriest for the old woman's blood. They would suck greedily from the witch's mark or teat—sometimes described in great detail as a nipplelike protuberance. Thus, examiners found on Elizabeth Wright "a thing much like the udder of a ewe that giveth suck with two teats, like unto two great warts, the one behind under her armhole, the other a handfull off toward the top of her shoulder."[47] But the familiars seem to have been willing to suck at almost any place on the body. Joan Prentice confessed to having a spirit named Bid, who came to her in the likeness of a ferret (see figure 4). He sucked blood from the forefinger of her left hand and from her left cheek; she summoned the spirit by calling "Bid, Bid, Bid, come Bid, come Bid, come suck, come suck, come suck."[48] Joan Robinson's maid reported seeing her mistress feed her cat by making her nose bleed.[49] The significance of blood as food is suggestive in more than one way. Mothers were believed to provide food to their infants

46. Examples are many; for a sampling, see ibid., pp. 143, 148 (butter making), 149, 187 (beer brewing), 98, 144 (cow milking), 154 (loss of brood goose's eggs).

47. Ewen, *Witchcraft and Demonianism*, p. 177.

48. Rosen, *Witchcraft*, pp. 187–88.

49. Ibid., p. 154. Note also that in some cases the witch would prick her body for the blood rather than allow the imp to suck.

Figure 2. Witch sending familiar into action against her neighbor, from *A Rehearsall both straung and true* (1579), STC 23267, by permission of The British Library.

Figure 3. Witch feeding familiars, from *A Rehearsall both straung and true* (1579), STC 23267, by permission of The British Library.

❡ Th e Apprehenſion and confeſsion

of three notorious Witches.

◢rreigned and by Iuſtice condemned and

executed at *Chelmeſ-forde*, in the Countye of
Eſſex, *the 5. day of Iulye, laſt paſt*.

1 5 8 9.

❡ With the manner of their diueliſh practices and keeping of their
ſpirits, whoſe fourmes are heerein truelye
proportioned.

Figure 4. Title page from *The Apprehension and confession of three notorious Witches* (1589), STC 5114, by permission of the Archbishop of Canterbury and the Trustees of Lambeth Palace Library.

by converting their blood into breast milk, through a mysterious process taking place deep within their bodies; the witch, usually beyond her child-bearing years, inverted that process, providing blood as a substitute for milk.[50] At the same time, the shedding of her own blood to nurture her followers was an unholy parody of the sacrifice of Christ.[51]

The Kleinian notion of the "bad breast" is especially suggested by the notion of the demonic imp sucking at a nipplelike witch's mark. As Klein has it, this infantile fantasy begins in the infant's own oral sadism; and the image of the demonic imp, sucking at a nipple until it bleeds, is a central feature in "confessions" and informants' statements that describe the witch's relation with her familiar. The breast becomes "bad" and persecutory when the child, as result of her envy and anger when the breast is withheld, projects this sadism on to the breast and fears its retaliation. The demonic imp seems to represent the infant's own dangerous sadistic impulses, but then becomes an extension of the "bad" breast's persecutory will. Oral desires of early childhood may play a significant role in the shaping of this aspect of witchcraft belief.

The witch's maternal care did not stop with feeding, however. She also provided her imps with a cozy place to sleep, most often in womblike earthen or wicker pots lined with wool.[52] The imps themselves appear with frequency in informants' statements, often Janus-like in aspect. On the one hand, they were extensions of the witch's malevolence, carrying illness to her victims, causing accidents, sometimes displaying hunger or nipping them; on the other hand, they made the witch herself a target of a good deal of oral greed, sucking blood, sometimes against the witch's will, leaving marks, and causing the witch pain, in one case even burning her.[53] Like children, the imps could get a little out of the witch's control. Elizabeth Bennett, for example, sent her imp to kill the animals of her neighbor, William Byett, but the spirit exceeded his instructions and "plagued Byett's wife to death."[54] If the imps enacted the witch's destruc-

---

50. Beliefs that constituted witchcraft as an inherited power may follow from the notion that witches' power over demonic spirits came from "blood."

51. One woman in her confession made this point explicitly, but her admission may represent the doctrinal concerns of the examiner. Ewen, *Witchcraft and Demonianism*, p. 167.

52. For examples, see Rosen, *Witchcraft*, pp. 95, 110, 112, 123–25, 128, 138–39.

53. Ewen, *Witchcraft and Demonianism*, pp. 157–58, 144, 145, 149, 159, 160, 167. See Rosen, *Witchcraft*, p. 123, for the burning incident. Elizabeth Bennett seems to have had an especially difficult time with her imps, Lierd and Suckin; they imposed themselves upon her despite her pleas to God to be delivered from these evil spirits.

54. Ewen, *Witchcraft and Demonianism*, p. 158. Another example is on p. 167.

tive will, they also in a sense enacted the child's rebellious resistance to the mother.

Sometimes, but by no means routinely, the witch was believed to employ wax images or doll-like figures to carry out her magic—that is, like Mrs. Dewse, she used sorcery. These images were called not only "puppets" (poppets) but also "child's babies" and "maumets" (mammets—a term for the breast-fed infant). Alice Hunt denied "having any puppets, spirits, or maumettes." Alice Manfield had an imp called "Puppet alias Mamet"—a name that raises the interesting question of the relation between familiars and image magic.[55] Both, in any case, linked the witch to the role of mother. In the case of the familiar, the witch was a mother whose sacrificial feeding of a childlike imp enabled her to acquire magical power. In the case of image magic, the "child" was the one sacrificed. Through sorcery the witch turned her adult target into a child in the hands of a deadly mother.

Imps seem sometimes to have been actual animals—pets perhaps—kept by an old woman or sighted in her vicinity; sometimes they were apparitions or fantasies. Testimony about imps comes from the witches' own "confessions," from a few adult accusers, but especially from children—some of whom were children of the accused. This testimony has often been considered the most "doctored"; children may have been easily led to say what their examiners wanted to hear.[56] But their statements may also have registered their own fantasies about the witch (fantasies undoubtedly influenced by stories and beliefs heard from adults),[57] in which

---

55. Ibid., pp. 158, 159. Ewen discusses "puppets" in his introduction, on p. 79.

56. Reginald Scot is especially contemptuous of the use of children's testimony in trials. Commenting specifically on W. W.'s pamphlet about the St. Osyth trials, he writes, "See whether the witnesses be not single, of what credit, sex, and age they are—namely, lewd, miserable, and envious poor people, most of them which speak to any purpose being old women, and children of the age of 4, 5, 6, 7, 8, or 9 years" (quoted in Rosen, *Witchcraft*, p. 161).

57. Thus, before the onset of the Throckmorton daughters' "fits," one of them had Alice Samuel already pegged as a witch. Brought in to tend upon ten-year-old Jane, who had fallen sick of a "strange kind of sickness and distemperature"—later to be diagnosed as the beginnings of her possession by the devil—Alice Samuel appeared to the child to be a witch merely because of her hat: "She had not been there long but the child grew something worse than she was at her coming, and on the sudden cried, saying, 'Grandmother, look where the old witch sitteth,' pointing to the said Mother Samuel. 'Did you ever see' said the child, 'one more like a witch than she is? Take off her black thrummed cap, for I cannot abide to look on her'" (Rosen, *Witchcraft*, p. 241). In addition, the second set of Lancashire trials was set in motion by a ten-year-old boy, who "having invented or assimilated some stories of witches, for the purposes of gain, was put forward as . . . a witch-finder" (Ewen, *Witchcraft and Demonianism*, p. 244. This case forms the basis of the play by Thomas Heywood and Richard Brome, *The Late Lancashire Witches*.

Anne Baker.   *Ioane Willimot.*   *Ellen Greene.*

Figure 5. Witches with familiars, from *The Wonderful Discoverie of the Witchcrafts of Margaret and Phillip Flower* (1619). Courtesy The Huntington Library, San Marino, California.

the imps formed a central concern. In one sense the imp was the child's "evil twin"; these fantasies seem informed by the child's desire to disassociate him- or herself from sadistic or devouring oral impulses that threatened the mother with injury. In another sense the demonic imp was the rival child the mother appeared to favor, who was pampered and fed special treats while her own or a neighbor's child was neglected. The child so well treated also became an extension of the mother's malevolent will.

It is difficult, of course, to tell from the statements what the child really experienced. Did the child witness the mother with actual pets or with creatures she really treated as her familiars? (See figure 5). Was the child reporting a fantasy or dream? Was the child merely saying what the examiner wanted to hear? Some of the statements do seem believable as children's fearful fantasies of mothers they have come to distrust. They can suggest also a troubled family environment. In the case of Cicely Celles, two of her accusers were in fact her own children.[58] Her two sons

58. Their statements, from which the following quotations are taken, may be found in W. W., *A true and iust Recorde*, sig. D–D2v.

testified that she fed and sheltered a rival set of demonic siblings, who threatened the sons in various ways. Henry, aged nine, described a spirit who came "one night about midnight" and took his younger brother John by "the left legge, and also by the litle toe." The spirit, he said, resembled his sister, "but that it was al blacke." John, according to the statement,

> cryed out and said, "Father, Father, come helpe me, there is a blacke thing hath me by the legge, as big as my sister": whereat his father said to his mother, "why thou whore cannot you keep your impes from my children": whereat shee presently called it away from her son, saying, "come away, come away," at which speech it did depart. . . . The next day he [Henry] tolde his mother hee was so afraid of the thing that had his brother by the legge that he sweat for feare, and that he could scarce get his shirt from his back: his mother answering "thou lyest, thou lyest, whoreson."

Henry also reported seeing his mother feed the imps "out of a blacke dish, ech other day with milke," and carry them out to a hiding place in the roots of a crabtree near the house. One, "a blacke one, a he," was called Hercules or Jack; the other, "a white one, a she," was Mercury, and they had "eyes like unto goose eyes." On the night that a neighbor's maid, Alice Baxter, reported a sudden but temporary illness, Henry said he heard his mother tell his father that she had sent Hercules to the maid, the father answering, "Ye are a trim fool."

John corroborated Henry's story, and though there are some discrepancies in their accounts, taken together, they suggest a sadly conflict-ridden family in which husband abuses wife, wife abuses children, and the children fear further abuse from a set of rival siblings. The cycle of conflict has undoubtedly intensified by poverty, and the family is suggestively fractured along sex lines: the father protects his sons—"*my* children"—from the mother's imps, who remind the sons of their sister. Did the mother neglect her sons while favoring a daughter as well as the alleged imps? Were the sons envious as well as afraid of the rival siblings whom their mother fed and set against them? Difficult as it is to draw any firm conclusions from such fragmentary evidence, it is hard to avoid the impression that the son's destructive impulses toward other siblings and toward the mother who seemingly favored them was being recycled in the form of fearful apparitions that enacted the will of a mother literally experienced as a witch—a witch who nourished her brood of demonic imps while tormenting her human children.

Statements from adults also contain descriptions of encounters with demonic imps. Adults too could be frightened, even paralyzed, by such encounters. Alice Baxter reported that while she was milking one of her master's cows, it suddenly started, kicking over the pail of milk, and she saw "all the rest to make a staring and a looking about." She then "felt a thing to pricke her under the right side, as if she had been striken with ones hande, and she saith that after, as she was going homewards with her milke . . . there came a thing all white like a Cat, and stroke her at the hart, in such sort as shee could not stand, goe, nor speake, and so she remained until her said master and two of his workmen did carry her home in a chaire: she saith, she saw the said thing to go into a bush by the style, and that she knew not her master when he came unto her." [59] Alice may have found in witchcraft a convenient explanation for this lapse on the job, or she may have been prompted by her master, another informant against Cicely, to come forward with this story. But the linkages are suggestive: the milk spilled, the pain in the region of the maid's breast, the cat white like milk. It is possible, at least, that anxiety about an injury to the maternal body—specifically to the breast—was here coming back to haunt Alice Baxter. Whatever its motivations, her story contributes to the construction of the witch as malevolent mother, enemy of her neighbor's access to maternal nurturance and its substitutes.

But sightings of demonic imps were not in themselves sufficient grounds for indicting someone as a witch. The witch must be believed responsible for death or at least serious illness to galvanize community opinion against her and elicit the interest of authorities. Throughout most of this period, she was not subject to the death penalty unless a human death had occurred. Nor did the emotions generated by a neighborly quarrel always trigger a witchcraft accusation. For some accusers, at least, the experience of terrible misfortune itself—for example, the death of a child or a loved one—may have produced a sense of bewitchment without any clear notion of its source. In such cases, what followed was truly a witch-"hunt," a search to "discover" a witch hidden in one's midst. The woman eventually selected for the role of witch may have been chosen for reasons even more superficial than usual. Quarrels recalled from months or even years back were given sinister significance once serious misfortune occurred.

59. Ibid, sig. D4v.

Especially in the post-Reformation context, the death of a child or loved one could be a deeply disturbing experience. In any period, grief can be accompanied by troubling feelings of anger at the dead person and a guilty sense of responsibility; such feelings are especially evident in children but can also be observed in adults. According to Melanie Klein, bereavement is an experience especially likely to revive persecutory anxieties, even in "normal" adults; the death of a loved one may revive infantile fears that one's hostile feelings can literally kill, producing guilt and anxiety that complicate the mourning process.[60] In early modern England, the Reformation transformed religious practice in ways that reinforced and intensified such feelings. Misfortunes were routinely characterized as God's tests of the faithful or, much more frequently, as his "corrections" for sin. When a child died, parents were exhorted to scrutinize their past behavior to discover the sin or lapse of faith that had warranted this display of divine wrath. Often, they were persuaded that their sins had in a sense "caused" the child's death.[61] Parents were also reminded that their child had only been "lent" to them. The child was a gift that God had every right to reclaim at his whim, its life a "bond" that could be canceled.[62] Grief then displayed one's possessiveness; it implied one's child was one's private property when the child "really" belonged to God, as land "belonged" to the feudal master or to the commons.

Other post-Reformation changes in religious practice may also have exacerbated the guilt experienced when a loved one died. The medieval church had tolerated and even encouraged lavish displays of grief, but Protestants discouraged them, even to the point of making grief itself a sign of a sinful lack of faith. The medieval church authorized a variety of practices by which one could ease the suffering of loved ones in the afterlife: almsgiving, bell ringing, the singing of masses for the dead—all provided means for persons close to the deceased to assuage any lingering guilt feelings about them. Through pilgrimages, flagellant societies, and other penitential practices sinners could atone for their sins and improve their standing in God's eyes. The Protestant denial of the existence of

---

60. See especially Klein, "Mourning and Its Relation to Manic-Depressive States" (1940), in *Writings*, 1:344–69.

61. Thomas, *Religion*, pp. 78–89. Note also Macduff's response to the death of his family in *Macbeth*: "Sinful Macduff / They were all struck for thee—naught that I am, / Not for their own demerits but for mine / Fell slaughter on their souls" (4.3.224–27).

62. Cf. *Richard III* 4.4.77: "Cancel his bond of life, dear God, I pray."

purgatory and of the efficacy of "works" led to the abolishment of all such practices.[63]

Protestant doctrine, moreover, reinforced people's sense of powerlessness to repair the damage caused by their sins. Protestant preachers not only sought to initiate a process of self-scrutiny which would lead to repentance and amendment of life; they also emphasized human inability to achieve salvation without God's help. The recognition of one's powerlessness in the face of sin was a necessary step in the Protestant conversion process, designed to make sinners aware of their utter helplessness and dependence on God and his Word for salvation and renewal. But "justification by faith" could be difficult to accept intellectually, not to mention emotionally. For many, perhaps especially the less educated, doctrinal changes led not to "new birth" but to melancholy, madness, and despair. According to Michael Macdonald, over 10 percent of the clients of the seventeenth-century doctor and clergyman Richard Napier consulted him for symptoms related to religious anxieties. Of these, a third came to him because doubts about salvation were causing them mental disturbances and suicidal thoughts.[64]

The death of a child, then, could leave some parents feeling not only guiltily responsible but even suicidal. Since women were in charge of child care, they might feel especially vulnerable to such feelings. Traditional beliefs joined forces with new ones to intensify the burdens of guilt for bereaved mothers and wives at the same time as older modes of making reparations to the deceased were being taken away. Women, as the weaker sex, were in any case believed to be more prone to sin; and the stereotype of the "natural" mother who felt only love, compassion, and pity for her children may have generated additional guilt when a woman's feelings were more ambivalent. As the person most directly involved with the child, the mother might also be the most likely to feel a resistant anger at God or a sense of responsibility when the child died. At least 134 persons sought medical help from Richard Napier for mental disturbances associated with bereavements. Of these cases, 58 involved the death of children, and 51 of the sufferers were their mothers. Another 42 cases involved the death of spouses; 33 of the distressed survivors were wives.[65]

---

63. Thomas, *Religion*, pp. 602–6.

64. See Macdonald, *Mystical Bedlam*, pp. 89, 136, 217–31. Napier's experiences with these patients made him critical of Puritan zeal in much the same way as his contemporary Richard Burton.

65. Macdonald, *Mystical Bedlam*, pp. 82, 103.

Others may have transformed or forestalled such mental disturbances by means of an accusation of witchcraft. As Thomas and Macfarlane have noted, using witchcraft to explain misfortune had its advantages. If an illness, say, was caused by witchcraft, there was hope that it could be alleviated once the witch was discovered and countermeasures were taken. If death had already occurred, the witch provided a target for one's anger and a way to share the blame. Citing witchcraft as the immediate cause of the death of one's child did not rule out the possibility that one's own sinful behavior was also a cause. Theologians maintained that God could be using the witch as his rod of correction, just as he also used more natural means. Nevertheless, blaming the witch might provide a means of diminishing the intensity of the bereaved person's self-blame; one could divert a self-destructive, possibly suicidal impulse by venting one's rage on the witch.

Moreover, the belief that one's child or spouse had been a victim of witchcraft may have been the explanation that most closely corresponded to the emotional state of the bereaved person. The death of a loved one might arouse feelings of persecution along with grief and guilt. Death places the human subject back in the position of the child, powerless, at the mercy of forces it cannot control. God himself may seem a persecutor when his "corrections" do not seem to fit the crime; the parent does not "deserve" to have the child taken away. Blaming the witch may protect one from the guilt of being angry at God as well as at the "good" mother one has internalized, encoding the fantasy— especially common to women—that the dead child or spouse has been "stolen" by a bad, retaliatory mother.[66] Beliefs about the witch and her demonic imp provided images that "made sense" of the bereaved per-

---

66. Melanie Klein comments, "If for instance a woman loses her child through death, along with sorrow and pain her early dread of being robbed by a 'bad' retaliatory mother is reactivated and confirmed. Her own early aggressive phantasies of robbing her mother of babies gave rise to fears and feelings of being punished." Klein goes on to discuss the dream of one patient following the death of her much loved son: "She saw two people, a mother and son. The mother was wearing a black dress. The dreamer knew that this boy had died, or was going to die. No sorrow entered into her feelings, but there was a trace of hostility towards the two people." In the course of analyzing the patient's associations with the dream, Klein finds embedded in it the patient's hostile wishes against her brother and the desire to punish her mother by means of his death. The patient experiences the death of her own son as retaliation for this hostile fantasy. "Compassion and love for the internal mother were denied, feelings of revenge and triumph . . . were reinforced, partly because, through her own revengeful feelings, they had turned into persecuting figures" (Klein, *Writings*, vol. 1, pp. 353–54).

son's feelings of persecution, giving them a local habitation and a name.

In transferring blame from self to witch, the accuser was not necessarily acting weakly or insincerely, as contemporaries sometimes charged.[67] Accusation of the witch can be seen in some cases as a form of resistance to the imposition of Protestant doctrine "from above." The bereaved mother who accused a witch may, among other things, have been rejecting the notion that she was to blame for her child's death and that every misfortune required anxious examination of her conscience and submission to a new clerical elite's interpretation of God's word. Moreover, it is important to keep in mind the very real fears of many village-level accusers. In coming to perceive another woman as a witch, the accuser may have been driven by unconscious processes over which she had little control; the impulse to defend the ego from excessive, self-destructive guilt through projection is enacted automatically, creating the impression of a magical persecution that seems quite real.

But if witchcraft accusation could provide a much-needed defense against a profoundly felt inner threat, it could also be a defense against an external one. It is likely that some women accused of witchcraft did in fact intend to harm or kill their neighbors and their children by magical means. And some of these women succeeded; they "caused" the symptoms of illness and perhaps even brought on death in neighbors who shared a belief in magic and whose personal histories had made them vul-

---

67. One comment on the accuser's "vulgar Plea" can be found in a poem of Sir Francis Hubert (d. 1629):

> Besides, when any Errour is committed
> Whereby wee may Incurre or losse or shame,
> That wee our selves thereof may be acquitted
> Wee are too ready to transferre the blame
> Upon some Witch: That made us doe the same.
> It is the vulgar Plea that weake ones use
> I was bewitch'd: I could nor will: nor chuse.

Quoted in Macfarlane, *Witchcraft*, p. vii. Nor did contemporaries think all witchcraft accusations sincere. Holinshed refers to Richard III's charges against Jane Shore and Queen Elizabeth as "but a quarrel." Just as in elite contexts the witchcraft accusation was sometimes a smear, so, undoubtedly, it sometimes was at the village level. Reginald Scot suggests that some witchcraft accusations derive not only from the ignorance of country "butter wives" and "dairie maides" but from their need for a convenient cover: the surest way to protect your butter from witches is "to looke well to your dairie maid or wife, that she neither eat up the creame, nor sell awaie your butter" (*Discoverie of Witchcraft*, p. 238).

nerable to the witch's craft. It is also possible, as Thomas suggests, that others found a reputation for witchcraft a useful means of pressuring recalcitrant neighbors into meeting their requests.[68] But many women undoubtedly were falsely accused. They were merely older women who "persecuted" their neighbors with no more than their economic need, their sharp tongues, or their associations with the maternal body, whose ability to arouse an excess of unconscious guilt in their neighbors gave them an unwitting magical power. Read as persecutors by their neighbors, they provoked persecution in response.

But it was especially the ambiguity of these women's behavior which made them a disturbing force in the village community. The women who ended up accused of witchcraft provoked both anger and anxious self-scrutiny, calling into question assumptions not only about good neighboring but also about good mothering, with which it intersected. Macfarlane and Thomas remind us that it took a long time—often years—for a woman to acquire a reputation as a witch. She was at first perceived as merely another neighbor, another gossip, another white witch. When a quarrel broke out between her and another women, it was not necessarily clear who rightfully occupied the position of "nurturing neighbor." The accuser must appeal to the larger community to confirm her choice. The witch trial helped a community move from ambiguity toward clarification, helped it draw many distinctions important to the village social order: good neighbor/bad neighbor, gossip/witch, cunning woman/witch, healing magic/maleficium, justice/revenge, curse/prayer, natural body/unnatural body, good mother/malevolent mother. But the events that led up to a trial showed the troubling ways such categories could overlap. The witch's power to awaken fear partly depended on the possibility that "right" was on her side. Once the community had made up its mind that a particular woman was clearly "bad," no longer confused with the "good" nurturing neighbor—that is, that she was a witch—her power dissolved.

The revelation of the witch's teat was usually among the last pieces of evidence to be entered against the accused woman.[69] It is as if the full fantasy—of witch as malevolent mother feeding a brood of rival chil-

---

68. Thomas, *Religion*, pp. 514, 565.

69. According to Ewen, the belief in the witch's teat was a peculiarly English variation on the notion of the devil's mark—sign of the witch's servitude to the devil, rather like the liveries worn by servants identifying them with their feudal masters. The belief in the witch's teat, moreover, became widespread in England only in the sixteenth century, just as witch-hunting was about to begin in earnest. See *Witchcraft and Demonianism*, pp. 63, 73–74.

dren—could be confronted only in the relative safety of the courtroom. Only then, in the presence of male authorities deemed to serve a power greater than that of the witch, and after a relative consensus about her danger to the community had been reached, could the ultimate source of conflict—the mother's breast—be confronted and allowed to become a target for aggression. That the witch's teat is an *extra* one seems significant; it can be destroyed while leaving the "good" mother's body intact. The grotesque body of the witch could be punished and executed, leaving the community the maternal body in its "natural" and purified form. And since the trial was also a demonstration of legal, paternal, and divinely sanctioned authority over the witch, the maternal bodies that remained, those of the female accusers, had in effect found access to an orthodox magic of the father's body far more powerful than that of the witch.

The Witch and the Early Modern Mother

The woman who was labeled a witch wanted things for herself or her household from her neighbors, but she had little to offer in return to those who were not much better off than she. Increasingly resented as an economic burden, she was also perceived by her neighbors to be the locus of a dangerous envy and verbal violence. It was unsettling as well as exasperating when her curses, uttered in response to the smallest frustrations, seemed to be backed up by an unseen power, when "bad" things happened to "good" people. For refusing her some milk, a child would die, a husband fall sick. When neighbors—often but not always other women—put their resentments and their fears into words, they represented the witch as a malevolent mother who used her power to suckle, feed, and nurture a brood of childlike demonic imps in order to bring sickness and death to the households of other mothers. In doing so they punished a woman who resembled the mother who had once punished them.

If witchcraft beliefs in an important sense construct the witch as a malevolent mother, does that mean witch-hunting in early modern England was related to new anxieties about mothers and the maternal role? There is a good deal of evidence to suggest that such anxieties were increasing during the sixteenth century. Mothers and other women in caretaking roles came under a new scrutiny, especially as the Reformation gathered force; elites located a dangerous potential in women's caretaking roles, requiring stricter forms of surveillance and social control. These efforts had implications for all social levels. Infanticide, for example, was newly criminalized at this time and, as in witchcraft cases, most trials involved lower-class women. There appears to be a surprisingly close correlation between infanticide and witchcraft cases, in fact; communities that hunted witches also prosecuted murderous mothers, in roughly similar numbers.[70] After 1512, regulation of midwives also increased, through licensing by local religious authorities; among other things, midwives had to swear oaths not to use magic and not to harm the infant.[71] Wet-nursing became a site of intensified controversy, as religious authorities and others decried the practice, encouraging mothers to feed their own infants, lest the lower-class wet nurse pass on diseases and unsatisfactory lower-class character traits to the nursing infant through her milk. Such anxieties combined with centuries-old attitudes about the maternal body. Even when the milk the child imbibed was its natural mother's, it might pose a variety of dangers. Some believed mother's milk to be unwholesome in the days immediately following birth; it too could be a medium of disease and undesirable character traits. The womb was another site of anxiety, a source of trouble and danger for both mother and child.[72] Through the womb, the mother could damage the fetus if she ate the wrong foods or too many of them or was given to unnatural imaginings; she could also deform the fetus with her sins. The empty womb could make trouble when it moved out of its proper place, causing *hysterica passio*, or the "suffocation of the mother"; sufferers experienced a choking sensation in the throat, extremes of emotion, and sometimes had fits or episodes of bizarre behavior.[73]

70. See Peter C. Hoffer and N. E. H. Hull, *Murdering Mothers: Infanticide in England and New England, 1558–1803* (New York: New York University Press, 1981). Perhaps cases sometimes overlapped; the case of Elizabeth Francis, accused of witchcraft, also involved self-induced abortion and infanticide. Rosen, *Witchcraft*, pp. 74–75.

71. See Thomas R. Forbes, "Midwifery and Witchcraft," *Journal of the History of Medicine* 17 (1962): 264–83, later expanded into the book *The Midwife and the Witch* (New Haven: Yale University Press, 1966); also see Jean Towler and Joan Bramell, *Midwives in History and Society* (London: Croom Helm, 1986), pp. 55–63.

72. Adelman, *Suffocating Mothers*, pp. 4–5; Paster, *The Body Embarrassed*, pp. 198–208; Cahn, *Industry of Devotion*, pp. 104–5; Patricia Crawford, " 'The Sucking Child': Adult Attitudes toward Childcare in the First Year of Life in Seventeenth-Century England," *Continuity and Change* 1 (1986): 23–54; Valerie Fildes, "The English Wet–Nurse and Her Role in Infant Care, 1538–1800," *Medical History* 32 (1988): 142–73.

73. Adelman, *Suffocating Mothers*, p. 300 n. 27, and see 5–7; For a guide to medical writings on the female body and its disorders, see Audrey Eccles, *Obstetrics and Gynaecology in Tudor and Stuart England* (London: Croom Helm, 1982), pp. 76–79 and esp.

Furthermore, the concern of Renaissance humanists with education brought new attention to the potentially negative influence of mothers in educating the young child. Juan Vives worried: "For children rounne unto theyr mother, and aske her advice in all thyng[s]: they inquire every thyng of her: what some ever she answereth, they beleve and regarde and take hit even for the gospell." Mothers, in his view, must limit themselves to instilling basic virtues. The "good" mother was the nurturing mother, often one who confined herself to the care of infants and very *young* children. She was warned to keep the bad influence of her doting nature from spoiling not only sons but daughters.[74] Among elites, male tutors would take over the more serious business of preparing sons for the public domain. Conduct books advising mothers on their "special vocation" appeared as a new genre around this time, putting a Protestant spin on many traditional ideas and weighting them with the authority of the printed book; in general, they stressed the importance of the mother's role in caring for infants and shaping the character of the young child, while downplaying her duties as a producer of domestic goods.[75] Yet they also suggested the mother's attentions to her child had to be carefully monitored. Mothers received sometimes contradictory advice to be devoted, sacrificing, loving, and tirelessly attentive, yet also to avoid indulgence and to insist upon the duty of children to obey their parents. The "bad" mother might either neglect her infant or spoil her older children, en-

---

pp. 43–57. See also Paster, *The Body Embarrassed*, pp. 168–97. As noted earlier, bewitchment was sometimes reinterpreted as suffocation of the mother. On p. 74, Eccles quotes William Harvey's mid-seventeenth-century summary of the womb's unruly effects: "No man (who is but never so litle versed in such matters) is ignorant, what grievous *Symptomes*, the Rising, Bearing down, and Perversion, and Convulsion of the *Womb* do excite; what horrid extravagancies of minde, what Phrensies, Melancholy Distempers, and Outragiousness, the *praeternatural Diseases* of the Womb do induce, as if the affected Persons were inchanted: as also how many difficult *Diseases*, the depraved effluxion of the Terms, or the use of Venus much intermitted, and long desired do foment." The womb's diseases hover on the borderline between natural and supernatural, creating wild disturbances in mind and body.

74. Quoted in Mary Beth Rose, "Where Are the Mothers in Shakespeare? Options for Gender Representation in the English Renaissance," *Shakespeare Quarterly* 42 (Fall 1991): 300; see her essay for a fuller discussion of Vives and his relation to sixteenth-century English conduct books for mothers.

75. For surveys of this literature, see Cahn, *Industry of Devotion*; Suzanne W. Hull, *Chaste, Silent, and Obedient: English Books for Women, 1475–1640* (San Marino: Huntington Library, 1982); Betty S. Travitsky, "The New Mother of the English Renaissance: Her Writings on Motherhood," in *The Lost Tradition: Mothers and Daughters in Literature*, ed. Cathy N. Davidson and E. M. Broner (New York: Frederick Ungar, 1980), pp. 33–43; and Elaine V. Beilin, *Redeeming Eve: Women Writers of the English Renaissance* (Princeton: Princeton University Press, 1987), pp. 266–87.

couraging a dependent, egocentric disposition; the "bad breast" provided either too much food or too little. Even the best mother could not escape the general curse of Eve. As a woman, she was the conduit for sin, passing on to her child the general condition of fallen man. A Protestant poetics of conversion elaborated the idea of a "new birth" in Christ, in which the milk of one's natural mother was to be replaced by the "marvelous sweete" milk of God's Word; by contrast, earthly mothers were the site of sin, ignorance, and general deficiency. Truly sustaining spiritual nourishment was to be had only from the Father, his Word, and his male representatives on earth, the Protestant clergy.[76]

If the mother's influence over her young children could be cause for concern, her effect on her grown children could be maddening. Among elite families in particular, patrilineal inheritance customs handed down from the Middle Ages restricted and yet empowered mothers in ways that could generate intense conflict between them and their children. Though a woman's property was ordinarily absorbed into her husband's estate upon marriage and she had no independent standing under the law, her dowry returned to her control upon his death and she was able to name her own heirs. Furthermore, husbands frequently named their wives executors and left them a portion of the family estate, to be enjoyed for the duration of their lives before it passed to male heirs. Under these conditions, conflict was structured into the relationship between mother and eldest son. Mothers could interfere with sons' control of their inheritance and their dowers could disadvantage them economically: bitter quarrels were frequently the result.[77] As the sixteenth century progressed, more mothers initiated legal struggles over property, as married women and widows gained significant rights to file suit on their own behalf in Chancery court. John Webster's early seventeenth-century play *The Devil's Law-Case* dramatizes one such legal battle. A mother, Leonora, seeks vengeance on her son by bringing a lawsuit to have him (falsely) named a bastard and thus to disinherit him. For those whose interests were threatened by women's new legal powers, gender provided a language with which to express their disapproval. Webster's subtitle exemplifies the demonizing strategies that could be used: *When women go to law, it is the Devil's Business*; within the play, Leonora's actions are

76. This was also a medieval theme; see Caroline Walker Bynum, *Jesus as Mother: Studies in the Spirituality of the High Middle Ages* (Berkeley: University of California, 1982).
77. See Barbara J. Harris, "Property, Power, and Personal Relations" and "Women and Politics in Early Tudor England."

specifically denigrated in terms of perverse maternity. Though Leonora also is at odds with her daughter, the success of her suit would mean that her daughter would inherit the son's lands. The wills of elite and "middling" families show that her attitude was not unusual. Mothers frequently thwarted primogenitural expectations, making provisions for daughters and younger sons which aroused the resentment of their eldest sons and kin with ties to the husband's patrilineage.[78] Inheritance customs thus empowered mothers to undermine strict patrilineality.

In a number of ways, even as a new emphasis was being placed on maternal power, it was likely to be experienced as dangerous or anger-provoking by children and by others with an interest in monitoring mother-child relations. Concerns about the dangers of mothering were tied in with broader post-Reformation efforts to monitor marriage and family life, which often involved what Lawrence Stone has called the "reinforcement of patriarchy": the father's authority was strengthened, his prerogatives extended, and a new symbolic importance was conferred upon his role.[79] Wives were to submit to their husbands' authority in all things; yet at the same time, they ran the household, and their mothering role was gaining a new importance and prestige. As the mother of her husband's children and mistress of his servants, the wife asserted authority over subordinates, issuing her own commands and demanding obedience. But the habits of a mother and domestic manager were in many ways opposed to those a husband was supposed to expect from a wife. Women had to shift roles deftly from playing the master to playing the servant. Linda Pollock has made the important point that a woman (at least an upper-class woman) had to learn in effect two roles—to be "the weaker vessel" in her husband's presence and yet "the best steward" in his absence. She must negotiate between submission and competence, be properly female and yet also have a masculine part. Susan Amussen has brought out the mixed messages women received in household manuals

---

78. See Amussen, *An Ordered Society*, pp. 78, 91–93. On women's suits in Chancery, see Cioni, *Women and Law in Elizabethan England*.

79. The phrase is from Lawrence Stone's widely influential but also much criticized book *The Family, Sex, and Marriage in England, 1500–1800* (Abridged edition; New York: Harper and Row, 1979), pp. 109–46. The "reinforcement of patriarchy," to the extent it took place, was not necessarily bad for women in all its aspects. See Rose, "Where Are the Mothers?" pp. 293–98. In addition, Margaret J. M. Ezell, *The Patriarch's Wife: Literary Evidence and the History of the Family* (Chapel Hill: University of North Carolina Press, 1987), pp. 1–61, offers an important look at the mother's contribution within a patriarchal family structure.

as they were advised to submit to their husbands and yet assist them in the management and supervision of the household.[80] Slippages were bound to occur, and the husband might find himself being spoken to and treated as if he were a child. The fear of such role reversal was expressed in the imagery associated with shrews and scolds. Woodcuts and drawings show the "husband-dominator" as the punitive mother, spanking her kneeling husband.[81] In turn, husbands may have had a special sensitivity to being treated like children. As many critics have observed, sons in this culture had an extended period of dependence on the mother and thus of identification with her, and they may have found the differentiation from the mother which patriarchy required of them especially difficult to achieve.[82] The wife who stepped out of place and asserted herself too vig-

80. Pollock, " 'Teach Her to Live under Obedience': The Making of Women in the Upper Ranks of Early Modern England," *Continuity and Change* 4 (1989): 231–58; Amussen, *An Ordered Society*, pp. 41–47.

81. See the illustrations that accompany Natalie Davis's essay "Woman on Top," in *Society and Culture in Early Modern France* (Stanford: Stanford University Press, 1975), pp. 124–51. For an English example, a woodcut from *The Deceyte of Women* (London, 1557) is included in Laura Gowing, "Gender and the Language of Insult."

82. That early modern culture rendered the patriarchal imperative for males to "disidentify with mother" particularly problematic is a point familiar to many Shakespeareans from the work of Adelman, Kahn, Sprengnether, and others. Adelman, for example, sees the "violent unmaking of the maternal body" as the point of origin for a tragic masculine selfhood not only in Shakespeare's plays but in his culture. *Suffocating Mothers*, pp. 7–10. See also Coppelia Kahn, *Man's Estate: Masculine Identity in Shakespeare* (Berkeley: University of California Press, 1981), pp. 1–20; and "The Absent Mother in *King Lear*," in *Rewriting the Renaissance: The Discourses of Sexual Difference in Early Modern Europe*, ed. Margaret W. Ferguson et al. (Chicago: University of Chicago Press, 1986), pp. 33–49; Madelon [Gohlke] Sprengnether, " 'I Wooed Thee with My Sword': Shakespeare's Tragic Paradigms," in *Representing Shakespeare: New Psychoanalytic Essays*, ed. Murray M. Schwartz and Coppelia Kahn (Baltimore: Johns Hopkins University Press, 1980), pp. 170–87; Valerie Traub, "Prince Hal's Falstaff: Positioning Psychoanalysis and the Female Reproductive Body," *Shakespeare Quarterly* 40 (1989): 456–74. Such claims depend for their historical force on early modern child-care practices, in particular that of "breeching" (Stone, *The Family, Sex, and Marriage*, p. 238), and on tensions between the single-sex and two-sex models of gender differentiation current at the time. See Thomas Laqueur, *Making Sex: Body and Gender from the Greeks to Freud* (Cambridge: Harvard University Press, 1990); and Paster, *The Body Embarrassed*, pp. 166–97. For their psychoanalytic argument they depend on the feminist recasting of the work of Robert Stoller, Ralph Greenson, and others by Nancy Chodorow in *The Reproduction of Mothering: Psychoanalysis and the Sociology of Gender* (Berkeley: University of California Press, 1978).

While ultimately this account of early modern male subjectivity needs to be complicated by a recognition of the sites in early modern culture where male identification with the mother (or the feminine) was tolerated or even encouraged, I am in substantial agreement with it. What I consider more problematic is the relatively serene and untroubled account of mother-daughter relations which sometimes surfaces alongside it.

orously brought the mother back into the masculine domain, challenging her husband's masculinity and even his adulthood: enraged by her violation of gender hierarchy, he must also resist the temptations of a regressive return to dependence on maternal power.

Anxieties about mothering, then, went hand in hand with anxieties about female power; the one often implied the other. When women, by virtue of the tensions inhering in early modern systems of gender and class, were catapulted into positions of power over men—as queens, as patrons, as stewards in their husband's absence, or as managers of households—their power might be a potent and potentially threatening reminder of the mother's power over her child and all the emotional freight that carried. However legitimate their claims to those positions, women who ruled over men were unsettling presences, in part because they threatened to bring a maternal subtext back into patriarchal view.[83] John Knox's "monstrous regiment of women" was in an important sense a monstrous regiment of *mothers*.[84]

Nevertheless, whereas these social practices and the anxieties with which they were associated have a good deal to do with the male interventions in witch-hunting I discuss in subsequent chapters—that is, with state prosecution of the witch—they have limited relevance to witch-hunting at the village level. As midwives, wet nurses, and unwed mothers, lower-class women were subjected to intensified regulation. At least some lower-class mothers would have been exposed to the new ideology of

83. I allude here to Kahn, "The Absent Mother in *King Lear*," p. 35: "Patriarchal structures loom obviously on the surface of many texts, structures of authority, control, force, logic, linearity, misogyny, male superiority. But beneath them, as in a palimpsest, we can find what I call 'the maternal subtext,' the imprint of mothering on the male psyche, the psychological presence of the mother whether or not mothers are literally represented as characters." Also see Louis Montrose's suggestive discussion of Simon Forman's dream about Queen Elizabeth in "*A Midsummer Night's Dream* and the Shaping Fantasies of Elizabethan Culture: Gender, Power, Form," in *Rewriting the Renaissance*, pp. 65–87. Montrose highlights the ambivalence toward Elizabeth as a quasi-maternal figure, tracing also the ways in which a tension between the impulse to submit to female power and the impulse to reassert male dominance similarly shapes Shakespeare's play.

84. Mary Beth Rose in fact shows that John Knox's argument in *The First Blast of the Trumpet against the Monstrous Regiment of Women* depends heavily on the idea that the "legal incapacities" of mothers show women to be unfit for political rule. "Where are the Mothers?" p. 303. The literature on early modern debates about the "female regiment" is now vast. See especially Linda Woodbridge, *Women and the English Renaissance: Literature and the Nature of Womankind, 1540–1620* (Urbana: University of Illinois Press, 1986); Pamela Benson, *The Invention of the Renaissance Woman: The Challenge of Female Independence in the Literature and Thought of Italy and England* (University Park: Pennsylvania State University Press, 1992), pp. 205–50.

mothering promulgated by a reform-minded clergy. Yet what is "new" about sixteenth-century discourses about mothers tends to bespeak the elite son's anxieties and not the village-level daughter's. Like magical beliefs in general, witch-hunting in some form was probably a regular feature of peasant culture for centuries before the Reformation; we would expect to find the main sources of village-level witch-hunting not in post-Reformation changes in child care or in discourses of mothering but in aspects of social practice continuous through the Middle Ages and into the early modern period.[85]

Unfortunately, data about peasant family relations in either period are hard to come by, and data about mother-daughter relations harder still. English peasant discourse is for the most part an oral tradition in effect "outside" of history because it produces no written texts. The written texts that report it, such as the documents related to witchcraft cases, are heavily mediated by the elites that make up "officialdom." Even upperclass mother-child relations have received little attention from the males who largely "make" history, who write and preserve in the records of the past the "line" of the patrilineage, passing from father to first son. What can be pieced together, however, does suggest that conflict was structured into the relations between children and mothers, stepmothers, and nurses in ways that, at least in some families, may have promoted persecutory anxieties and fueled witchcraft accusations.[86]

Gail Paster has noted one irony of child-rearing practices: whereas aristocratic and gentry-level mothers frequently employed wet nurses to feed and care for their infants and young children, mothers of the lower classes tended to do their own breast-feeding—a physically and perhaps psychologically healthier situation for mother and child alike. Moreover, they generally did not deny their infants the valuable colostrum that flowed from their breasts in the first few days following birth, as was recommended to upper-class mothers.[87] Still, other features of early and premodern child care suggest that babies of all classes might experience

---

85. On the longevity of witchcraft beliefs, see Thomas, *Religion*, pp. 437–38; Clive Holmes, "Popular Culture?" pp. 85–111, esp. 94–99.

86. For general accounts of family structure and the position of daughters within that structure, see Wrightson, *English Society*, pp. 66–118; Amussen, *An Ordered Society*, pp. 38–49, 91–93; Stone, *Family, Sex, and Marriage*, pp. 81–89, 113–27. For education of daughters in more well-to-do families, see Cahn, *Industry of Devotion*, pp. 109–18; Pollock, " 'Teach Her to Live under Obedience' "; and Harris, "Property, Power, and Personal Relations."

87. Paster, *The Body Embarrassed*, p. 201.

disruptions in nurture, deprivations of the sort likely to intensify their sense of the breast's importance. Lower-class children might not be sent out to nurse, but they might be displaced by a nurse-child if their mothers found such employment. Peasant mothers, in any case, had to be busy with many domestic or farm-related tasks, and economic pressures could make hunger and competition for food a significant factor in poorer families. The period of breast-feeding was often prolonged—mothers could use it as a form of birth control—encouraging strong attachment. When weaning came, it tended to be abrupt and involved not only frightening the child but also inculcating shame about its oral desires.

Such experiences could heighten the aggressive and envious fantasies about the breast which Melanie Klein has identified as sources of retaliatory fears. As the child grew older, envy of the mother's attention to other siblings might also contribute to the intensity of aggressive fantasies. This envy assumed a historically specific form in a patriarchal, primogenitural culture, moreover. Privileges were often meted out according to birth order and gender, and parents also appear to have had relatively few inhibitions about openly selecting favorites. Whatever anger the child felt about these or other experiences of deprivation, he or she (and for gender reasons especially she) was probably allowed few opportunities to express it. Historians of the family who are otherwise at odds agree that families at all social levels strongly stressed children's obedience and deference to adults. Aggression might be directed toward peers or social inferiors and even take violent form, but it could not be allowed to flow upward, towards mothers, fathers, or other "masters."

If anger toward mothers was largely unspeakable, it might come to seem to the child even unthinkable when it was followed by loss or separation. During premodern and early modern times mothers frequently died in childbirth as well as from other causes; a majority of children, Lawrence Stone has concluded, were bereaved of at least one parent before they reached adulthood.[88] Serious illnesses and accidents were common as well. Such losses or misfortunes were likely to reinforce the child's (particularly the *young* child's) sense of the "magical" quality of its anger, hence also the fear of its destructive power.

Situations that heightened a child's hostile fantasies about the breast and the mother and then reinforced their magical character might make the child especially subject to persecutory anxiety; such fears would be

88. Stone, *Family, Sex, and Marriage*, p. 48.

confirmed and intensified if the mother were actually punitive in her behavior. Early death, moreover, meant remarriage was frequent, and resultant family structures could encourage splitting: a lost, idealized mother could be replaced by a "wicked stepmother," an alien presence especially suited to step into the role of persecutor. In many a fairy or folk tale, her alter ego is clearly the witch.

Some evidence from the early modern period suggests that the mother-daughter relationship could be particularly untroubled and warm. But it is clear that there were also many conflict-ridden, "dysfunctional" families, especially at lower social levels and when remarriage brought together unrelated children and stepparents. We have glimpsed conflict along gender lines in the Celles family, in which sons harbored resentments against their sister and mother, and husband fought with wife. Other witchcraft cases show evidence of fractious mother-daughter relations: daughters accused mothers of witchcraft in several cases recorded by Ewen. In one seventeenth-century case, a cunning woman became caught in the cross fire between a mother and her two stepdaughters, each side at first suspecting the other of murderous intentions. As the conflict unfolded, it became convenient for both mother and stepdaughters to transfer their anger and suspicion onto the cunning woman, who eventually was executed as a witch.[89]

Perhaps especially pertinent to witchcraft quarrels between women were the relations between young mothers and their aging parents (or parents-in-law). On these women could fall the burdens not only of child rearing and domestic management but care of elderly kin who might be sick or incapacitated. Maintenance agreements allowed for the transfer of property from aging parents to children in exchange for the children's support; such agreements suggest, among other things, that parents could not rely on mere gratitude.[90] Children of both sexes might feel resentment, but even if the parents were still healthy, the burdens of day-to-day feeding and other forms of care would fall most heavily upon their

89. For example, Ewen, *Witchcraft and Demonianism*, pp. 214, 220, 223. See also Edmond Bower, *Dr. Lamb Revived; or, Witchcraft Condemn'd in Anne Bodenham a Servant of His* (London, 1653), discussed in Frances E. Dolan, *Dangerous Familiars: Representations of Domestic Crime in England 1550–1700* (Ithaca: Cornell University Press, 1994), pp. 232–34.
90. On care of aging parents, see especially Stephen Greenblatt, "The Cultivation of Anxiety: King Lear and His Heirs," *Raritan* 2 (Summer 1982): 92–114; and Lucinda McCray Beier, *Sufferers and Healers: The Experience of Illness in Seventeenth Century England* (London: Routledge and Kegan Paul, 1987), p. 5.

daughter or their son's wife. Affectionate ties might be weaker and resentment stronger when in-laws were involved, but there is plentiful evidence of tensions between those bound by ties of blood. "Old fools are
babes again," complain Goneril and Regan when their father becomes
their unwanted responsibility: *King Lear* provides an aristocratic example of a situation common among the lower classes, except that then, as
now, women tended to live longer; widowed mothers were thus more
likely to end up dependent on the "kind nursery" of their children.

The mother of young children who also had to provide food and shel-
ter for elderly relatives had particularly good reason to want to limit her
care-giving responsibilities; she might thus be especially resentful of demands made by a needy older female neighbor not her kin. The unacceptable anger she felt toward a dependent, aging parent could readily be
transferred to this neighbor, but not without anxiety and fear of retaliatory attack. Though the younger woman might now possess the life-giv-
ing breast that gave her value and made family members depend on her,
she confronted in the old woman not only a "bad" mother but also a version of the envious child she once was and of the postmenopausal "hag"
she would become. To reject and accuse her was in a sense also to reject
and accuse herself. The anxiety produced by this set of unconscious identifications was legible as bewitchment. Lacking milk, the old woman nevertheless had excess blood in her postmenopausal body. Following a
cultural logic of inversion as well as an intrapsychic logic of retaliatory
fantasy, with this blood she could feed her imps and magically retaliate
against the recalcitrant "daughter"-neighbor who refused to mother her.

Informants' statements taken in witchcraft cases, distorted as they may
be by their interlocutors' expectations, provide some of the only textual
traces of peasant mother-daughter relationships. To an extent, they support the idea that tension or conflict was structured into the relations of
female accusers with mothers or other women in mothering roles. But
witchcraft documents provide evidence of women's alliances as well as
quarrels: the women accused of witchcraft may have come from families
that encouraged strong mother-daughter bonds. Witches were often believed to have learned their craft from their mothers and sometimes came
in mother-daughter pairs.[91] They sometimes shared imps or knowledge of
their craft with other female friends. Ursula Kemp confessed to sharing
her spirits with Alice Newman after first quarreling with her, and Eliza-

91. Holmes, "Popular Culture?" Rosen, *Witchcraft*, pp. 94, 127–28.

beth Francis reported sharing with Mother Waterhouse.[92] It is well to remember that such statements may testify more to animosity than to amity, since they call down the suspicion of authorities on the other woman. Neverthelesss, if the statements of women who "confessed" to witchcraft are at least to some extent indicative of their actual beliefs and practices, it would appear that "real" witches were poor women who passed on to their daughters and friends strategies designed to help them survive psychically as well as pragmatically in a world where they had few opportunities, especially as they grew older and lost the husbands or other connections that had provided them with support and status. Such mothers taught their daughters to locate deprivation outside the home, to perceive female neighbors as, in effect, split-off "bad mothers" who denied them the food and nurture they were entitled to. At the same time, witches passed on to their daughters an alternative maternal identity, the witch's role, with its own powers and compensations.

The witch's care and feeding of her familiars might provide her with at least the illusion of control over a world in which she was largely powerless; moreover, they gave her a sense of companionship, a surrogate family. Women who confessed to the crime of witchcraft dwelled in detail on their maternal care of their imps, and they described conversations with them. Thus Alice Manfield, who had four imps serving her (Robin, Jack, William, and Puppet alias Mommet), confessed to hearing from them what might be thought of as gossip about the activities of other witches; she also described their polite requests to make trouble for her neighbors.

> This examinate saith, that little before Michaelmas last, her said four imps said unto her, "I pray you, Dame, give us leave to go unto Little Clacton to Sellis," saying, they would burn barns and also kill cattle; and she saith, that after their return they told her that Sellis his wife [that is, Cicely Celles] knew of it, and that all they four were fed at Sellis' house by her all the time they were away from this examinate, which she saith was about a sevennight; and that Puppet sucked upon this examinate's left shoulder at their return unto her, and the rest had beer.[93]

Witches shared their imps with other witches and cared for them, just as women linked in village networks helped one another and cared for one another's children; upon their imps' return, touchingly, they welcomed

92. Rosen, *Witchcraft*, pp. 116, 75.
93. Ibid., p. 139.

them with blood and beer. Imps at times even became the witch's advo-
cates. Thus Elizabeth Bennett, though at first harried by her spirits into
adopting them against her will, found that one of them had acted on her
behalf without her instructions. After she fell out with William Byatt and
his wife, she asked her spirit Lierd to kill their livestock, but her other
spirit, Suckin, took it upon himself to "plague" Byatt's wife to death. "I
know that Byatt and his wife have wronged thee greatly," he told his mistress, "and done thee several hurts, and beaten thy swine and thrust a
pitchfork in one of them." Bennett was skeptical of his motives, however,
and told the examiner he was merely attempting "to win credit."[94] Bennett's reluctance to accept her spirits' assistance may have been a sign of
her own ambivalence about her vengeful wishes, or it may have been designed to win sympathy from the authorities. But witches less conflicted
about their craft may have considered their spirits consoling allies, who in
exchange for a mother's care returned loyalty and gratitude as well as a
means to "get even" with hostile neighbors.

Such descriptions appear in many statements taken in different times
and places; they suggest, if not a shared set of practices, at least a shared
fantasy life, in which marginalized women dreamed of an "oppositional"
female network paralleling those of the female villagers who had come to
exclude them.[95] Like infants, supernatural spirits were above all hungry—
hungry for food, attention, and care. A witch could feel as needed by
them as any neighbor was by her human child. Indeed, it is striking how
much the witch had in common with her female accuser. Both got angry
and sought vengeance when they felt wronged. Both shared many assumptions about maternal identity and a fantasy of maternal omnipo-
tence. Whether these women were "blaming the mother" or exploiting
her powers, witchcraft beliefs allowed escape from a patriarchal symbolic
that located deficiency in the female. The witch gained magical power
through her powers of maternal nurture. The mother of merely human
children could use a variety of antiwitchcraft techniques as well as the
legal process to reclaim a magic of her own by defeating the witch.

But what of the sons who were subject to bewitchment and could also
become accusers of the village witch? If I am right to believe that a majority of quarrels leading to witchcraft accusations took place between

94. Rosen, *Witchcraft*, p. 124.
95. This discussion of female networks is mainly inferred from the witchcraft documents
themselves—with help from accounts of village-level relations between neighbors cited earlier. See also Quaife, *Godly Zeal*, p. 108.

women, it is nevertheless true that many men also quarreled with old women and displayed anxieties and symptoms similar to those of their female counterparts. In many village-level cases, the intrapsychic dimension of bewitchment does not appear to have been markedly gender-differentiated, and fear of the witch's retaliatory anger seems to have been capable of producing persecutory anxiety or hysterical symptoms in a man as well as in a woman. Though Klein stresses that persecutory fantasies about the preoedipal mother lead to a "primary female anxiety situation," she believes such fantasies also create problems for males.[96] Klein (in contrast to Freud) postulates an early "femininity" phase for boys, whose earliest sense of self is modeled on the mother, and she maintains that they display a strong envy of the maternal body. As the son shifts to identifying more strongly with his father, his earlier identifications with the mother tend to be absorbed and obscured; afterward, persecutory anxieties are more likely to be linked to a father-figure or to a male-female pair (such as the witch-devil partnership I discuss in later chapters). But many variations are possible; ultimately there is no hard and fast line between "male" and "female" fantasies or developmental histories. It may also be that in agricultural communities (where women's labor is more obviously central to survival and where male and female work spaces often overlap), less emphasis is placed upon the son's identification with the patriarchal father.

At the village level, in other words, the son's story about the witch could closely resemble the daughter's; a refusal to nurture or aid an older female neighbor, unconsciously experienced as an attack on the mother, could make a man or his household a target of her retaliatory magic. We may, however, note a few differences. Though both men and women had investments in their own health and that of their children, men, because they performed different tasks in a village economy, in some cases blamed the witch for different types of misfortune than women did—for example, the sickness of cattle or other livestock, often tended by men.[97] A more significant difference is that when a witch quarreled with men she may in-

---

96. See *The Selected Melanie Klein*, pp. 50, 69–83; Hinshelwood, *A Dictionary*, pp. 84–93. See note 40 for some examples of possible male hysteria. Others include an ostler, victim of Mother Stile, in Rosen, *Witchcraft*, p. 89, and the son of a vicar, victim of Margaret Simons, in Ewen, *Witchcraft and Demonianism*, p. 154.

97. It may be that fear of a witch's retaliation was especially likely to be felt by men whose occupational identities had a quasi-maternal aspect; as caretakers of cattle, horses, or sheep, male accusers had a certain resemblance to mothers taking care of children.

deed have been challenging gender hierarchy in some sense. Elizabeth Francis, for example, confessed to using her witchcraft against a man who refused to marry her after having sex with her. She married another man and then caused his lameness when it turned out "they lived not so quietly as she desired, being stirred, as she said, to much unquietness, and moved to swearing and cursing."[98] Even when a quarrel involved more "typical" violations of neighborliness, a new element could be introduced when a man was the target of the witch's anger. The witch might not only arouse retaliatory fears about an injury to the maternal body, she might also challenge the man's right as husband or master to control that body. When the milk wouldn't come or the butter wouldn't churn, when wives or children or milkmaids fell sick, an occult maternal malevolence was undermining his control over those aspects of his household most closely associated with the maternal function. A witch's attack on another woman, moreover, was also an attack on the husband (or father) whose "property" she was. For men so affected, the witch was not only a malev-

---

98. Rosen, *Witchcraft*, pp. 74–75. This case has other features that suggest Elizabeth Francis's transgression of gender norms and gender hierarchy; she appears to have been the initiator of the relationship with Andrew, the man she first desires; she induced an abortion when she became illegitimately pregnant; she had sex with the man she married before they were married and got pregnant; she killed this child when it was one and a half. In this case, there are certainly grounds for seeing the witch as an embodiment of "proto-feminist" resistance to patriarchal control. The case also has a few problematic features, however. While asserting her right to control her body and choose her own sexual partners, she killed her child for causing them to live "not so quietly as she desired" or perhaps (Medea-like) to get back at her husband. It is difficult to tell whether her husband abused her or whether they abused each other. Finally, despite her confession of causing the death of her ex-lover, her fetus, and her child, she was not convicted for any of these crimes, but was imprisoned for one year for causing the illness of a neighbor's child. That was not the end of her story, however. Six years later she was again given a one-year sentence for bewitching a female neighbor; and she may be the same Elizabeth Francis who was convicted and hanged in 1579 for causing the death of Alice Poole. Ewen, *Witchcraft and Demonianism*, pp. 145, 150; Rosen, *Witchcraft*, pp. 92–94.

Other cases with proto-feminist potential include that of Mother Waterhouse, who appears in the same pamphlet as Elizabeth Francis at the time of her first arrest. She also confessed to bewitching her husband to death but was executed for the death of a neighbor. Rosen, *Witchcraft*, pp. 76–82; Ewen, *Witchcraft and Demonianism*, p. 145. Ellen Smith quarreled with her stepfather, John Chandler, over an inheritance from her mother. Rosen, p. 94; Ewen, p. 150. Elizabeth Bennet's possibly "romantic friendship" with William Bonner's wife enraged the husband. Rosen, pp. 120–21. Nevertheless, such cases were exceptional, I believe. It is not surprising, though, that conflicts about the limits of women's rights in a patriarchal culture would sometimes provide the basis of a witchcraft quarrel, especially when the quarrel was between a man and a woman.

olent mother but also a disorderly woman who threatened patriarchal control.

Because a woman was almost always the property of some man, was embedded in a network of patriarchal rights and privileges, to attack another woman was inevitably to attack her husband or father or master. Quarrels between women extended to the men who had rights in those women. Similarly, quarrels between neighbors—relative equals of lowly social status—affected the masters or authorities who were responsible for them. "Masters" became concerned when witchcraft seemed to be causing disturbances among their servants just as they did when their immediate families were affected. Just as husbands came forward on behalf of wives, masters came forward to give information about bewitched servants. They had a stake in seeing the witch subdued, for bewitchment might cause a work slowdown, so to speak, or compromise a master's reputation for godliness or keeping good order.

In the chapters that follow, I explore what happened when "masters" were affected by or intervened in witchcraft quarrels, when, in short, the village-level witch was rewritten by male elites, producing a strikingly different sort of discourse. To a large extent in this discourse the witch is stripped of her powers as malevolent mother and featured more prominently as a transgressor of state, religious, and gender hierarchies. Here, however, in the village-level quarrels between women which made up half to two-thirds of witchcraft cases in this period, witch and accuser tended to meet as relative social equals, each insisting on an aspect of neighborliness which the other denied: the witch's rudeness and failure to reciprocate confronted the accuser's less than satisfactory charity; what one perceived as "getting even" the other saw as excess. Both were felt to fail each other as nurturing neighbors—in a sense, as mothers. Given the similarities between witch and accuser, it is not surprising that in some cases we find a good deal of slippage between the two roles: witches accuse other witches, accusers are accused. These anger-driven quarrels took place in a world that lacked a satisfactory solution to the problems of aging, dependent women and, more broadly, to the problems of the poor in general. One woman's "right" to charity clashed with another woman's "right" to limit giving. The women who turned to a "real" witchcraft invented their own solution, becoming victims who enacted (or at least intended) further victimization, holding an individual neighbor responsible for a collective problem, sometimes, perhaps, taking out their frustrations on the very neighbors who had given most in the past.

For the feminist critic rereading the witch-hunts in search of exemplary instances of female resistance, neither the position of witch nor that of accuser, it seems to me, should be uncritically endorsed. Their clashes called out for a rethinking of neighborliness and women's identities which their culture could not deliver at that time. But in the end it can hardly help but appear to those of us who lack a theory of magical causation that ultimately the accuser was the agent of excess. For a few words mumbled in anger, she did her best to send her difficult neighbor to a cold imprisonment, a cruel and untimely death.

CHAPTER THREE

REWRITING
THE WITCH

What happens when witch-hunting becomes a male "story" instead of a female one, when governing elites intervene in village quarrels? And what motivated these elites to do so? During the Middle Ages, the state pursued only a handful of witchcraft cases, most of them involving treasonous plots against the king or other highly placed officials. Not until the mid-sixteenth century did authorities become interested in prosecuting the witch whose victims were merely other peasants.[1] Could it be that male elites had developed a new concern for the village inhabitants—

---

1. Thomas, *Religion*, p. 454. Studies of medieval witchcraft cases include H. A. Kelly, "English Kings and the Fear of Sorcery," *Mediaeval Studies* 39 (1977): 206–38; and William R. Jones, "Political Uses of Sorcery in Medieval Europe," *The Historian* 34 (1972): 670–87. The shift from "treason-cum-sorcery" trials (Christina Larner's phrase) to trials of witches whose victims were members of the lower classes can be illustrated by contrasting the 1441 case of Eleanor, duchess of Gloucester, to those of the North Berwick witches in Scotland, 1590–91. Eleanor was alleged to have consulted Margery Jourdain, known as the Witch of Eye, in the course of a plot against Henry VI's life (an incident treated in Shakespeare's 2 *Henry VI*). Her arrest led the king to open a major inquiry into "all manner treasons, sorcery, and all other things that might in any wise touch or concern harmfully the king's person" (Kelly, "English Kings," p. 224). Inquests were opened in London and in the surrounding countryside, but only a handful of witches were ever indicted. In 1590 the arrests of some witches in North Berwick, similarly charged with practicing a treasonous magic against the king's person, led to the indictment of over a hundred persons, many of them villagers unconnected to the original plot or to other treasonous activities; their alleged *maleficium* merely harmed other villagers. The much greater *scale* of the North Berwick prosecutions is partly to be explained by Scotland's much different legal traditions, but the shift to cases involving lower-class victims took place in both countries. Larner, *Witchcraft and Religion*, pp. 10, 69–78.

women, men, and children—who were targets of the witch's maleficium? Or if not exactly a new concern, a new capacity for fear, which enabled elites to identify, to a greater or lesser extent, with villagers' anxiety about the witch's maternal malevolence?

In a sermon preached before Queen Elizabeth shortly before the passage of the 1563 anti-witchcraft law, John Jewel appealed to such sentiments, vividly describing the horrible effects of witchcraft upon her majesty's "poor subjects":

> This kind of people (I mean witches and sorcerers) within these few last years are marvellously increased within this your grace's realm. These eyes have seen most evident and manifest marks of their wickedness. Your grace's subjects pine away even unto death, their colour fadeth, their flesh rotteth, their speech is benumbed, their senses are bereft. Wherefore, your poor subjects' most humble petition unto your highness is, that the laws touching such malefactors may be put in due execution. For the shoal of them is great, their doings horrible, their malice intolerable, the examples most miserable. And I pray God they never practise further than upon the subject.[2]

Although Jewel mentions his concern for her majesty's person, his deeper concern is with the health of her majesty's kingdom. Not only their suffering but her reputation is at stake. The passage occurs as almost a digression in a sermon devoted to defending the Protestant reformers against "Romanist" charges of heresy and issuing a counterattack. The "marvellous increase" in witches and sorcerers was of course due to the Catholic rule of Mary I; Elizabeth was being called upon to distinguish herself from her sister. Jewel's concern for subjects, however genuine, was embedded in larger ideological struggles. By promoting the witchcraft laws, an emergent Protestant elite could display a greater piety and "biblical correctness" than its Catholic predecessors. New modes of reading the Bible led to new conceptualizations of the witch's crime. Witch prosecutions became part of a larger campaign carried out by state and religious authorities against many varieties of "false belief," including papistry, skepticism, mere ignorance, and popular magical traditions both black and white.

Along with this post-Reformation campaign for greater religious conformity went a more secular campaign for "good order" in many areas of

---

2. Quoted and discussed in Kittredge, *Witchcraft in Old and New England*, p. 252.

village life.[3] Ideological reform had implications for everyday social practice: clerics and magistrates concerned with promulgating Reformation doctrine were also overtaken by a new zeal for the policing of public morality and "keeping the peace," as new laws were introduced and enforcement of the old expanded in matters such as public drunkenness, churchgoing, vagrancy, rowdy behavior, illegitimate births, and the like. In this light, the witch with her sharp tongue and quarrelsome behavior can be thought of as yet another disturber of the peace, akin to the male "brawler" and the female scold. And in disturbing "good order" she also disrupted social hierarchy; her attacks on other women (not to mention those on men) injured the male "masters" to whom they were connected.

It seems clear that in some regions, at least, justices of the peace saw it as part of their role to be on guard against the witch. They may have been active in identifying suspects and in encouraging villagers to come forward when they suspected a neighbor of witchcraft.[4] Brian Darcy, justice of the peace for the St. Osyth trials, seems to have been well known in his community for his willingness to take action against witches. Alice Newman, for example, after a quarrel with Ursula Kemp, threatened to go to Darcy and expose her witchery.[5] In a pamphlet about another case, we hear that the "eye of Mr. Arthur Robinson, a worthy Justice of the Peace, was watchfull" over Elizabeth Sawyer, a woman whom he had long suspected as a witch, "not without just cause." From suspicion he proceeded to "great presumptions" after gaining information from her neighbors

3. On the emergence of a Protestant governing class and its concern for social order, see the chapter "Magistracy and Ministry" in Patrick Collinson, *The Religion of Protestants: The Church in English Society, 1559–1625* (Oxford: Clarendon Press, 1982), pp. 141–88. See also the essays collected in *Order and Disorder in Early Modern England,* ed. Anthony Fletcher and John Stevenson (Cambridge: Cambridge University Press, 1985).

4. On the role of the justice of the peace and the legal process more generally, see Cynthia B. Herrup, *The Common Peace: Participation and the Criminal Law in Seventeenth-Century England* (Cambridge: Cambridge University Press, 1987). Her book stresses the interplay between local magistrates and "ordinary people" in pursuing a criminal investigation (p. 68). Although I have found no evidence to support the idea, it also seems possible that clergy encouraged villagers from the pulpit to inform on suspected witches. At least one introduction to a witchcraft pamphlet makes such an exhortation: "If, therefore, thou be assured that thy neighbour either in body, family or goods, is impaired by damnable witchcraft or perceivest by information or otherwise of such devices intended to be practised, or likely presumption of such devilish deeds contrived, for charity to thy Christian brother and tender regard of thine own state, prevent or stop the mischief by all possible means" (*A detection of damnable drifts* (1579), quoted in Rosen, *Witchcraft,* pp. 92). The author seems to be encouraging the equivalent of the modern "vigilance committee."

5. Rosen, *Witchcraft,* p. 116.

and "seeing the death of Nurse-children and Cattell, strangely and suddenly to happen."[6] Without the encouragement of these local officials, it is possible that villagers would have continued to deal with the witch by traditional methods—that is, by visiting a cunning person for magical protection, by employing anti-witchcraft measures such as "scratching" the witch, by social ostracism, and the like. The justice of the peace offered villagers a new, more effective means of protection, an orderly method to assuage local fears. Though witchcraft trials could not have proceeded without active support "from below," the justice of the peace may have performed a key role in transforming informal village-level witch-hunting into formal prosecution by the state.

The text of the 1563 statute against witchcraft registers a similar concern for "good order," making it a national as well as a local issue. The law, it explains, first passed at the end of Henry VIII's reign and repealed five years later, is being revived not only because "many fantasticall and devilishe persons" are using and practicing witchcraft "to the Destrucčõon of the Psons and Goodes of their Neighebours" but also because they bring "great Infamye and Disquietnes" to "this Realme."[7] As to the realm, so to the local household, village, or county: reputations were on the line and trouble was in store for masters and magistrates when the "infamye" and "disquietnes" occurred within local jurisdictions. The witch's maleficium is perceived both to humiliate elites and to cause them practical problems. In harming neighbors, the witch also harms the nation. She is not only, or even primarily, a malevolent mother who hurts other mothers and their households; she is an enemy of God and a rebel against the state.

The villagers who accused women of witchcraft were interested in purging their community of a specific threat to specific individuals. Governing elites, however, tended to be more interested in curing the whole country; for them the witch was an abstraction more than a danger personally experienced, and her punishment sent a number of important messages far and wide. A case in point is the pamphlet about the St. Osyth witches, attributed to one W. W., which is almost wholly composed of "informations" taken by Brian Darcy, the justice of the peace for this series of trials. These documents, however, are preceded by a title page and a dedicatory note by W. W. which provide something of a "frame

6. Henry Goodcole, *The wonderfull discoverie of Elizabeth Sawyer, a Witch, late of Edmonton* (London, 1621), sig. A4v.

7. Ewen, *Witch Hunting and Witch Trials*, pp. 15–16.

story."[8] The pamphlet is dedicated to the head of the ennobled branch of the Darcy family, distant relation of Brian Darcy, and the title page sets forth its purpose: to show "what a pestilent people witches are, and how unworthy to live in a Christian Commonwealth." Punishing the witch rigorously, the author claims in the dedicatory note that follows, is the most likely means to "appease the wrath of God, to obtain his blessing, to terrifie secreete offenders by open transgressors punishments, to withdraw honest natures from the corruption of evil company, to diminish the great multitude of wicked people, to increase the small number of virtuous persons, and to reforme all the detestable abuses, which the perverse witt and will of man doth dayly devise." Hanging, in fact, is too good for the witch; the penalty that suits the ordinary felon and murderer is hardly severe enough for one who defies "the Lorde God to his face . . . trampling the precious blood of that immaculate lambe Iesus Christ most despitefully underfeete." To do less than burn the witch, as do the "magistrates of forren lands," is to eclipse the "honour of God . . . and the glorye due to his inviolable name." The witch here is not the malevolent mother feeding demonic imps but the servant of Satan and blasphemer against "the person of the most high God." Satan is suggestively represented both as rebellious feudal lord and as false deity: witches "worshippe" Satan, to whom they have "sworne allegiance," joining his "hellish liverie." Not maleficium but "idolatrie" makes witches deserving of the cruelest torments. Severe punishment not only keeps "a due analogie and proportion" with the crime; it also sends a message about a whole host of sins for which idolatry can stand as a general term. The dedicatory note closes with hints of praise for Brian Darcy's conduct in presiding over the "orderly processe" of examination as the author humbly submits himself to the "Right Honorable" Lord Darcy's judgment and patronage.

8. W. W., *A true and iust Recorde*, "W. W." in fact, may have been Brian Darcy himself; if so, the pamphlet in a sense has a "single author." Macfarlane makes this suggestion, although I do not find his reasons fully convincing (*Witchcraft*, pp. 85, 92 n. 14). The lapses into first person which Macfarlane cites in support of this idea occur in the informants' statements that form the body of the pamphlet and do not necessarily indicate anything about the author of the preface, which is ostentatiously signed "Your Honours to Commaund W.W." Macfarlane also claims the Lord Darcy to whom the pamphlet is dedicated is Brain Darcy's father. Not so, according to Barbara Rosen (*Witchcraft*, pp. 103–4) or to Anthony Harris, the author of the introduction to the Scholars' Facsimile edition of *A true and iust Recorde*, whose argument I follow in my subsequent discussion. Anthony Harris identifies W. W. as William Lowth, publisher of a translation of Bartholomew Batty, *The Christian Man's Closet*, which contained a similar dedicatory epistle (p. vi).

Yet the informants' statements or summaries of indictments which make up the body of these pamphlets continue to tell the story of the malevolent mother. They foreground exactly the type of case I have examined so far, featuring quarrels, usually between women, over sources of nourishment, milk, feeding, and child care, in which the witch is typically portrayed as the caretaker and nurse of demonic imps who bring death and disease to the community's children. Inside the enemy of God and rebel against the state lurks still another threat; though the "frame story" obscures the witch's gender (she is not prominently designated as female, and the term "witch" is regularly coupled with "sorcerer") and stresses the rivalry between God and Satan, the body of the pamphlet foregrounds the witch as mother. It is as if, despite the confident assertion of patriarchal authority by God, magistrate, and the Right Honorable Lord Darcy, the male author still finds himself vulnerable to a threat associated with this earlier figure of authority. The patriarchal fantasy encoded in the introduction is not, after all, enough to contain the threat of the malevolent mother.

Other introductions to witchcraft pamphlets from this period similarly foreground the witch as enemy of God or rebel against the state and yet bracket tales of the witch as malevolent mother. Like W.W.'s pamphlet about the St. Osyth witches, pamphlets about Chelmsford and Windsor witches, among others, are strung together from transcripts of informants' statements and "confessions" or from lists of indictments, prefaced by short addresses to the reader stressing religious and social concerns.[9] The "collage" of voices in these pamphlets suggests that beliefs

---

9. See especially *A Rehearsall both straung and true*, reprinted in Rosen, *Witchcraft*, p. 84; *A Detection of damnable driftes* (1579); and *The Apprehension and confession of three notorious Witches* (1589). In *The examination and confession of certaine Wytches at Chensforde* (1566) the contrast between the attitudes expressed in the prefatory material and those in the body of the pamphlet is less striking, in part because the preface is very convoluted. Interestingly, although the witch is not portrayed as malevolent mother, the verse preface invites "patrones with your babes" and "matrones mild" to "behold" what follows; tellingly, mothers are explicitly specified as an audience for these stories about the crime and punishment of witches. But later in the preface, the witches are described not as mothers with childlike familiars but as women "whom Sathan had infect / with Belial's spirite whose sorcery did, / the simple so molest." That is, the witches' deeds are referred to Satan's overriding control.

Rosen's anthology *Witchcraft in England* reprints the body of these pamphlets but only small fragments of the prefaces; her selection from *A Rehearsall both straung and true* offers the most complete example. Macfarlane discusses the reliability of the material incorporated in the pamphlet accounts and finds them generally consistent with other surviving documents; see *Witchcraft*, pp. 81–86. In "Popular Culture?" Clive Holmes notes the hybrid aspect of these pamphlets, commenting, "Each of the tracts commences with a preface or dedication in which the editor emphasizes the satanic origin of witchcraft. Yet the

representing the witch as malevolent mother could readily coexist with other modes of representation; she appears to fascinate readers of many different social levels. The pamphlets also stand as a reminder that the boundaries between "elite" and "village-level" belief were permeable. Many members of the gentry and aristocracy—perhaps especially those who had not received a stringently Calvinist education—shared beliefs that were in circulation at the village level. And later in the seventeenth century there is evidence that elite views had begun to filter down to lower social levels. Clive Holmes is surely right to speak of a "complex dialogue" between popular and elite views, rather than sharply opposed distinctions.[10]

Nevertheless, these pamphlets, I believe, ultimately foreground the *discontinuities* between elite and village-level beliefs about the witch. While village-level informants and accused women dwell on the witch's maternal malevolence and her animal familiars, gentry-level and aristocratic writers about the witch typically are concerned with promoting a new religious orthodoxy and maintaining social order. For them, the witch is a heretic, a class upstart, a traitor, and an unruly woman more than a malevolent mother. Elite texts appropriate some aspects of village-level representations of the witch but also significantly rewrite them, in ways that carry different implications for gender as well as for the political and theological controversies in which they were usually embedded.

Most striking, elite discourse transforms the meanings attached to the witch's malevolent mothering. In some texts, her maternal aspects are effaced altogether. Either way the effect is the same: elite discourse worked to undo the association of the witch's maternal attributes with *power*. In village-level discourse, the witch acquires supernatural power in exchange for the maternal care—food and comfort—she provides to needy, childlike imps in the form of small animals, allowing them to nurse from her witch's teat. In elite discourse, the imps front for or are completely replaced by an adult male devil—Satan himself. Satan controls all; it is a

doctrine makes at most a peripheral appearance in the cases and . . . is entwined with the popular tradition of the witch's familiar" (p. 100). Holmes's broader discussion of the interaction between popular and elite beliefs is germane to my argument at many points.

10. As Thomas points out, the wording of English antiwitchcraft laws and the practices of individual magistrates show the influence of popular belief; he also provides many examples of upper-class persons whose magical beliefs resemble those at the village level. *Religion*, pp. 441–45. On the filtering down of elite views to lower social levels, see especially Sharpe, *Witchcraft in Seventeenth-Century Yorkshire*, pp. 6–7. On "complex dialogue," see Holmes, "Popular Culture?" p. 89.

mistake to think the witch has any independent power of her own. In one introduction to a witchcraft pamphlet, the witch's imp is rewritten as "Belial's sprite"; another reminds us, "For it is Satan that doeth all, that plagueth with sickness, that maimeth, murdereth, and robbeth, and at his lust restoreth. The witch beareth the name, but the devil dispatcheth the deeds—without him the witch can contrive no mischief."[11] Satan is no mere imp but an adult male master, a canny con artist, an aristocratic warlord. Though he may appear in animal form, he is more accurately represented as a "fierce Dragon" than a ferret or toad. He may be hungry, but his hunger is for the souls of men, not for the powers of nurture located in the witch's body.

At the same time the witch herself is demoted; elite discourse emphasizes her dependence on Satan. She is a subordinate under Satan's control, a mere servant or "drudge." Her "witch's teat" is often replaced by the gender-neutral "devil's mark," sign of her compliance in the diabolic pact; like the colors that identify a servant's master, the devil's mark shows her to be enlisted in Satan's "hellish liverie." The witch's crime is no longer the doing of magical harm so much as the act of betrayal. Having no autonomous power of her own to kill or spread sickness, she nevertheless injures "good order" by her disloyalty. Her service ought to be rendered to God, ruler, and local magistrate. Instead, she turns against these male "masters" to aid, abet, and honor a transgressive male rival, often imagined as a virile and rebellious aristocratic lord.

The representation of Satan as aristocratic lord would receive its most memorable expression a century after the start of the witch-hunts, in book 1 of Milton's *Paradise Lost*. But his precursors can be glimpsed in many sixteenth-century texts, including those of George Gifford, to be examined more fully later in this chapter. It is a notion implicit in continental theories of the diabolic pact, in which the witch explicitly makes a deal with the devil reminiscent of a feudal contract. Such theories did find their way into elite discourse in England, though they were never as influential as in other European countries.[12] The pact, however, is not cru-

---

11. Rosen, *Witchcraft*, pp. 73, 84.

12. Seminal continental texts include the *Malleus Maleficarum* (Cologne, 1486), by the Dominican inquisitors Heinrich Kramer and Jacob Sprenger; and Jean Bodin, *De la Demonomanie des Sorciers* (Paris, 1580). A long section of the *Malleus Maleficarum* and a very short selection from Bodin are included in *Witchcraft in Europe: A Documentary History*, ed. Alan C. Kors and Edward Peters (Philadelphia: University of Pennsylvania, 1972). Their key ideas include not only the demonic pact but also the witches' sabbath. Though the sabbath quickly became a feature of Scottish trials and is mentioned in the pamphlet *Newes*

cial: what is more important and pervasive is the reassigning of diabolic power to a dominant adult male. To the mother-child dyad suggested by the pairing of witch with familiar is added a third figure, a Satanic "master" who embodies what resembles a child's fantasies of the father's phallic-aggressive powers. Elite beliefs about the witch reimagined her as part of a perverse but patriarchal family, in which the mother's powers were clearly inferior.

In village-level discourse, the witch's familiars were not directly linked with Satan; rather, they were part of the "third world" of the medieval cosmos, an intermediate realm between heaven and hell, populated also by mischief-making fairies, ghosts, spirits of "bad luck," and other supernatural denizens of the byways, forests, wild spaces, bogs, and fens of rural England. Reformation doctrine did away with the sycretistic multiplicity of this realm, along with the intercessory spirits of saints and the Virgin Mary associated with Catholic Christianity. The supernatural was recast as a stark binary opposition between God's angelic hosts and the dark forces of Satan. The power to control sickness and health, life and death, was associated with a heavenly paternal body rather than a human maternal one. Yet, Satan, though a retaliatory "bad" father and the proximate cause of misfortune, acted only as God's "rod of correction." As these authors remind us, Satan was able to exercise his destructive power only insofar as it "pleaseth God." Ultimately, supernatural power was the monopoly of the divine father who underwrote patriarchal male identities.

If the witch lost her access to the supernatural, so did the conjurer and the cunning folk. They too were Satan's dupes and lackeys. In elite rewritings of the witch, the maternal body lost its magical healing and protective powers along with its malevolent ones. Protestant doctrine implied that the white witch and black should be equally condemned. In this case, however, doctrine did not translate into legal action to any great extent. Though white witches came under increased surveillance and received small penalties, they were seldom subject to the more severe punishments

<hr />

from Scotland (London, 1591), it did not become a feature of English trials until well into the seventeenth century, and then only rarely. These texts were read by many educated Englishmen, including Reginald Scot and William Perkins. Interestingly, Perkins accepts the notion of the pact (calling it a "league or covenant") but considers the witches' sabbath a "mere fable." Neither Scot nor George Gifford accepts either idea. See Kittredge, *Witchcraft in Old and New England*, pp. 249–53, for some discussion of the circulation of these texts in England. Rosen notes that Bodin influenced Brian Darcy's interrogation methods in the St. Osyth trials. See Rosen, *Witchcraft*, pp. 104, 121 n. 24. Bodin also made a speech to Queen Elizabeth during a visit to England in 1581.

that in theory they deserved. But as propaganda, the Protestant campaign was more successful. The cunning folk increasingly lost credit among the better educated classes as the period of the witch-hunts wore on. Consulting them came to be seen as backward "superstition," if not something darker.

Surprisingly, gentry-level critics of witchcraft prosecution were at one with witch-hunters in divesting the witch of maternal power. Skeptics who did not believe in the threat posed by witchcraft found it necessary to account for witches' confessions and the symptoms of bewitchment experienced by their alleged victims. Reginald Scot and others ascribed these matters to the infirmities of the maternal body rather than its powers. Witches who confessed were the victims of their own diseased imaginations, subject to the melancholy brought on by menopause. The afflictions experienced as bewitchment were not caused by the witch's magic but were instead instances of *hysterica passio*—"suffocation of the mother." So doctors testified in the 1600 case against Margaret Francis and again in the 1602 case against Elizabeth Jackson, who was accused of causing Mary Glover to "languish," suffer periods of blindness, and have "strange fits."[13] As it was medicalized, the witch's malevolent maternal power disappeared, to be replaced by the weaknesses and diseases associated with the female reproductive body—site of inferior unruliness, in need of male diagnosis, aid, and "good government."[14]

The benevolent paternalism of these gentlemen skeptics is certainly to be preferred to the punitive rigor of those who promoted witch-hunting, who saw in the witch's rebellious submission to Satanic power something worse than mere infirmity. Yet both groups share a distinctly patriarchal view of the female body. Though largely shaped by theological and political concerns, elite discourse about the witch also promotes an agenda related to gender. As if to help sons get on with their developmental tasks, this patriarchal discourse enacts the devaluation of the maternal body as a primary source of nourishment and safety. Written by men and aimed at a largely male audience, it seeks in effect the dissolution of the son's dependent attachment to the preoedipal mother, encouraging him to "dis-

13. Ewen, *Witchcraft and Demonianism*, pp. 190–93, 196–99. On the medicalization of witchcraft beliefs, see Carol Thomas Neely, " 'Documents in Madness': Reading Madness and Gender in Shakespeare's Tragedies and Early Modern Culture," *Shakespeare Quarterly* 42 (Fall 1991): 321.

14. With weakness and infirmity also went a loss of agency, as Frances Dolan shows; see *Dangerous Familiars*, pp. 194–210.

identify" with her and take on the father's role. Rendered less magically powerful, the maternal body—more specifically the maternal breast—need no longer be envied, attacked, or feared for its retaliatory power. For some, such as Reginald Scot, the old women upon whom such fantasies were projected could then be seen in more human terms, and thus more sympathetically. Such men believed that those accused of witchcraft ought not to be subject to punishment and even maintained that their poverty and age made even their ill temper and diseases understandable up to a point. But for others, persecutory anxiety was merely relocated as the maternal body was reconceived as an erotic object. Elite texts about the witch suggest fantasies associated with oedipal rather than preoedipal conflicts. The oedipal son's hostile fantasies focus no longer on the mother's envied breast but on the father's phallic power: it is thus from a "bad father," Satan, that he primarily fears retaliation. But the "bad father" is joined by a mother who maddeningly complies with him, who allows him access to her "open" body in ways forbidden to the son. The son may experience the mother's dutiful submission to the father as a powerfully humiliating rejection and betrayal. The mother, moreover, may actively support the father in frustrating the son's continuing need and desire for her, becoming a source of further humiliation. His rage shifts back to her, the mother who has divided him from the father in the first place. Satan and God are ultimately too powerful to confront. The witch, however, may be dominated and destroyed.

But whatever the intrapsychic implications of texts about witchcraft for their elite male authors—undoubtedly more varied and complex than my schematic summary can suggest—it is nevertheless clear that the witch's malevolent maternal power is not seen by gentry-level witch-hunters as the primary source of injury and threat. Not the mother's breast but the permeability of her body and soul, her shifting affections and loyalties are at issue. In her very subservience she has the power to ratify the identity of those whom she serves, to proclaim who is "master." Her turning away from a "godly" master to a diabolic one constitutes a wounding "failure of deference," a narcissistic blow, an enraging betrayal, which in effect writes godliness as lack by complying with a transgressive rival.[15] The witch's betrayals, moreover, might be a reminder of

---

15. On the significance of "refusals of deference" in early modern culture, see Amussen, *An Ordered Society*, pp. 144–66. On the precariousness of the master's position and his dependence on subordinates, see Frances E. Dolan, "The Subordinate('s) Plot: Petty Treason and the Forms of Domestic Rebellion," *Shakespeare Quarterly* 43 (Fall 1992): 317–40.

more than troubling childhood fantasies: they might also echo the betrayals of everyday life, and they had a class as well as a gender content. The witch resembled the disloyal servant as well as the unfaithful wife, the all-too-yielding whore who spiritually cuckolds "legitimate" male authority. For children in elite families, the witch also would have had affinities with the wet nurse. Not only a potential source of a contaminating lower-class "otherness," the wet nurse might be experienced as betraying her elite nurse-children when she abruptly abandoned them after their weaning to return to her own family.[16]

In order to elaborate upon these claims, I examine several gentry-level and aristocratic texts about the witch in greater detail in this and the following chapters. Here, I focus on two religious tracts about witchcraft produced by the Protestant clergyman George Gifford and compare them briefly with writings by his close contemporary William Perkins. Gifford sought to shift the emphasis of witch-hunting away from the legal prosecution of witches and toward a biblically based critique of white witchcraft in its many forms. In so doing, he directly engaged village-level beliefs about the witch; divesting the witch of her malevolent maternity is part of his explicit strategy. Perkins, though he shared many of Gifford's theological assumptions, saw the witch as a clear and present danger and promoted prosecutions; his discourse elides the village-level witch almost entirely, replacing her with the betraying servant of Satan.

In the next chapter, I deal primarily with aristocratic discourse about the witch, first examining the events surrounding the reinstatement of the witchcraft law at the beginning of Elizabeth's reign and noting the uncanny replication of village women's quarrels at the heights of power, as Elizabeth sought to differentiate herself from her Catholic predecessor, Mary I, and her primary rival, Mary Queen of Scots. The bulk of the chapter, however, discusses James VI and I's extensive involvement in the first large-scale witchcraft trials in Scotland, an involvement, as I hope to show, that may have been significantly shaped by his difficult relationships with his two powerful "mothers," Mary Queen of Scots and Eliza-

---

16. Or when she sent them away: children were sometimes farmed out to a family rather than nursed at home. At the village level, the wet nurse may have left her own children feeling neglected, her attention directed instead toward the upper-class child who brought income to the family—thus playing into the village-level idea of the witch as the nurse of rival children. On wet nursing more generally, see Fildes, "The English Wet-Nurse"; and Crawford, "The Construction and Experience of Maternity," esp. 25–27. See also Janet Adelman's remarks in *Suffocating Mothers*, pp. 4–5.

beth I, who frequently "betrayed" him in his confrontations with an unruly Scottish aristocracy. Dependent for his power on these political mothers in some obvious and unavoidable ways, James could play out his resentments and reassert patriarchal dominance over the maternal by prosecuting witches in the North Berwick trials.

Elite discourse about the witch rewrites village-level representations in important respects, stripping the witch of her perverse powers of nurture, turning her into a betraying servant of a diabolic male "master." Yet even in elite texts, the malevolent mother never entirely disappears. Her persecutory power is redefined along oedipal lines but not fully dissolved; it lingers in the wounding effects of her disloyalty. She haunts the peripheries, arousing anxieties not confined to the village level. Yet it is also noteworthy that governing elites directed their concern especially *to* that level. It was primarily lower-class witches, not women of their own class, who ended up on trial. The malevolent mother was always someone else's mother, at a distance from one's own.

Two Protestant Clergyman

Though the pamphlet about the St. Osyth witches foregrounds the witch as mother in its main section, its preface elides all traces of her maternity. Do the prosecuting classes have a stake in masking the malevolent maternity of the witch? Another gentry-level text, *A Dialogue concerning Witches and Witchcraftes*, written by the Essex clergyman George Gifford and published in 1593, both reveals and conceals the witch's associations with the mother (see figure 6).[17] Gifford's text, however, reverses the order in the pamphlet by W. W., first displaying, then stripping, the

17. Available in a facsimile edition by Beatrice White (Warwick Square, E.C.: Oxford University Press, 1931). Gifford's views about witchcraft in some respects resemble those of Reginald Scot, the great English critic of the witchcraft trials and of continental demonological writings. Gifford may, in fact, have attended the same college at Oxford as Scot, but it seems he finished his education at Cambridge in 1573. In 1582, the year of the St. Osyth trials, he received a living at a church in Maldon, Essex, twenty miles away. Although he lost his living in 1584 for his nonconformist beliefs (he refused to endorse all of the Thirty-nine Articles), he remained active in Maldon as a preacher and author of a number of religious tracts or dialogues. Unlike Scot, Gifford concentrates on common English beliefs rather than continental antiwitchcraft texts; this text, along with another work on witchcraft written a few years earlier, demonstrates his familiarity with local attitudes and is full of examples that closely resemble those described in the Essex trial documents (though historians have not been able to link them to specific cases). For an overview of his life and work, see the entry on him in the *Dictionary of National Biography*, ed. Leslie Stephen and Sidney Lee (1908–9).

A
DIALOGVE

concerning Witches
and *Witchcraftes.*

In which is laide open how craftely
the Diuell deceiueth not onely the Witches
but many other and so leadeth them
awrie into many great
errours.

By George Giffard Minister of Gods
word in Maldon.

LOND

Printed by *Iohn Windet* for T   Cooke and Mi-
hil Hart, and are to be fold   Church-
yard, at the Tygers head.   9 3.

Ames p. 411. Wt.p. 1230.

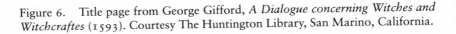

Figure 6.   Title page from George Gifford, *A Dialogue concerning Witches and Witchcraftes* (1593). Courtesy The Huntington Library, San Marino, California.

witch of her maternal power over supernatural spirits and, through them, over the households of her neighbors.

The dialogue begins with an encounter between two old acquaintances, "Daniell" and "Samuell," who have not seen each other for some time. Samuel, complaining of mental troubles, tells his friend that he suspects he has been bewitched: "For I see nowe and then a hare; which my conscience giveth me is a witch, or some witches spirite, shee stareth so uppon me. And sometimes I see an ugly weasell runne through my yard, and there is a foule great catte sometimes in my Barne, which I have no liking unto."[18] When asked whether he has yet suffered any real harm, Samuel replies: "Trust me I cannot tell, but I feare me I have, for there be two or three in our towne which I like not, but especially an old woman, I have been as careful to please her as ever I was to please mine own mother, and to give her ever anon one thing or another, and yet me thinkes she frownes at me now and then" (A4v–B). Thus, from the outset, the witch is explicitly associated with a mother's demands. Samuel quite obviously and anxiously experiences the old woman as a mother who is impossible to please, suspecting her of witchcraft merely for frowning at him. The animals he believes to be her familiars, moreover, become for him extensions of her persecutory gaze: the hare is a "she" who stares at him accusingly.

Samuel has also failed to please his wife. In greeting the two men she angrily chastises her husband for his failure to take action against the witch, an "olde filth," as she calls her. By now Samuel should have sought help from the cunning folk, as the husband of Goodwife R. has done. As in many of the cases discussed in Chapter 2, Samuel's witchcraft accusation turns out to have roots in a quarrel between women. Here, however, the husband is represented as henpecked, caught in the cross fire of a quarrel between two angry, overcritical women, one his wife, the other resembling his mother. Samuel himself seems fearful and indecisive. His wife shows little personal sympathy for him, though she is ostensibly on his side; her concern is for the death of her hens. Although the enemy of the witch, she also resembles her in accusative behavior and in calling attention to Samuel's inadequacy. Samuel is at sea in a world of women. Goodwife R. later joins his wife, and both urge him to seek magical pro-

---

18. Note the slippage in the term "conscience": for Daniel it has a meaning that corresponds to modern usage (conscience as voice of guilt or self-regulation); for Samuel the older meaning (conscience as consciousness, as mind interpreting the external as well as internal world and not necessarily engaged in self-accusation).

tection from the cunning "woman at R. H." The task of the dialogue as a whole is to wean Samuel away from his overdependence on women—on both the "bad mother" who threatens and the "good mother" who offers (illusory) protection.

The heart of the debate takes place at Samuel's house, where Daniel is introduced to "M. B.," a schoolmaster well acquainted not only with Latin and logic but also with local beliefs about witches and the cunning folk. In debating this more formidable adversary, Daniel—clearly Gifford's mouthpiece—lays out his central argument. Samuel has misinterpreted his mental troubles. It is not the old woman but the devil who has afflicted his mind "with blindnes and unbeleefe, to draw you from God, even to worship himselfe" (Br–B2). Witches do exist, as Scripture plainly says, and the devil works through them, but not in the manner commonly supposed. The witch has no power to command the devil; she is his servant and not he hers (B3r). Satan and his followers are not mere childlike imps who come and go at the witch's command but mighty and to be feared, "full of power, rage, and crueltie," comparable to "a great fierce red dragon," as Scripture sets forth. A devil is not like a hungry infant or a pet that needs the food and care only a witch-mother can give. Its hunger is that of a "greedie . . . lion, that roreth after the pray." If the devil sometimes takes on the guise of "paltrie vermine," such as cats, toads, and weasels, it is "even of subtiltie to cover and hide his mightie tyrannie and power which he exerciseth over the heartes of the wicked" (C2). Satan tricks the witch into thinking she has a power that in fact she does not. "Can you be so simple," Daniel asks M. B.,

> as to imagine that the devill lieth in a pot of wooll, soft and warme, and stirreth not, but when he is hired and sent? The devils conspire together in their worke, they bestirre them, and never take rest night nor day; they are never wearie, they be not a colde, they care not for lying soft; These be fooleries by which hee deceiveth the witches, and bewitcheth the mindes of many ignorant people. (C4v)

The witch's words of command are empty; the food and maternal care she offers to her imps have no real value to them. The devil fosters the illusion of power to ensnare her soul, but in reality he is "Lord and commaundeth," while "she is his drudge and obeyeth." The witch is the devil's "vassal" because he "rules in her heart," inflaming her mind with malice and the will to be revenged upon her neighbors (C4v). Then he tricks her into believing she has power to hurt them by cleverly exploiting coincidences; if the butter won't turn or a child dies, it is the result of natural causes.

Though she has no real power of her own, the witch nevertheless deserves punishment. She deserves the death sentence mandated in Exodus not because she kills men and livestock but because she "deals with devils" and because she imagines that her spirits actually do those harms that she requests them to (D2v). The cunning folk who claim to offer remedies for the harm done by the witch are just as deceived—and just as guilty—as she is. They too are tricked by the devil into believing that they have nonexistent powers; they too are inflamed with malice, often against old women who are really innocent. The cunning folk are in effect the devil's "other sort of witches" (D3r). They offer a false sense of protection, for they cannot drive the devil away by thrusting a red-hot spit into the cream any more than the witch can command the devil to stop the cream from turning to butter.

Ultimately, the devil can do nothing without God's permission. Misfortunes come from God, sent to try the faithful or to punish men for their sins. When one's hens die or one's child sickens, one may try all "natural" means to remedy the situation, but Scripture clearly forbids those means that involve dealing with devils. In blaming misfortunes on the witch, in turning for help to the cunning folk, people like Samuel and M. B. are missing the only true remedy. They must recognize the high sovereignty and providence of God over all things; they must see that their troubles are caused by their own sins and most likely indicate God's displeasure (D2). Above all, they must "heare the voyce of God, to be taught of him by his lively word . . . full of pure light" (M2v).

In expanding the category of "witch" to include the cunning folk, it would appear that Daniel is also expanding the potential scope of the witch-hunts. Indeed, Daniel believes that it is the cunning folk most of all who deserve to be rooted out and destroyed, for in seeming to do good, they are most likely to seduce the people into error. Yet at the same time the thrust of his argument makes conviction in a witchcraft trial almost impossible. It is clear that Daniel thinks most old women indicted for performing acts of harmful magic are in fact falsely accused. As M. B. and Samuel offer various examples from trials they have heard about or from their own experience on juries, Daniel demolishes the "proofs" upon which conviction depends. It is untenable to conclude that an old woman is a witch merely because misfortunes followed her angry curses, and sightings of her imps are also suspect, for in feare, in the darke men take some litle cat or dog to be an uglie devill. As not long since a rugged water Spaniell having a chaine, came to a mans doore . . . and some espied him in the darke, and said it was a thing as big as a colt, and had eyes as great as saucers. Hereupon some came . . . and did charge him in the name of the Father, the Sonne, and the holy Ghost, to tell what he was. The dogge at the last told them, for he spake in his language, and said, bowgh. (K4–K4v)

Daniel dismisses with similar contempt most other types of evidence used in and out of the law courts against a suspected witch—including not only the so-called devil's mark but also the cunning man's use of divination to identify the witch and the naming of a witch by a possessed person (Jv–J2). Though he states a witch's confession may be taken as a valid "proof" against her, even that must be viewed with suspicion; it may be the result of melancholy. When M. B. and Samuel protest that no one could be convicted given his standards, Daniel emphasizes the horrors of shedding innocent blood, which is "one special cause why Satan dealeth by witches: for he laboureth to wrappe in many guiltlesse persons upon suspitions . . . and thus whole Juries must become guiltie of innocent blood, by condemning as guiltie, and that upon their solemne oath, such as be suspected upon vaine surmises and imaginations, and illusions" (H3v–H4). Daniel will accept as proof only the witch's own confession or the sworn testimony of at least two witnesses who actually catch the witch "dealing with devils." Convicting an innocent woman is far worse than allowing a guilty one go free.

Daniel comes close to construing the whole legal apparatus for witch prosecutions as the work of Satan. Contrary to common opinion, the devil profits from the spectacle of punishment. He gains more from a witch's confession than from her denial, for how else would he "make men think that he doth so many harmes at the request of the witch? howe should he draw so many to runne after devils, to seek help at their handes? Or how should he draw the people into manifold errours and to thirst even in rage after innocent blood?" (J). To prosecute a witch for her alleged harmful acts is in any case a distraction from the more important business of recognizing one's own sins and turning to God.

It is less clear, however, how Daniel would feel about prosecuting the cunning folk. Daniel correctly sees that the cunning folk function as an informal branch of the legal apparatus, insofar as they help to identify a particular individual as a witch or offer the "testimony of devils" against her in court. But his objections to them extend to all their activities. When

M. B. points out that the law allows the death penalty to be applied only to those witches who have caused someone's death, it appears that Daniel favors a revision: "It wer to be wished, that the law were more perfect in that respect, even to cut off all such abhominations," including those of the cunning folk (K3–K3v). The crime should be defined as "dealing with devils" rather than causing injury by magical means. Would anyone who witnessed a cunning woman's use of divination then be able to provide reliable testimony against her? Daniel does not answer such a question directly; so it is difficult to say. What is clear is that the techniques of the cunning folk are to be shunned by all good Christians. If it is not Daniel's intention to make them objects of formal prosecution, certainly he wants to subject them to community censure and to drive them out of business.[19] They and all who seek them out are to be termed "witches" no less than those who cause harm (G).

In order to drive this point home at the end of the dialogue, Gifford exploits gender difference to mark a distinction between superior and inferior beliefs, using a female figure to embody the attitudes that Samuel and M. B. have now learned to reject. Having won the day, Daniel departs— just as "the good wife R." comes to pay a call (M3). Samuel's wife (present but silent throughout the dialogue with Daniel) tells her friend that, according to their recent guest, she is a witch. "I a Witch?" Goodwife R. responds, "I defie him that sayth it, though he be a Lord. I would all the witches in the land were hanged, and their spirits by them."[20] Samuel's wife explains that Daniel would call her a witch because she has done such things as put a red-hot spit into her cream when it would not turn to butter. "Is that witchcraft?" Goodwife R. retorts. "Some Scripture man hath told you so. Did the devil teach it? Nay, the good woman at R.H. taught it my husband: she doeth more good in one yeare, than all these Scripture men will doe so long as they live." Goodwife R. is a clear embodiment of exactly the beliefs Daniel has been condemning. She is quick to blame witches for her troubles and thinks those troubles would end if all witches were hanged; she employs "white" magical techniques and seeks out the cunning folk to protect herself from the witch's maleficium; she defends the practical remedies they recommend and dismisses the

19. Some pamphlet introductions make the same point.
20. At this point M. B. teases her as if she were a sixteenth-century version of Disney's Cruella Deville: "Would you not be glad if their spirites were hanged up with them to have a gowne furred with some of their skinnes"? he asks. "Out upon them, there were furre," she responds.

remedy supposedly residing in a close reading of Scripture. At the same time she considers herself a godly woman, believing that the cunning woman at R.H. is inspired by the "holie Spirite" of God.[21] When M. B. and Samuel make fun of her belief that the devil is somehow "in" her cream and is frightened by a spit, she retorts "I know he was driven away, and we have bene rid of him ever since." Results are what count; she cares little that she cannot explain the means. In her view, M. B. and Samuel have been "turned" by the Scripture man, becoming "defenders of witches," that is, scum of the earth. For this they deserve to become victims of the witch themselves: "I would you might loose all your hens one after an other, and then I would she would let her spirite upon your duckes and your geese, and leave you not one alive. Will you come to defend witches? . . . Yes, yes, there be too many that take their part, I would they might witch some of them even into hell, to teach others to defend them" (M3v–M4). The speech of Goodwife R. shows graphically how the accuser of the witch, as her verbal violence escalates, comes to resemble the very thing she denounces. Goodwife R. in effect calls down a curse, wishing harm to the neighbors who have angered her.

Gifford's dialogue ends rather equivocally. Goodwife R. cannot be persuaded; as she leaves, M. B. remarks, "she is willfull indeede." Nor has she persuaded them; they remain converts of the "Scripture man." The choice is clear: the goodwife or the Scripture man—"superstitious" belief to which an illiterate, ignorant country wife clings obstinately or correct Protestant doctrine, learned, logical, masculine, based on a careful reading of the relevant biblical texts. We are clearly invited to dismiss the goodwife as another Eve-like victim of the devil's subtlety. Yet she has been given the last word, and there is something about her stubborn insistence on the practical benefits of white magic to which M. B. and Samuel have no real answer. Would the devil "tarrie to be sent or intreated by a woman?" M. B. asks, rather desperately, at the last. Can a mere woman hope to control the evils in her environment? For Goodwife R., the answer is yes.

---

21. Goodwife R.'s view may be in the mainstream of English belief, for elites as well as for villagers. Conjurers and maguses such as John Dee or Richard Napier (an Anglican clergyman as well as a doctor) believed they were aided by angels or other good spirits sent from God and that without prayer and a holy life their healing magic or divinations would not be effective. The tenacity of such beliefs is probably one reason the white witches were never prosecuted to the same extent as the black, even when the laws allowed it and Calvinists such as Gifford recommended it. See Thomas, *Religion*, pp. 267–72; and Macdonald, *Mystical Bedlam*, pp. 16–32, 156–57, 210–11. And maguses too found scriptural support for their practices.

What is at stake here? Gifford's ultimate goal is nothing less than a radical re-formation of the subject, a "new birth" that requires people to turn away from all superstition and belief in devilish magic: only when people give up running to the cunning folk and blaming witches for their troubles will they have a chance to be saved from real misfortune. They must recognize that true help will come only through the new process of disciplining the subject advanced by Protestant reformers, which placed the close reading of Scripture at its center.[22] Like many others, Gifford invited Christians to commit themselves to an ongoing project of self-fashioning through submission to the biblical text, as mediated by men such as himself. The alternative to witch-hunting, in other words, is conversion. For these reformers, conversion takes place in the context of a masculinized supernatural landscape, in which the diverse range of beings recognized in popular belief had been reduced and reconceived in the light of the all-important battle between God and the devil, directly related to the battle against sin and error going on in every individual soul. Not only did this rethinking of the supernatural involve the expulsion of a host of beings with no foundation in Scripture (fairies, ghosts, and saints with intercessory powers); it also involved a new notion of Satan and his powers, a much greater emphasis on God's sovereignty, and a recoding of the meaning of misfortune. For Gifford, the devil's name is Legion, but the idea of spirits operating semiautonomously and limited to producing very specific effects, sometimes good, sometimes evil, was alien to him: "Though the devils be manie, yet they be all caried with such hatred against God . . . that they bend their studie all together, one helping and furthering another what they can in their worke"; therefore, Scripture speaks of them "as if they were but one devil" (C2v). One will animates them, and that will is utterly opposed to God's. The Christian confronting this eternal agon between two mighty males must oppose the devil just as vigorously, aligning his own will with God's, refashioning himself in the image of a divinity represented in patriarchal terms as father, judge, and sovereign lord. Given God's ultimate sovereignty, one's misfortunes cannot be blamed on the witch. Rather, they are to be accepted and understood as loving "corrections," the work of a firm but benevolent father, who punishes his children for their own good, remind-

---

22. That Gifford's rejection of the cunning folk is carefully grounded in Scripture is evident from the many biblical citations incorporated into Daniel's arguments, but even more evident in Gifford's earlier treatise, A Discourse of the subtill Practises of Devilles by Witches and Sorcerers (1587).

ing them of their sins and spurring them on to a conversion of the will and a perpetual struggle to amend their lives.

Clearly, this aspect of Gifford's rewriting of popular belief works to the advantage of the angry old women who tended to be accused of witchcraft. They are no longer to be blamed for the sickness of one's child or the death of one's hens; their angry words are not magically dangerous; and punishing them will not make one safe from further misfortune. Gifford removes these strong incentives to witch-hunting; yet his demystification of their powers also has a cost. He goes, in effect, to the opposite extreme, rewriting maternal power as self-delusion. Woman's ability to feed, nurse, or provide maternal care is not needed in this newly masculinized supernatural realm. The devil is not a hungry child who depends on something only a witch-mother can give him but a "dragon," a "mighty tyrant," or "God's executioner," feeding only on violence and destruction. The witch is not the devil's mother but his servant. The devil rules her through his superior male intellect, artful trickery, and ability to "enkindle" sinful passions. God, in turn, rules the devil. As God's executioner, he unwittingly carries out God's decrees; the Great Deceiver is ultimately the greatly deceived. Thus Gifford recodes the supernatural exclusively in terms of a male power structure; maternal power becomes irrelevant instead of dangerous.

Insofar as the maternal has any place at all in Gifford's conception of the supernatural, it is as an aspect of the divine Father. The child's fantasy of the magically powerful breast, encoded in the notion of the witch's nipple or teat, resurfaces in connection with God's holy Word—if not in the *Dialogue*, in some of Gifford's sermons. Here, for example, is a passage on the conversion process, in which Gifford makes an extended comparison of the "spiritual birth" to the natural:

It is good for us to consider that the spiritual birth is compared and likened to the naturall birth: for as in the naturall birth there is first brought forth a little weake babe, which hath life, and doth in tyme by degrees, even by little and little grow up unto mans estate, so in the spirituall birth, such as be borne againe in Christ, they be first as little babes, they have indeede the life of GOD in them but they be marvelous weake. . . . Most true it is also, as no man can deny, that in the naturall things men do grow up from babes to mans estate by food and sustenance, they growe also in knowledge and understanding by practice and meanes. The same is to be saide of the babes in Christ: they cannot grow up without the Spirituall food, they cannot come to more assured knowledge of their salvation but by the means which God hath ordained. . . . [F]irst seeing the word of GOD is the sincere milke by which we are to be nourished, it is our part . . . to covet the same. Wee doe all know this, that when a childe is borne, if it be alive and in health, howe much it doth covet the mothers breast, and how sweete the milke is unto it: in like manner, when a man is borne of God in the new and heavenly birth, he hath a vehement desire and longing after Gods word, it is marvellous sweete and delectable unto him. And questionles, all such as care not nor labor not to know the heavenly oracles, are void of the spiritual life: they be like unto those children which are born dead, which care not for the mothers breast. We must labour therefore by reading and by hearing the word preached, by meditation and earnest prayer to come to the true understanding and right use of the sacred word of God.[23]

Here, then, is an expansive vision of God the Father; along with his many lordly and paternal attributes, he metaphorically acquires both the mother's power to give birth and the mother's breast, his Word becoming the "sincere milke by which we are to be nourished."[24] Female is converted into male; God is mother and father both, hermaphroditically complete.[25] At the same time, the spiritually reborn subject becomes an infant again, a "little babe" who is "marvelous weake." God provides him with the "food and sustenance" of his Word, and by "practice and meanes"—by reading, absorbing, and applying the biblical text in his daily life—the spiritually reborn subject slowly comes again to "mans estate." Imagining God as a mother thus is necessary only temporarily, as the process of self-refashioning gets under way.

Elsewhere in Gifford's writings, God is emphatically masculinized, and the "babe" who grows to "mans estate" is to become a "valiant souldier"

23. Gifford, *Foure Sermons* (London, 1598), sig. F–F2.

24. In other ways as well the divine Father may be said to incorporate—one might say appropriate—traits associated with the feminine or the maternal: the God of judgment is of course also a God of love and mercy; and the Holy Spirit has been associated with the feminine since the early days of Christianity. The association of the maternal with God is not new either: it found rich expression in many forms of medieval spirituality. See especially Bynum, *Jesus as Mother*. It should also be remembered, however, that these traditions coexisted with others focused on the maternity of sacred females as well as males—most obviously Mary but also many female saints. After the Reformation, these figures lost much of their numinous power. The point here is that the more expansive vision of divine paternity suggested by the metaphors emphasized in Reformation discourse—attractive as it is taken in itself—coincides with the banishing of female presences from the supernatural realm.

25. The Galenic "one-sex" model of the body may be relevant here. See Laqueur, *Making Sex*. This way of conceiving of divinity also provides a spiritual equivalent for the child's fantasy of bisexual completeness, as described by Irene Fast, *Gender Identity: A Differentiation Model* (Hillsdale, N.J.: Analytic Press, 1984), pp. 12–23.

(*Dialogue*, D4) in the battle against Satan. The last chapter of Gifford's earlier tract on witchcraft, *A Discourse of the subtill Practises of Devilles by Witches and Sorcerers* (1587; see figure 7), ends with a passage in which the language of war and warriors is used extensively. Men who seek protection from all the "hurt and danger" imagined to come from witches must turn not to the cunning folk but to God. The real danger comes only from Satan:

> And . . . that the exhortation may the more affect us, Saint Paule doth expresse the whole matter under the likenesse and termes of warre. For thereby appeareth that there is neede of Gods power, that we may escape out of the great perill. The Apostle as a chiefe Captaine in the Lords Armie, doth stirre up and prepare all Christian souldiers. . . . The souldier had his head and all parts of his bodie with his legges and feete armed: then had he his sword in his right hand, and his shield in the left. Even so in this spirituall armour applyed by similitude unto the soule, here is armour for the head, for the feet and legges, and for al the whole bodie, and then the shield of faith to hold forth in the one hand, and the spirituall sword which is the word of God in the other hand. The summe of the whole is, that by faith in the Gospell of Jesus Christ we are armed with power of grace, with true knowledge and light, with sincere integritie of heart, and with a godly life, with zeale, with patience, and with all other heavenly vertues, so that the fierie darts of the devill, neither in tempting unto filthie sinnes, nor yet in damnable heresies and opinions, can fasten upon us. . . . For all those which despise the glorious Gospell of Christ, or the publishing of the same, and most especially such as fight against it, doe to their power set up the kingdome of the devill, and bring in all witcherie. The light of the Gospell doth beate him downe: and therefore when Christ sent forth his Disciples at the first to preach, and they returning rejoyced, that even the devilles were made subject unto them: he saith, I saw Satan fall downe from heaven like lightning. (I3v–I4r)

Thus the spiritual rebirth that initially makes men into babes again increasingly infuses them with God's "mightie power," turning them into nearly invincible warriors, making them over in God's image. The "whole armour of God" becomes their own, and shielded from head to toe and carrying the sword of faith, their spiritual bodies are immune to injury from the malevolent power they previously attributed to witches. This armored spiritual body is patterned on the father's, not the mother's; it has no vulnerable openings, and the Word associated with the mother's breast has now become a phallic sword. Such metaphors also suggest the new "activist" identity to be acquired after one's spiritual infancy and passive

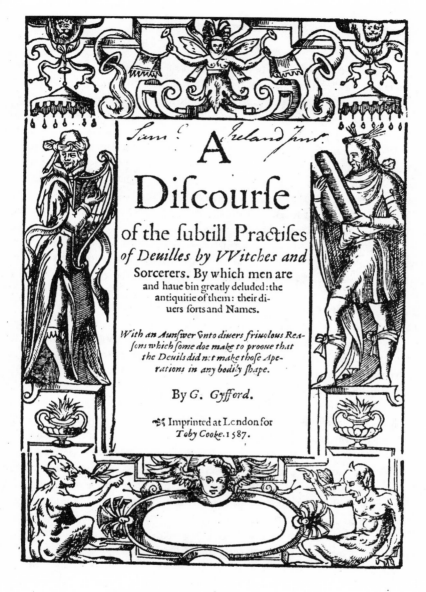

Sam: Ireland Jun:

A
Discourse

of the subtill Practises
of Deuilles by VVitches and
Sorcerers. By which men are
and haue bin greatly deluded : the
antiquitie of them: their diuers sorts and Names.

*With an Aunswer vnto diuers friuolous Rea-
sons which some doe make to prooue that
the Deuils did not make those Ape-
rations in any bodily shape.*

By *G. Gyfford.*

Imprinted at London for
Toby Cooke. 1587.

WH page 1262

A-p. A21.

Figure 7.   Title page from George Gifford, *A Discourse of the subtill Practises of Devilles by Witches and Sorcerers* (1587). Courtesy The Huntington Library, San Marino, California.

dependence on the biblical text: after "often hearing" of the Word, after afflictions have "driven" one to godly meditation, one may become a "publisher" of the Word, empowered as a speaking subject to preach it and "beat down" Satan, a disciple going forth as a triumphant Christian soldier.

Gifford, then, along with many other Protestant reformers, wanted the Samuels of the countryside to recognize that God's power was far greater than they had previously understood, that his governance extended into every corner of their lives, that he was mighty and to be feared as a sovereign lord and stern father, and that as a father, he could show a mother's tender care for his spiritual children as well as sternly "correct" them. The reformers used this vision of God to authorize new versions of identity which limited aggression, inculcated increased self-regulation and restraint, and mandated a more thoroughgoing internalization of the biblical text and submission to it. To triumph over Satan is to triumph over his violent masculinity—that is, to resist his attempt "to harden the heart, to blinde the eies of the mind, and from the lustes and concupiscences which are in them, to inflame them unto wrath, malice, envy, and cruell murthers: to puffe them up in pride, arrogancy and vaine glory: to entice them unto wantonnesse, and whoredomes, and all uncleannesse" (*Dialogue*, C2). Aggression was not, however, to be wholly repressed; rather, it was to be converted into a Christian activism, such as that displayed by Daniel in his learned, energetic debates—or, for that matter, by Gifford himself, who did not hesitate to speak out against secular authorities when they advocated a different reading of biblical precepts. As a preacher, Gifford was a critic of the rich and powerful as well as a "nonconformist" who lost his living as a parish priest because he refused to accept the Thirty-nine Articles. He was also arrested and imprisoned on charges of preaching limited obedience to civil magistrates and for other potentially seditious activities; though acquitted, he remained for many years under government suspicion as a "ringleader" of nonconformists.

Yet, at least in Gifford's writings on witchcraft, the discourse of conversion turns maternal power into powerlessness and denigrates the female as a speaking subject. As the threat of a persecutory maternal gaze associated with the witch's look is evacuated from the supernatural realm, it resurfaces in the human realm, not dissolved so much as disguised, diminished, and relocated: the witch reappears as cunning woman and willful wife. Whereas in Gifford's *Dialogue* the active will of the male has both positive and negative manifestations (God vs. devil, Scripture man vs. the sinner "inflamed" with lust, wrath, malice, envy, and the like), the active female will is represented in almost entirely negative terms. It is expressed primarily through women's angry speech as malice, accusation, and curse; men's anger, by contrast, is expressed through controlled debate and learned argument. Perhaps the only female subject position portrayed as positive is Samuel's wife's almost complete silence throughout the exchange among the three men, and perhaps also her brief application of Daniel's teachings to her friend. Even that contribution is ambiguous, however, for it is not clear that she has actually accepted Daniel's views.

It is important to do Gifford justice. If judges and juries in witchcraft trials had subjected the evidence to such a skeptical critique, it would have been far more difficult to convict and execute a woman (or man for that matter) for witchcraft. In both of his treatises on witchcraft, we glimpse briefly what may be a genuine sympathy for the old women who ended up on trial and criticism of the lack of charity often shown them.[26] Nor does he resort to Eve baiting; his text makes little overt reference to the inferiority of women. Although he addresses primarily a male readership and constructs the community of the faithful as one of male speakers and female listeners (as if prefiguring Milton's "He for God only, she for God in him"), in the broader context Protestant reformers unsettled older modes of subordinating women by advocating the extension of literacy to them so as to make them into interpreters of the biblical text. Women too were invited to put on the "whole armour of God" and become valiant soldiers, were empowered to speak and even to criticize husbands and other "masters" in some limited contexts (though not, of course, to become priests or preachers). Moreover, draining the maternal from the supernatural realm might have positive as well as negative consequences for women, opening up possibilities for cross-gender identifications with the Father and for the construction of roles for women that move them beyond the narrow confines of their maternal function.

At the same time, historians need to do more than celebrate Gifford for his critique of witch-hunting. Macfarlane considers Gifford's work "one of the most humane and rational attacks on current beliefs about the evil power of witches. . . . In his two witchcraft works we are watching a mind trying to rise above the limitations of his time, to argue its way out

---

26. This sympathy is easier to see in Scot, however. What comes across most powerfully in Gifford is his conviction that executing the innocent is a clear violation of God's will.

of a closed and circular system."[27] Perhaps so. Yet Gifford's construction of the cunning folk and of the country goodwife should also be taken into account in making such judgments. Arguably, Gifford advocated not so much a discontinuation as a transformation of the hunts. He wanted to shift the focus away from witches who supposedly practiced harmful magic and toward the cunning folk and those who patronized them. Gifford in at least one sense was very much a man of his time. In this dialogue and elsewhere, we see a mind rigorously following out the logic of a particular reading of the biblical text and its categories. Gifford's two works on witchcraft contributed to the climate of opinion which led to the revision of the witchcraft statute in 1604 and put the cunning folk (as well as others) at increased risk. If Gifford did not really mean to promote their formal prosecution, he did want to see these traditional methods of "self-help" among peasants (and presumably their elite counterparts) come to an end and their practitioners be put out of business. In seeking to reduce conflict between neighbors by discouraging them from blaming the witch, he was also in effect encouraging that informal, village-based methods for dealing with neighborly conflicts be replaced by the mediation of clergy and secular authorities. He demonized healing techniques that may have had therapeutic value, may even have been as effective as the medicine of the time. He demonized divinatory and other magical practices that may have done important "cultural work" in village communities. In place of cunning folk's syncretistic combinations of lingering medieval habits, magical traditions, and Christian doctrine, Gifford sought to substitute a text-based, puritan conformity to the divine Word; in the place of the cunning man or woman, he put the preacher who was "cunning in the Scriptures."

Gifford's opposition to conventional witch-hunting, moreover, can be overstated. Though stressing the flimsiness of evidence which made most convictions suspect, Gifford still believed witches who intended harm did exist. They were not capable of magical retaliation; they were not to blame for their neighbors' misfortunes; yet they deserved death for "dealing with devils" and for allowing Satan to inflame them with malice. The witch who intentionally tried to injure her neighbor, to "hire" spirits as

---

27. Alan Macfarlane, "A Tudor Anthropologist: George Gifford's *Discourse* and *Dialogue*," in *The Damned Art: Essays in the Literature of Witchcraft*, ed. Sydney Anglo (London: Routledge and Kegan Paul, 1977), pp. 140–55. Similar sentiments are also expressed in James Hitchcock, "George Gifford and Puritan Witch Beliefs," *Archiv fur Reformationsgeschichte* 58 (1967): 90–99.

her hit men, so to speak, was as guilty as if she had actually caused their misfortunes. But what did Gifford think of the old woman who felt malice, who perhaps even threatened to "get even" with her neighbor, yet did not actually seek out spirits to turn her anger into destructive acts? What was the status of "ill wishing," of wrathful thoughts or fantasies? Could women's angry speech ever take positive form? Gifford clearly wanted to prevent the deaths of innocent women; he believed many were falsely convicted. He was concerned about the plight of the poor, and delivered sermons that stressed the importance of almsgiving. Yet what options did he give the needy old women who tended to be accused? As passive sufferers they could be objects of pity, but could they voice their grievances, could they act to improve their lot? Gifford's text is vague on this point; he makes it difficult to distinguish between a premeditated decision to commit a destructive act and a mere angry thought. That vagueness may have been deadly; some women who "confessed" to witchcraft seem to have been motivated mainly by guilt feelings for such thoughts. Women's anger is not magical in Gifford's view, but it is still sinful.

Gifford contributes to a discourse that reinscribed the witch's maternal malevolence in the goodwife, making woman's tongue, will, and influence over her husband the object of increased suspicion, regulation, and punishment. Through M. B., he implicitly devalues the housewife's role, ridiculing her for her trivial concern with her hens and her butter rather than with the "Tyrants and wicked men" who persecute the godly and cause wars and division (C2v). He does not recognize or speak to the sources of friction between village women which led to rivalry, hate, and witchcraft accusations. His attack on the cunning folk, had it been successful, would have closed off an important option for women; becoming a white witch was one of the few ways a woman might earn extra money and status in a village community. Gifford, while enriching alternatives for male identities, restricts those available to women in some significant ways.

Ultimately, however, Gifford's intervention in the discourse of witch-hunting was indeed more "humane" than that of many of his contemporaries. It is useful, for example, to compare his views with those of William Perkins, with whom Gifford had much in common. Perkins, also a clergyman and thoroughgoing Calvinist, wrote sermons and an often-reprinted tract on witchcraft and the conversion process. His views, laid out in *A Discourse of the Damned Art of Witchcraft*, parallel those of Gifford in most respects; he too defines the sin of witchcraft as "dealing with devils" rather than causing harm by magical means, and he too considers the "good witch" to be worse than the witch believed to harm her neighbors: she is the more "horrible and detestable monster" because better able to fool the ignorant people.[28]

> Now howsoever both these [the good witch and the bad witch] be evil, yet of the two the more horrible and detestable monster is the good witch. For look in what place soever there be bad witches that hurt only, there also the devil hath his good ones who are better known than the bad, being commonly called Wisemen or Wisewomen. . . . It is in [the nature of ignorant and superstitious people] to abhor hurtful persons such as bad witches be and to count them execrable, but those that do them good they honour and reverence as wise men and women, yea, seek and sue unto them in times of extremity, though of all persons in the world they be most odious: and Satan in them seems the greatest friend, when he is most like himself and intendeth greatest mischief. Let all ignorant persons be advised . . . and learn to know God and his word. (P. 598)

Like Gifford, Perkins wants people to see that all misfortunes come from God and that those who suspect that they are afflicted by witchcraft should "enter into serious examination of themselves and consider the cause which it pleaseth God to suffer Satan to exercise them with that kind of cross" (p. 608). Their recognition that their afflictions are the result of their own sins should initiate them into the conversion process.

But whereas Gifford believes witch-hunting distracts people from conversion and is for the most part to be replaced by it, Perkins considers witch-hunting a supplement to conversion. Perkins sees the witch as a genuine danger; she does not merely "deal" with devils but makes an explicit "league" or "covenant," becoming a vehicle of real harm to others. Very few of the village witch's maternal aspects are mentioned at all; Perkins simply replaces beliefs about the witch as nurse to childlike imps with beliefs about the dangers of the "open" female body. Satan is especially drawn to women because they are "weaker vessels" like Eve and have a quasi-sexual susceptibility: with them he "findeth easiest entrance and best entertainment" (p. 596). Perkins replaces the witch's teat with the devil's mark: "When the devil maketh his covenant with them, he always leaveth his mark behind him, whereby he knows them for his own" (p. 603). Perkins is also far more open to circumstantial evidence than Gifford, accepting as "presumptions"—that is, as evidence sufficient to

28. Reprinted and abridged in *The Work of William Perkins*, pp. 579–610.

cause an investigation to be opened and an indictment to be handed down—matters Gifford would dismiss as "testimony of devils," such as information from another witch or magician, cursing or quarreling followed by death or "mischief," even the devil's mark when "no evident reason in nature" can be given for it. For conviction, confession is always desirable, and Perkins has no objection to the use of torture, believing that it "may no doubt lawfully and with good conscience be used" when there are "great presumptions going before" and the accused is "obstinate." When there is no confession, sufficient proof can be found in the testimony of two witnesses "of good and reliable report" that the accused has made a pact with the devil or that she has "done some known practices of witchcraft." And here—again unlike Gifford—Perkins is willing to leave much to inference: along with testimony that the accused has invoked or called upon the devil directly, Perkins will accept testimony that she has "entertained a familiar spirit and had conference with [it] in form or likeness of a mouse, cat, or some other visible creature" (pp. 604–5).[29] If a diviner has "showed the face of a man . . . in a glass, or used enchantment, or such like feats," that too can be taken as sufficient proof of witchcraft.

Clearly, both the cunning folk and the cursing, quarreling old women sighted in the company of small animals are at risk in Perkins's formulation. If accusers who believe themselves to be victimized by witchcraft must recognize that their own sins are the ultimate cause of their suffering, they may take some comfort in the belief that the witch too deserves punishment; not all the anger and frustration they feel need be subject to restraint or redirected onto the self. Accusing the witch—"good" or "bad"—and pursuing her punishment reinforces conversion by enacting God's will as revealed through biblical injunctions; if prosecution will not bring to an end the misfortunes conventionally believed to be caused by the witch, it will nevertheless restore order to the land by destroying the enemies of God and his church. For Gifford, the scaffold is a stage upon which the devil may "publish" his false text and win new converts; for Perkins, it is exactly the opposite, the place where God's righteous wrath is displayed against those who are guilty of the "horrible impiety" of joining "in confederacy with Satan" (p. 600).

29. Note here also how Perkins subtly eroticizes the witch's relations with the devil: she "entertains" a "familiar" spirit and "has conference" with it. The appearance of spirits in the shape of small animals seems to function as a disguise for a quasi-sexual liaison rather than to reveal anything childlike or petlike about their natures.

In one respect, however, Perkins's views work to the advantage of the white witch. For Gifford, being unaware that she is "dealing with devils" in working her cures and protections does not exculpate the white witch: "ignorance" Daniel warns, "doeth not excuse. For what though the witch suppose it is the soul of Moses, which appeareth in his Chrystal, is he not therefore a witch[?]: Your neighbor, whose butter wold not come, which heat a spit red hoat and thrust into the creame, using certaine wordes, doth thinke she did by the power of God fray away the devill, is she not therefore a witch, dealing with that which the devil, and not God hath taught?" (G) The ignorance of the white witch and those that consult her merely reveals their refractory attitude toward being instructed in God's word: when people "will not be taught of God, but dispise his doctrine, then are they iustly given over to be disciples of the devill" (Hv, and see F2v).

For Perkins, by contrast, both insanity and ignorance are extenuating circumstances. Perkins (adhering more closely to continental theory) substitutes the notion of a formal covenant between witch and devil, made "wittingly and willingly," for Gifford's vaguer notion of "dealing with devils." As a result, conscious consent is required to make one a witch. Those "tainted with frenzy or madness" cannot "give their consent to use his aid truly, but only in imagination"; they are thus excluded from the definition of a witch. Similarly,

> all such superstitious persons, men or women, as use charms and enchantment for the effecting of anything upon a superstitious and erroneous persuasion that the charms have virtue in them to do such things, not knowing that it is the action of the devil by those means, but thinking that God hath put virtue into them, as he hath done into herbs for physick [are expressly excluded from being witches]. Of such persons we have, no doubt, abundance in this our land, who though they deal wickedly and sin grievously in using charms, yet becuase they intend not to join league with the devil, either secretly or formally, they are not to be counted witches. Nevertheless, they are to be advertised in the meantime that their estate is fearful, for their present ungodly practices have prepared them already to this cursed trade and may bring them in time to be the rankest witches that can be. (Pp. 596–97)

Perkins, more "modern" here than Gifford in his emphasis on consent, does not take ignorance itself as a sign of sinful rejection of God's word. Yet the thrust of Gifford's dialogue works to make all legal prosecution of the witch suspect, whereas Perkins's tract works to reinforce it with minor modifications. As M. B. points out, "dealing with devils" is hard to prove in court without the sort of indirect evidence that Daniel disallows: witches seldom confess, and "they deal so secretely with their spirits, that very seldome they can be convinced by flat testimonies of men, as to say directly they have heard or seen them send their spirits" (H2v). Daniel acknowledges the difficulty but insists that likelihood, suspicions, and common fame ("notorious defamation" in Perkins's phrase) can never be sufficient for a conviction. It is, he repeatedly stresses, a terrible thing to be guilty of innocent blood; juries should avoid it at all costs, even at the risk of letting the guilty go free. For Gifford, it would seem, a witness must actually see the witch consult her spirit. For Perkins, however, the witch's pact with the devil may be inferred from the practices she uses.

Gifford spends much of his dialogue detailing the inadequacy of most (if not all) testimony commonly used to convict witches in trials at the time. Although his definition of the white witch's crime is more ominously inclusive than Perkins's, Gifford, through Daniel, criticizes only in passing the law that allowed the white witch to go free (K3–K3v). In its 1593 context, Gifford's dialogue functioned primarily as an intervention on behalf of women falsely accused. In its context Perkins's tract, written after the scope of the witchcraft law was expanded in 1604, could have facilitated prosecution of both the witch accused of maleficium and the white witch accused of employing devils to do good. As we know, white witches were never pursued; only the witches charged with the practice of maleficium ended up in court.

Ultimately both Perkins and Gifford engender the witch in similar terms. Gifford displays the witch's maternal aspects only to reveal them as derivative and illusory; Perkins barely mentions the witch's maternal aspects, substituting instead language that suggests the sexual openess of the female body. But both rewrite the witch as servant or drudge of an adult male devil and his superior transgressive power. If woman's anger, conjoined with her ability to feed and nourish, no longer invites blame for a variety of misfortunes associated with domestic life, neither is it to be respected or given much credit, even when directed against another woman suspected of practicing maleficium. The witch's crime, no longer defined as the production of injury or death by magical means, is instead constructed as a rebellious allegiance to God's chief rival and a rejection of God's divine Word—at once passive submission and defiance. In a sense, witchcraft (dealing with devils) arises from believing in witchcraft (maleficium), from believing that witches can cause misfortunes through their magic instead of seeing misfortune as God's "loving correction" for particular sins. The witch fails to read misfortune properly, as does the villager who consults or fears her. To this extent Gifford and Perkins agree. Yet these men, who share so many assumptions, nevertheless construct divine justice in some significantly different ways—different enough that Gifford might see the devil at work even in Perkins's recommendations, not to mention in those of Goodwife R. and the cunning folk. Puckishly, inexorably, the devil rises up from an excess in the biblical text itself.

CHAPTER FOUR
JAMES AMONG THE WITCH-HUNTERS

L ittle is known about the circumstances surrounding the passage
of the 1563 witchcraft legislation. The "Act against conjurations enchantments and witchcrafts" went through initial readings in both houses of Parliament in 1559, the very first year of
Queen Elizabeth's reign. Overshadowed by momentous issues such as the
Act of Supremacy (which made the queen supreme head of the English
church) and the Act of Uniformity (which set the English church back on
a Protestant course by mandating revision of the Book of Common
Prayer), the legislation was not passed until Parliament was reconvened
in 1563. Disputing some earlier scholars, G. L. Kittredge has maintained
that the witchcraft legislation was not influenced by continental theory,
nor was it exclusively the work of the Calvinist-minded Marian exiles;
rather, it drew upon native traditions of popular belief and represented
common ground between "romanist" holdovers and reformers.[1] It may
thus have helped Elizabeth to maintain these potential enemies in uneasy
alliance and to consolidate her power in the early years of her reign. Kittredge further contends that the immediate impetus for the legislation
came from a perceived increase in reports of actual instances of witchcraft
and sorcery—a rationale the statute itself suggests. Kittredge lists many
examples of such reports, a number of them involving aristocratic victims. Perhaps the most significant is the case of Anthony Fortescue and
his five confederates, indicted early in 1563 for treason. They allegedly

1. Kittredge, *Witchcraft in Old and New England*, pp. 23–72, 250–59. Kittredge is responding to Wallace Notestein, among others; see Notestein, *A History of Witchcraft in
England from 1558 to 1718* (1911; rpt. New York: Russell and Russell, 1965), pp. 14–20.

had conspired to depose Elizabeth and replace her on the throne with Mary Queen of Scots, having been encouraged in their plot by a horoscope that predicted a timely "natural death" for Elizabeth. Two of the conspirators had, according to the indictment, "practised various incantations and conjurations of evil spirits in working their said affairs; and inquired of an evil spirit how to carry their treasons into effect."[2]

The 1563 Act against witchcraft, then, was established during the tense and difficult years when a Catholic regime gave way to a Protestant one, a time when Elizabeth and her supporters were understandably anxious about any signs of conspiracy against her. Legislation, moreover, took shape largely along traditional lines: witchcraft was defined as maleficium, as it had been for centuries, and a powerful motive behind the passage of the law may have been the very traditional one of fear of harm to the sovereign's person. For secular authorities anxious about treasonous plotting against the queen, the witch's use of magic to cause illness or death loomed as the most immediate threat; conjuration that resulted in knowledge about the queen, her health, or her probable time of death was also a source of anxiety. While it was assumed that such practices required diabolic assistance to be effective, the essence of the crime of witchcraft seemed, at least at first, adequately summed up in the idea of maleficium.

Though there was little in the text that marked it as a special product of Protestant doctrine, once the legislation was in place, a growing Protestant majority could find in the witch a propaganda lesson that made enforcement of the law a compelling reiteration of an antipapist lesson.[3] Elizabeth's regime could, among other things, display its moral purity in contrast to a decadent Catholic laxity. Gentlemen reformers such as John Jewel, architect of early Anglicanism, aided in this process. As he wrote to Peter Martyr in 1559, "It is incredible how great a crop and forest of superstitions has sprung up in the darkness of the Marian time. Everywhere we found relics of the saints, nails by which foolish persons imagined that Christ had been crucified, and I know not what

2. Kittredge, *Witchcraft in Old and New England*, pp. 260–61. Also mentioned in Notestein, *History of Witchcraft*, pp. 25–26. The case of the Windsor witches seems to have begun in the fear that these witches were practicing image magic against the queen; this later proved to be a false assumption, and Reginald Scot found in it another opportunity to mock the whole proceeding. See Rosen, *Witchcraft*, pp. 83–91. Mrs. Dewse, of course, is another example of a would-be witch who had aristocratic victims in mind.

3. For the complete text of the law, see Ewen, *Witch Hunting and Witch Trials*, pp. 15–16.

fragments of the holy cross. The number of sorceresses and witches had increased immensely everywhere."[4] For Jewel, as for most Protestant reformers, witchcraft was inevitably associated with an empty and idolatrous Catholic sacramentalism. The rituals associated with the cult of the saints, like many Catholic practices including the Mass itself, seemed to these reformers little more than acts of blasphemous magic.[5] The implications of such rituals were blasphemous because they attributed a mechanistic supernatural power to words, objects, or persons; not only were such practices without foundation in Scripture but they also suggested that God could be coerced, that he would automatically allow his power to be manipulated at the whim of the priest or Catholic practitioner. The proper posture of the Christian was on his or her knees, humbly beseeching God for his favor but not presuming any mere "work" could guarantee a favorable response. The "magic" of the Catholic church presumed mere mortals could master supernatural power, could make God himself their subject. In effect, Catholics, like the witch, worshiped a false god, a devil. Such polemic enlisted the witch in the propaganda war against papistry, without, however, going so far as to redefine the essence of her crime as a pact with the devil.

Thus, to prosecute the witch was useful as Protestant propaganda and legitimating device in this time of religious controversy. Jewel's letter also suggests how gender could be enlisted in the service of a politics of religion: he implicitly links the Catholic threat to a sinister female power by feminizing the witch. Jewel emphasizes the association of witchcraft with the feminine by writing of "sorceresses" rather than "sorcerers"—this despite the fact that many of the reports of witchcraft or sorcery circulating at this time involved males. Jewel is perhaps underscoring his animus against Mary I: witches are extensions of this pernicious Catholic queen—dead a few years after a false pregnancy—who quite naturally let "sorceresses and witches" run riot in her kingdom. (That the cult of the saints often focused on female saints perhaps also contributes to the linkage of witch, woman, and Catholic practice.)

4. Quoted in Kittredge, *Witchcraft in Old and New England*, p. 250.
5. For an extended discussion of the intersection of witchcraft and anti-Catholic polemic, see Thomas, *Religion*, pp. 50–77. The earliest witchcraft pamphlets often displayed a pronounced anti-Catholic bias. See especially *The examination of John Walsh . . . upon certayne Interrogatories touchyng Wytchcrafte and Sorcerye* (London, 1566) and *The examination and confession of certaine Wytches at Chensforde* (London, 1566), reprinted in Rosen, *Witchcraft*, pp. 64–82.

But in a world where religious and political power struggles are waged through the female, a polemic that relies too heavily on sexual difference to underwrite its distinctions between "good" and "bad" categories will not be very useful, as John Knox had learned upon the untimely publication of *The First Blast of the Trumpet against the Monstrous Regiment of Women* the year of Elizabeth's accession. What are needed are not metaphors that set an evil and inferior female against a virtuous and superior male but metaphors that split the female into "good" and "bad." For this purpose, the figure of the witch (along with that of whore or seductress) could be opposed to that of virgin queen, natural mother, godly prince, and so forth. Such paired opposites in their varied combinations informed not only the polemics against Mary I but also those generated by the unfolding drama between Elizabeth and Mary Queen of Scots. Elizabeth presented herself and was presented by the men whose interests converged with hers as a brilliant contrast to both Marys. Here, Jewel's letter implicitly creates a space for Elizabeth to rewrite Mary I's reign as the "antimasque" to her "masque," in which she restores Protestant order by purging the realm of the magical practices and Catholic sacramentalism allowed to proliferate during Mary's reign, at the same time embodying a positive female power. As the memory of Mary I faded, the living threat of Mary Queen of Scots rose to take its place.

Strikingly, at this time England and its nearest neighbors were experiencing an unprecedented number of women in positions of power. Not only did Protestant Elizabeth come to power after her Catholic sister, Mary I, but her chief rivals for the succession, Mary Queen of Scots (Catholic) and Catherine Grey (suspected of Catholic leanings), were also female. Mary of Guise (Catholic) ruled as regent of Scotland until her death in 1560, when her daughter Mary Queen of Scots succeeded her; in that same year, the latter Mary's husband, Francis II of France died (precipitating Mary's return to Scotland) and was succeeded by his ten-year-old brother, Charles IX. His mother, Catherine de Medici, powerful enemy of the Protestant Huguenots, became regent of France. Ultimately, these women ruled in the name of their male patrilineage. Yet for the duration of their reigns, male-dominated religious and national rivalries circulated through the female personae they projected.

Thus, at the very heights of power, England was experiencing the uncanny likeness of the village women's quarrels. As in those quarrels, Elizabeth's conflicts with her rivals at the beginning of her reign also came to focus on maternal power, complicated by religious and political factors.

It was just around the time of the passage of the witchcraft statute that Elizabeth began to fashion for herself the persona of "natural" mother of her country. Pressured by her nobles to marry and produce an heir, Elizabeth was especially incensed when Catherine Grey was discovered to have married in secret and given birth to a son in 1561. Two years later, a second son arrived, just after the Commons had petitioned Elizabeth to name a successor and allay their fears about the return of a Catholic ruler (that is, Mary Queen of Scots) to power. She put them off, saying that though after her death they might have "many stepdames, yet shall you never have a more natural mother than I mean to be unto you all."[6] Elizabeth steadfastly refused to do the seemingly sensible thing and marry, fashioning instead an identity for herself as virgin queen and "natural mother" of the nation as a whole—her subjects her children, her rule a form of maternal nurturance.

Jewel's theme of "sorceresses everywhere on the rise" was echoed in the pamphlets and tracts on witchcraft from this early phase of the hunts. Does this claim perhaps gain part of its force from the fact that women in positions of dominance seemed to be everywhere on the rise as well? The monstrous regiment marched on. Both Protestant and Catholic men looked to a woman to advance their cause and feared a woman might check it; moreover, the intensely masculinist English nobility had to rein in its pride and defer to a woman on an almost daily basis. Many have written about the ambivalent feelings that female rule may have generated in aristocratic males.[7] Did such feelings also find expression in fear of the witch? The dominance of women in certain prominent positions may have also raised anxieties about women in less visible positions of

---

6. Quoted in Maria Perry, *The Word of a Prince: A Life of Elizabeth I from Contemporary Documents* (Woodbridge: Boydell Press, 1990), p. 177.

7. There is a growing body of work on female rule and its implications. On the impact of female rule on male subjects, see especially Montrose, "*A Midsummer Night's Dream* and the Shaping Fantasies"; Leah S. Marcus, *Puzzling Shakespeare: Local Reading and Its Discontents* (Berkeley: University of California Press, 1988), pp. 51–105; and Mervyn James on the gender implications of Elizabeth and Essex's interactions during the Essex revolt in *Society, Politics, and Culture: Studies in Early Modern England* (Cambridge: Cambridge University Press, 1986), pp. 416–65. For broader discussions of the controversies generated by female rule, see Pamela Joseph Benson, *The Invention of the Renaissance Woman: The Challenge of Female Independence in the Literature and Thought of Italy and England* (University Park: Pennsylvania State University Press, 1992), pp. 205–306; Susan Frye, *Elizabeth I: The Competition for Representation* (Oxford: Oxford University Press, 1993); and Constance Jordan, *Renaissance Feminism: Literary Texts and Political Models* (Ithaca: Cornell University Press, 1990).

power. Women's ad hoc powers were many. While elite wives were always subordinate to their husbands, they nevertheless frequently replaced them as "masters" in the absences created by war, illness, or visits to court.[8] Some were becoming well known as patrons at this time, helping—and refusing to help—men dependent upon them for advancement. Aristocratic mothers and mothers-in-law had considerable power in the brokering of marriages and other matters affecting their adult children.[9] Even Elizabeth's waiting women at court, whom the queen did her best to constrain, could exert a power of influence through gossip and the trading of information. Such ad hoc powers could seem sinister. As patrons, women blocked male advancement as well as promoted it. As mothers, they came into conflict with sons over marriage and inheritance. And the waiting women, Raleigh remarked, were "like witches . . . capable of doing great harm but no good."[10] Women's ad hoc powers, never fully acknowledged within prevailing cultural codes, were vulnerable to demonization when exercised in ways that conflicted with male desires.

As the century advanced, the understanding of witchcraft as maleficium came to be complicated if not replaced by continental notions about the demonic pact. The witch as an autonomous agent, a sorceress exerting powers over the supernatural (powers that might be understood as in some way inextricably linked to the maternal body), became in the new formulation the denigrated servant of a devil, a mere vessel of a distinctively male power. Visible not only in tracts such as those of George Gifford and William Perkins but also in pamphlets and stage plays, the continental formulation influenced the 1604 statute, instituted after James I came to the throne.[11] The new law redefined the crime of witchcraft, shifting the emphasis from those who practice harmful magic to those who "use practise or exercise any invocation or conjuration of any evil and wicked spirit, or shall consult covenant with entertain employ feed or reward any evil and wicked spirit." Significantly, the malevolent mother never fully disappeared; here we still glimpse her among those

8. On women as "good stewards" in their husbands' absence, see Pollock, " 'Teach Her to Live under Obedience.'" On the constraints imposed on women as officeholders, see Mortimer Levine, "The Place of Women in Tudor Government," in *Tudor Rule and Revolution: Essays for G. R. Elton from His American Friends*, ed. Delloyd J. Guth and John McKenna (Cambridge: Cambridge University Press, 1982), pp. 109–23.

9. See Harris, "Property, Power, and Personal Relations."

10. Quoted in Carolly Erickson, *The First Elizabeth* (New York: Macmillan, 1983), p. 350.

11. For the text of the statutes, see Ewen, *Witch Hunting and Witch Trials*, pp. 19–21.

who "feed" evil spirits, and to "covenant with" an evil spirit is only one of several other possibilities. But increasingly in representations of the witch, she is demoted to the position of Satan's servant. Did this reformulation serve a defensive function for men, enabling a consolidation of male identity along masculinist lines by writing out the possibility of a special female power over the supernatural? Was this reformulation especially attractive to aristocratic men resentful of female rule?

In what follows, I examine aristocratic witch-hunting as practiced by one individual, James VI of Scotland, soon also to be James I of England. Legislation against witchcraft which echoed the English statute of 1563 were instituted in Scotland in that same year, and the early course of Scottish witch-hunting, like that of England, consisted mainly of scattered cases against individuals. In some respects, however, Scottish witchcraft beliefs and especially the legal procedures involved in witch-hunting differed from those in England—increasingly so as the years wore on.[12] From the first, both "white" and "black" magic may have been more pervasive in Scotland, among elites as well as at the village level. Gentry-level clergy were more uniformly rooted in Calvinist doctrine and, in determined opposition to such practices, took up continental ideas about the demonic pact and the witches' sabbath more readily. Such doctrinal concerns combined with different rules regarding due process to create a state machinery more willing to prosecute not only "black" witches but also "white" witches and those who merely "consulted" them. Unlike their English counterparts, Scottish officials frequently employed torture to procure confessions and encouraged one suspected witch to name others. After 1590, witch-hunting in Scotland moved closer to the model of continental "panics" as large-scale trials involving hundreds of people at a time became common. At the same time an understanding of witchcraft as maleficium was transformed by the idea of the demonic pact. In those watershed years of the 1590s, what happened in England in a slower, less complete, and ultimately less lethal fashion happened in Scotland in condensed, intensified form.

Thus, keeping these differences in mind, James's involvement in the Scottish witch-hunts may provide us with insight into aristocratic witch-hunting in England as well. In particular, I offer James as the telling prod-

---

12. For a summary of the crucial differences and similiarities between English and Scottish witch-hunting, see especially Larner, "Witch Beliefs and Accusations in England and Scotland," in *Witchcraft and Religion*, pp. 69–78; and *Enemies of God*, pp. 9, 15–28, 103–19.

uct of a social and psychological positioning that may have had parallels for many among the English nobility and their affiliates. Though James was a king, his power was in significant ways limited by and dependent on queens who outranked him. Like the English nobility under Elizabeth, he too felt—perhaps especially acutely—the effects of a system in which the caprices of patrilineality occasionally brought women into positions of dominance and made men their subordinates, inverting gender order to preserve class hierarchy and, in so doing, disturbingly recalling the power of mothers over their male children and importing it into the public sphere. In both England and Scotland, it was within the anomalous context created by female rule that the witch was to a significant extent reconfigured, transformed from malevolent mother into betraying servant, her crime a covenant with the devil, not maleficium. What connections might there be between the effects of female government on male elites within a patriarchal culture and this reconfiguration of the witch? Did the increasing popularity of the theory of the demonic pact in both countries enact a reassertion of patriarchal power at the same time that it responded to other factors? James's involvement in witch-hunting makes it possible to consider such questions with a greater degree of specificity than usual. This is not to say that a history of James's involvement in the North Berwick trials is transparently self-evident—far from it. Reconstructing the events surrounding these trials, insofar as it is possible, must be done by looking through keyholes and peering around corners. The surviving state papers and trial records have many gaps; of themselves, they produce not a cohesive narrative but something far more fragmented.

Nevertheless, although we know little about the events that led to a witchcraft accusation in most village-level cases and even less about the personal histories of individual accusers, we have access to a good deal of information about James and his involvement in the trials, as well as the events, relationships, and gendered cultural practices that provide a broader context for his involvement. It is to his "story" of the witch that I now turn.

James VI and I and the North Berwick Witches

James's zeal for witchcraft prosecutions in Scotland was confined, it appears, to the years 1590–1597. His attention was first captured by investigations into charges of witchcraft against a group of women and some men in North Berwick; by 1597, after the publication of *Dae-monologie*, his tract on the subject, accumulating doubts about the evidence used to convict some witches persuaded him to overturn their convictions, and he withdrew from active involvement in trials or witchcraft-related scholarship. Historians have scrutinized James's infatuation with witchcraft in this period, interpreting it in the light of his developing views on kingship, his exposure to continental witchcraft beliefs at the time of his marriage, his dependence on the support of the Protestant clergy, and his conflicts with the Scottish nobility, particularly Francis Stewart, fifth earl of Bothwell.[13] I suggest that James's interest in prosecuting witches may also have been related to his ambivalent relations with his two "mothers"—his literal mother, Mary Queen of Scots, and his older cousin, Elizabeth I, whose heir James hoped to be. Beholden to both of these women in important ways, James also experienced them as threats to his secure possession of the crown and as instigators of aristocratic conspiracies against him. His construction of the witch and his involvement in witchcraft prosecutions, I suggest, was influenced by the complex history of his relations with these two powerful women, a history in which gender, family tensions, and intrapsychic factors played significant roles, along with politics and religion.

13. For the most detailed account of the trials and surviving documents, see Helen Stafford, "Notes on Scottish Witchcraft Cases, 1590–91," in *Essays in Honour of Conyers Read*, ed. Norton Downs (Chicago: University of Chicago Press, 1953), pp. 96–118. For a cogent study of James's exposure to continental beliefs and of the broader political context of his involvement, see Christina Larner, "James VI and I and Witchcraft," in *Witchcraft and Religion*, pp. 3–22. For a study of James and witchcraft in the context of his views on kingship, see Stuart Clark, "King James's *Daemonologie*: Witchcraft and Kingship," in *The Damned Art: Essays in the Literature of Witchcraft*, ed. Sydney Anglo (London: Routledge and Kegan Paul, 1977), pp. 156–81. For a treatment of James's relations with Bothwell, see Edward J. Cowan, "The Darker Vision of the Scottish Renaissance: The Devil and Francis Stewart," in *The Renaissance and Reformation in Scotland*, ed. Ian B. Cowan and Duncan Shaw (Edinburgh: Scottish Academic Press, 1983), pp. 125–40. For a study of the tensions between the king's government and Scottish Protestant reformers, with remarks on their implications for the North Berwick witchcraft trials, see Arthur H. Williamson, "The Failure of Antichrist and the Emergence of Satan," in *Scottish National Consciousness in the Age of James VI: The Apocalypse, the Union, and the Shaping of Scotland's Public Culture*, ed. Williamson (Edinburgh: John Donald, 1979), pp. 48–63. In addition, most of James's major biographers treat the subject at least in passing; perhaps the most detailed, if curmudgeonly, is David Harris Willson, *King James VI and I* (New York: Oxford University Press, 1956), pp. 96–115. Despite this rather lengthy list of studies (for what is really a rather brief episode in James's career), none even superficially relates James's views on witchcraft to gender issues.

The North Berwick trials apparently got under way when a deputy bailiff became suspicious about the activities of his maidservant, one Jill (Geillis) Duncan. Even before the allegations of witchcraft came to the attention of the king and other high-level officials, there was a "top-down" aspect to the investigations that set them apart from many English witchcraft trials. It was not the fear-driven complaints of neighbors which roused this bailiff to action but his own discovery of Jill's secret nighttime disappearances from his house and her acquisition "upon a sudden" of a seemingly miraculous healing power. The deputy bailiff subjected her to an examination, employing "the torture of the Pilliwincks" and other torments, but Jill did not confess until a witch's mark on her throat was discovered. She then admitted to dealings with the devil and named many others as "notorious witches." In the examinations that followed, authorities heard accusations and procured confessions containing descriptions not only of local attempts to use witchcraft against neighbors but also of treasonous attempts against the king's own life. Witches had met in "conventions" to perform ungodly rites, employing the body of a cat and the "ioynts" of a dead man to raise storms at the time of the king's return voyage from Denmark. One such storm was credited with sinking a ship carrying jewels for James's new bride; another with raising the "contrary wind" that plagued the king's own ship, part of an attempt to drown him. Shortly thereafter, on Lammas Eve 1590, a group of nearly forty witches met at Newhaven. Agnes Sampson, a midwife described as "the eldest Witch of them all," asked Satan to help them kill the king. He instructed some in the making of a wax image and a concoction of "toad, adderskin, and other vile materials," to be used to poison the king if the image magic failed; others were told to try to fetch a piece of the king's linen. Finally, on All Hallows' Eve, an even larger group, "to the number of seven score," met at the North Berwick Kirk. Reports vary as to what exactly went on. According to the pamphlet *Newes from Scotland* (see figure 8), the devil appeared "in the habit or likenes of a man" and enjoined them to "kiss his Buttocks, in signe of duetye to him," which all did after he had placed his hinder parts over the pulpit bar. He then delivered "ungodly exhortations," denouncing the king at length from the pulpit and terming him the greatest enemy he had in the world. Afterward, he received "oaths for their good and true service" to himself and departed.[14]

14. This reconstruction of the sequence of events is based on the anonymous pamphlet *Newes from Scotland* (1591), reprinted along with James I's *Daemonologie* (London, 1597) in *Elizabethan and Jacobean Quartos*, ed. G. B. Harrison (New York: Barnes and Noble,

Figure 8.   Scenes from *Newes from Scotland* (1591). Courtesy The Huntington Library, San Marino, California.

1966); and the dittays (indictments) contained in *Ancient Criminal Trials in Scotland*, part III, ed. Robert Pitcairn (Edinburgh: Maitland Club, 1829–33), especially those against John Fian (pp. 209–13), Agnes Sampson (pp. 230–41), Barbara Napier (pp. 242–44) and the jurors who subsequently acquitted her of some charges (pp. 244–47), and Eufame Mak-Calzane (pp. 249–57). The pamphlet is the only document that describes the events leading to the arrest of Jill Duncan, and there are discrepancies among the different accounts; for example, in the dittays against Fian and Sampson, tried earliest in the investigations, the description of what went on at the All Hallows' Eve "convention" contains no mention of treasonable activities against the king; instead, the witches gathered to pay homage to the devil and to engage in necromancy. Under the devil's instruction, they open up three graves ("twa within and ane without the kirk") and collect the joints of fingers, toes, and knees from the dead bodies—for what purpose is left unstated. But in the later trials of Napier and MakCalzane, the main purpose of the gathering is to carry out image magic against the king: "And this mater of hie hienes pictour wes the caus of that assemblie" (p. 246). Fian and Sampson were charged with other acts of treasonous magic (mainly the rite at sea involving the dead cat), but it seems that it took a while for the various gatherings to be understood as a continous series of attempts against the king's life. My reconstruction reflects what the king appears to have believed at least by May 1590. Other discrepancies among the accounts are discussed later in the chapter.

As investigations progressed, aristocratic involvement in the witches' activities was increasingly alleged. By mid-April, suspicions had become focused on the earl of Bothwell. The testimony linking Bothwell to the witches came from a male witch, Richard Graham, who claimed that Bothwell had met with him on several occasions to inquire about means of killing the king. Graham then met with the other witches, leading to the series of gatherings I have described. Bothwell conceded that he had indeed consulted Graham to make use of his magical expertise, but for personal reasons only; he denied all allegations of treason. Arrested and imprisoned in April 1591, Bothwell nevertheless avoided trial: James could not assemble an assize of Bothwell's peers willing to hear a case that depended solely on the allegations of an admitted witch.[15]

Whereas the powerful earl eluded the full force of the king's justice, many lower-class women and men continued to be examined, convicted, and sent to their death. In the months that followed, a hundred or more were questioned and a significant percentage executed in what turned out to be the first of a wave of large-scale witch-hunts in Scotland. As Christina Larner has pointed out, the investigation was also the last of the great "treason-cum-sorcery" trials familiar from the Middle Ages.[16] In such trials, proceedings were initiated primarily for political reasons, and harm to the king's royal person—rather than to lower-class victims—was the major concern. They frequently became vehicles for factional struggles and court intrigue, as rivals schemed to incriminate each other by means of a witchcraft smear. Clearly, there were strong political motives for pursuing the prosecution of the North Berwick witches so assiduously. Almost certainly the threat to the king was a major catalyst, and Graham's testimony linking the treasonous witchcraft to Bothwell may have been solicited by his enemies, as Bothwell claimed and others believed. Yet at the same time certain elements mark these prosecutions as products of a new age. In the past, the "treason-cum-sorcery" trials had stopped once the direct threat to the king was met, and they seldom involved more than a handful of cases at one time. The prosecutions instigated by James, by contrast, spawned an ever-widening series of trials, most of which had no overtly treasonous content. In Scotland as in En-

15. For the accusations against Bothwell and the events surrounding his arrest, see especially *Calendar of Scottish Papers*, vol. 10 (1589–1593), ed. William K. Boyd and Henry W. Meikle (Edinburgh, 1936), pp. 501–507ff, hereafter *CSP*. In addition, Stafford, Willson, and Cowan all provide overviews of Bothwell's activities as they relate to the witchcraft trials.

16. Larner, *Witchcraft and Religion*, p. 10.

gland, the "harm" of maleficium was central in legal definitions of the witch's crime, but for James and other authorities the crime took on an additional meaning in the light of continental demonological theory: maleficium also involved—in fact was made possible by—an act of disloyalty. In order for her magic to work, the witch had to enter into a pact with the devil; in doing so she betrayed both God and godly nation. By shifting loyalties from God to his worst enemy, she defied not only divine authority but also the earthly "chain of command" it authorized, stretching from king to magistrate to local master. The witch was thus by definition a traitor, always already the enemy of any king who aligned himself with God. Whether her magic was directed against the king or merely her neighbor, she was of the devil's party, aiding his enterprise and helping to extend his rule.

Larner credits James with introducing the concept of the demonic pact to Scotland, and she sees it as a key factor in turning Scotland into a witch-hunting state. But why did this concept take root in James's imagination, seem credible to him, become so emotionally compelling that he felt moved to spend months actively participating in investigations normally handled by lesser officials? He personally examined many of the North Berwick witches in time-consuming interrogations and was so invested in seeing them convicted that he lectured one jury at length after its decision to acquit; over the next few years, he devoted considerable kingly energy to writing his own demonological tract. Did this work merely reflect his tendency to "pick up and play around with fashionable ideas," as Larner suggests, intensified by fears for his personal safety? As Larner herself argues elsewhere, attitudes toward gender are not irrelevant to the study of the witch-hunts.[17] It thus seems worth considering how James's own attitudes in this area affected his response. Demonological theory was hardly gender neutral; it came heavily laden with often misogynist assumptions about women, and its revision of popular beliefs about witches also carried new implications for gender. Moreover, James's reading of demonological theory and of the allegations made by and about the North Berwick witches would have been mediated not only by his culture's preexisting gender norms but also by his own personal history of relations with women.

As king, James has often come in for harsh treatment. English contempt for the Scottish "barbarian," homophobia, and a variety of polit-

17. Ibid., pp. 5, 84–88.

ical agendas have underwritten many constructions of James as a "bad king," from his earliest biographers on. D. H. Willson's biography, which many still consider the best overall account of his life and reign, views James for the most part as an ineffective ruler with a multitude of character flaws. In literary and cultural studies, he has often been portrayed as not so much ineffectual as overbearingly oppressive. As architect of the theory of divine right, he has symbolized the very essence of royal absolutism; as heir to Elizabeth I, he has been held responsible for the "reinforcement of patriarchy" alleged to have followed her reign. Among some historians, however, James has been undergoing reevaluation. Maurice Lee Jr. and Jenny Wormald, for example, have called attention to the problematic assumptions underlying many earlier negative portraits of James and have demonstrated his strengths as a ruler in a number of areas.[18]

Yet however one assesses his overall career, in 1590 James was a young man, merely twenty-four years old, and his royal powers were sharply limited. Because he was king in name before he was old enough to rule, in his adolescence and early adulthood he had to struggle to

18. Anthony Weldon set the tone of much James bashing to come in *The Court and Character of King James* (1650), as Jenny Wormald has shown in "James VI and I: Two Kings or One?" *History* 68 (1983): 187–209. This disgruntled Englishman deprived of office by James took revenge through a "brilliant and deeply biased character sketch [that] has never quite failed to influence later attitudes," despite refutations by two contemporaries (p. 191). Wormald goes on to show that historians who have focused on James's reign in Scotland have evaluated him in much more favorable terms than those who have written primarily on his English reign. Maurice Lee Jr. reevaluates James in "James and the Historians: Not a Bad King after All?" *Albion* 16 (Summer 1984): 151–63, and also in his subsequent collection of essays, *Great Britain's Solomon: James VI and I in His Three Kingdoms* (Urbana: University of Illinois Press, 1990). For an overview of the existing scholarship on James, see the very helpful bibliographical essay by Susanne Collier, "Recent Studies in James VI and I," *English Literary Renaissance* 23 (Autumn 1993): 509–19. Discussions of James by literary critics include Jonathan Goldberg, *James I and the Politics of Literature: Jonson, Shakespeare, Donne, and Their Contemporaries* (Baltimore: Johns Hopkins University Press, 1983); and Leonard Tennenhouse, *Power on Display: The Politics of Shakespeare's Genres* (New York: Methuen, 1986), pp. 134–86. Both are important and sophisticated studies that nevertheless focus rather narrowly on James's absolutism and patriarchalism.

Most of the biographical work I have mentioned concentrates on James's *political* role. Yet there is another genre of biography (often written with a more popular audience in mind) that tends to emphasize interpersonal relations, including those cited herein by David Bergeron, Caroline Bingham, Antonia Fraser, and Alison Plowdon. In general, my own evaluation of James as king is closer to that of Wormald and Lee than to Willson's *King James VI and I*. But part of my purpose here is to juxtapose domains that have traditionally been kept separate: an analysis of gender, especially in the early modern period, requires that we examine the *intersection* of "the personal" and "the political."

establish himself and earn the respect of counselors and lords who were often much older. His nobles, when their own rights or interests were threatened, showed little respect for royal authority or the royal presence—and little fear of being denounced as traitors. On many occasions, James had reason to fear for his life; some nobles, when especially aggravated, did not hesitate to use the threat of violence or imprisonment to get their way. Royal survival depended on the strategic balancing of one faction against another, on careful management through concession, capitulation, and promises of patronage. From 1587 on, through policies devised by his principal adviser, James Maitland, the king managed to chip away at some of the rights that made the feudal aristocracy so powerful, among other things centralizing a court system that had been under the control of local lords, increasing his own power to give honors and offices (again at the expense of the nobility), and making lords more accountable for the misdeeds of their followers. The kirk, too, throughout this period, could be an unruly force. If the Protestant Reformation had freed the king's secular government from subordination to the pope and foreign interference, the kirk's "new men" demanded not only independence from the state but the right to instruct rulers in how to rule. All godly princes and magistrates ought to hear and obey the clergy, who were best able to interpret the will of God. Through the "Black Acts" in 1584, king and kirk had come to an agreement that checked the advance of such presbyterian thinking, naming the king head of the church and giving him the right to appoint bishops and to control the ecclesiastical courts. But such control by no means ended the kirk's criticism of the king when he was thought to be pursuing an ungodly course; though individuals who went too far risked punishment, the kirk's power to influence policy remained strong.[19]

Kingship in Scotland was a delicate balancing act, and James had had to become skillful in negotiating the conflicts that circulated among himself, a faction-ridden nobility, and an outspoken church hierarchy—not to mention a neighboring nation that assumed a strong controlling interest in Scottish affairs. Throughout his youth and early adulthood, two of the most powerful players in these conflicts were women—his mother, Mary Queen

19. For some treatments of James's struggles with the aristocracy and the kirk in the 1580s and 1590s, see Lee, *Great Britain's Solomon*, pp. 63–92; Jenny Wormald, *Court, Kirk, and Community* (Toronto: Toronto University Press, 1981), pp. 143–59; and Willson, *James VI and I*, pp. 49–50, 96–101.

of Scots and his (much) older cousin, Elizabeth I. Both alternately supported and blocked James's kingship and future hopes, forming alliances with members of the Scottish nobility, working through networks of secret "intelligencers" as well as through public representatives, attempting to influence and at times coerce events from behind the scenes in order to bring James's policies in line with their own. James never met either woman face to face, but hardly a week passed without significant communication from one or the other in the form of letters or ambassadorial address. From afar they exerted a power that James may have experienced as hidden, controlling, and malign as well as beneficial and (occasionally) maternally supportive. Although James's titles and rights of office were grounded in their own, these women also had the power to check, interfere with, and call into question James's ambitions and assertions of kingly prerogative.

In Mary, James confronted a mother who from the first was likely to provoke ambivalence—to say the least. The story of Mary at the time of James's infancy is a familiar one: less than a year after James's birth, she had eloped with James Hepburn, fourth earl of Bothwell, probable murderer of James's father, Lord Darnley.[20] Her knowledge of and complicity in Darnley's murder was widely assumed at the time, as it has been by many historians since then. Forced by the nobility to abdicate her crown, she fled to England and left her son to the guardianship of the earl of Mar and his wife, to be raised as a Protestant and crowned king before he was two years old. James was raised by a group of surrogate mothers—four nurses and the countess of Mar, a vociferous enemy of Mary who, as James Melville later described her in his *Memoirs*, was "wise and sharp, and held the king in great awe"—and two male tutors, the king's close companions in these early years, Peter Young and George Buchanan.[21] Buchanan was a particularly severe critic of James's mother and vilified her to her young son as a murderous adulteress, encouraging him to turn to Darnley for a better emblem of parenthood. Though in life Darnley had hardly been an exemplary role model, in death his aggrieved ghost became a powerful tool of propaganda; thus Mary's opponents had met Bothwell's forces with a banner bearing the image of the baby James at

20. For an introductory telling, see J. E. Neale, *Queen Elizabeth I: A Biography* (1934; rpt. Garden City, N.Y.: Doubleday, 1957), pp. 157–76; for a more detailed treatment, see Antonia Fraser, *Mary Queen of Scots* (New York: Delacorte Press, 1969), pp. 280–360.

21. For James's early childhood and education, see Caroline Bingham, *James VI of Scotland* (London: Weidenfeld and Nicolson, 1979), pp. 27–49; the line quoted from Melville is on p. 32. See also Lee, *Great Britain's Solomon*, pp. 31–41.

the side of his murdered father's body, holding up a scroll that said "Judge and avenge my cause, O Lord."[22]

Mary's elopement, abdication, and possible complicity in murder was a mixed legacy for James. It catapulted him early to the crown, first in name only but very quickly in substance; by the middle years of his adolescence he already wielded considerable real power. It made him a Protestant, thus solidifying friendly relations with England and increasing his chances to be Elizabeth's successor, king of England as well as Scotland. But Mary's actions could be interpreted as confirmation that James was a bastard; he might, given the new example of wanton sexuality provided by her elopement, be the son not of Darnley after all but of David Riccio, Mary's former secretary, as rumor had it. If no bastard, his blood, however royal, could nevertheless be construed as tainted with Mary's unreliable and murderous temperament. Buchanan, for example, angry at his pupil over the death of a sparrow, lectured James as the "true bird of the bloody nest to which he belonged."[23]

Finally, Mary's abdication, forced by nobles upon whom James depended yet whom he ruled over, left him with ongoing legitimacy problems (see figure 9). In James's evolving sense of kingly prerogative, no subjects had the right to sit in judgment upon their sovereign and force such an abdication. Yet those who had wronged his mother in this fashion were James's own friends and supporters, and to follow the logic of this position to its conclusion would require James to insist upon his mother's return from England, thereupon to step down in her favor—or at least accept co-rule. Joint rule is exactly what Mary herself pushed for during the early 1580s. In 1581 she proposed an "association" of mother and son.[24] James, perhaps influenced by his early favorite Esme Stuart, a Catholic and a supporter of Mary, was open to the idea at first. As the implications were spelled out to him, however, he turned against it. "Association" would mean that he would need his mother's approval for major decisions, that she would in effect "have the chief place before him."[25] The proposal to so limit his powers may have in-

22. See Alison Plowdon, *Two Queens in One Isle: The Deadly Relationship of Elizabeth I and Mary Queen of Scots* (Sussex: Harvester Press, 1984), p. 127.
23. Lee, *Great Britain's Solomon*, p. 33.
24. For accounts of the "Association" and its vagaries, see David Bergeron, *Royal Family, Royal Lovers: King James of England and Scotland* (Columbia: University of Missouri Press, 1991), pp. 39–42; Fraser, *Mary Queen of Scots*, 459–62.
25. *CSP* 6:262 (Robert Bowes to Walsingham).

Figure 9.   Mary Queen of Scots and her son James, here characterized as prince, not king, by one of Mary's supporters, from John Leslie, bishop of Ross, *Ad Nobilitatem Populumq, Scoticum* (1578). Courtesy The Huntington Library, San Marino, California.

sulted sensitivities observers noted much earlier in James. In 1579, for example, the thirteen-year-old king "stormed vehemently" after receiving "haughty Letters" from his mother—"haughty" because she had addressed him as prince instead of king. In any case, by 1583 James appears to have rejected his mother's offer, on the grounds that "she seeketh to have a quality and joint interest with him in those weighty matters, and prefereth herself before him . . . with such prejudice and danger to him and his estate as he cannot agree to join with her therein."[26]

By 1584 it was also clear to James that Elizabeth viewed the idea with great suspicion. The association would inevitably increase the power of Catholics within Scotland, creating a new potential for friction with England. But James's views were not clear to Mary until he and his council officially rejected the proposal in March 1585. She reacted sharply to this filial ingratitude, denouncing James as a "usurper" and threatening to disinherit him and bequeath his crown to someone else. In December of that year, she interpreted Scotland's internal troubles (over the earl of Arran, during which James was briefly forced to surrender to Arran's enemies) as "a just judgment of God upon my child, chastising him to bring him back, as I hope, to repentance for having failed in his duty, faith, and promises to his true and natural and very affectionate mother, allowing himself to separate from her to entrust himself, destitute of all protection, to the ambushes and perfidy of his enemies." This just judgment should force James to recall that he held the crown of Scotland by "the force, violence, and rebellion of subjects alone." In rejecting the association she had offered him, he was also rejecting the chance to become "lawful possessor" of his crown, as had always been her "main scope and intention." He had left the door open for subjects to use him as they had used her. "For if a son is entitled to dispossess his mother, a lawful queen, . . . what cannot our said subjects dare against a child rebellious, ungrateful, and tyrannical, such as in their consciences I am sure that they hold him to be, although in his infancy some have lent him the name of king, to possess themselves in effect of the entire authority by means of it?"[27]

Far from regretting his unfilial behavior, James moved to distance himself from Mary ever more decisively, and the breach lasted to the end of her life. It did not help that rumors reached James that Mary had indeed disinherited him in a will that named Philip II of Spain her successor (a

26. Quoted in Bergeron, *Royal Family, Royal Lovers*, pp. 38, 40.
27. *Letters of Mary Stuart, Queen of Scotland, Selected from the "Recueil des Lettres de Marie Stuart,"* ed. William Turnbull (London: Charles Dolman, 1845), p. 329. The quotation is from a letter to the French ambassador.

will that though it was never disclosed may in fact have existed).[28] Though he publicly protested when it became clear that Elizabeth was going to execute Mary, and though the Scottish nobility pressed him to avenge her death afterward, it seems clear that James accepted the situation and even felt some relief. "I am now sole king," he reportedly said on the evening of the day he received news of her death.[29] Though Mary had often presented herself as her son's "true and natural and very affectionate mother," a protector who acted unselfishly to make him a lawful king, James, it appears, perceived her as a threat to his own best interests. Her association would have clipped his wings and subjected his will to her own; her actions, thus, before and after had come to seem a direct assault on his kingly identity and powers.

During the year in which he broke off relations with his mother, James was busy improving his ties with Elizabeth, finding in her an alternative mother with greater powers and more to give than his own. In June 1585 after Elizabeth had sent him loving letters, presents, and a new, charming ambassador, James wrote back to thank her not only for "the wordis thairof most loving" but also for the "kinde cairfulness" toward himself he discerned in her, which "seamid rather to have proceidit from sum *alter ego* than from any strainge and forraine prince, quhich I can on no wayes requyte bot by ofring unto you my person, and all that is myne, to be used and imployed by you as a loving mother would use her natural and devoted chylde."[30] In several subsequent letters, James continued to address her as "Madame and mother," signing himself as "Your most loving and devoted brother and son."[31] The "natural, affectionate" mother who acts only for her child's good—the mother that Mary represented herself to be—James now found, rhetorically at least, only in Elizabeth.

We may note in passing that James's generous gesture of gratitude, his offering up of self in devoted service, can be read also as its opposite: it is Elizabeth who must continue to be generous, to nurture her new "son" with presents and handsome ambassadors, to "use and employ" him as a

28. Willson takes the opposite view in *King James VI and I*, p. 80.
29. Bergeron, *Royal Family, Royal Lovers*, p. 44; Fraser, *Mary Queen of Scots*, p. 545.
30. *Letters of Queen Elizabeth and King James VI of Scotland*, ed. John Bruce ([London?]: Camden Society, 1849), p. 15.
31. Akrigg, *Letters*, pp. 64, 66. These forms of address are part of a formal language of flattery and may tell us more about James's skill as a political strategist than about his actual attitudes or feelings. Yet it is also suggestive that James uses them at this particular juncture—and then gives them up in favor of "cousin" later on. See also Bergeron, *Royal Families, Royal Lovers*, p. 47.

"loving mother" would use her "natural and devoted child." James's language could facilitate a fantasy of a mother who is a second self, whose will and interests effortlessly converge with those of her child—a fantasy, however, that could not be entertained for long in the realpolitik of inter-state affairs. Mary had warned James not to be taken in by Elizabeth, by "the food of her fine promises," which would end up depriving him of the more reliable assistance and support that only she and her friends could provide. "I make no doubt that she will feed my son, as she has done myself, with the hope of the succession of this crown; but it is only an artifice, solely to keep us in leading strings after her. . . . [S]he is more resolved than ever, never to declare while she lives any heir, or to suffer her subjects to turn their eyes from herself to those who are to reign after her."[32] Mary's imagery represents Elizabeth as a mother whose "food" paradoxically arouses hunger, whose power to nurture is used as a manipulative tool to make puppets of those who are dependent on her. Mary proved to be quite right that Elizabeth would never name James as her heir. Instead, Elizabeth used the succession as a means of keeping James pliable; he would never risk too violent a divergence from her will with the crown in the balance.

The opposite of the all-nurturing mother who acts as her child's second self is, James's letter suggests, the "strange and foreign prince," mysterious, separate, aloof, an "other" clearly marked as outside the self, indifferent and distant. But when James's rhetorical evocation of happy accord between mother and son was disrupted by the reality of their conflicts over the succession and other matters, no such return to strangeness and distance was possible; James depended too much on her. Rather, the seemingly all-nurturing mother alternated with the mother who starved and reprimanded her son, a second self who could turn hostile, taking James at his word and threatening to "use and employ" him for her own private ends. After the failure of the Spanish Armada, James reluctantly admitted that if she refused to name him her successor when the enemy was at her doorstep, she would refuse him always; yet he never completely gave up hope. She maintained her power over him by playing both roles—giving and withholding, supporting him as king and undermining his authority.

Elizabeth, in fact, at times went so far as to encourage virtual rebellion against the king when his policies were at odds with her own, enacting

<hr>

32. *Letters of Mary Stuart*, pp. 313, 314.

her will by supporting those nobles whom James came to detest as his most arrogant and troublesome. James's policies toward Catholics especially aroused Elizabeth's ire. Because James could not count on being named Elizabeth's heir, he had pursued a policy of appeasing his Catholic lords rather than more severely restraining them, in order to keep the door open to their support. James developed, moreover, a tendency to choose "favorites" who, if not actually Catholic, were perceived by England, by the kirk, and by many Protestant Scottish lords, to be sympathetic to the Catholic powers within Scotland or abroad. Esme Stuart was the first of these. Older, Catholic, cultivated in arts and sciences, he had been an important influence on James at a young age. Though James believed he had succeeded in converting him to the Protestant faith, Elizabeth and many Scottish Protestants believed him to be an agent of the Guises and the pope. A coalition, supported by Elizabeth and spearheaded by the Ruthven lords, forced Esme Stuart from power in a manner greatly humiliating to the young king. The lords took James captive and threatened him at sword point, mocking him for his powerlessness and his youth. Two years later James took a new favorite, James Stewart, earl of Arran; though apparently without religion himself, Arran had Catholic connections and was hated by the kirk. He too was forced from power by the Ruthven lords, whose return from banishment in England Elizabeth had helped arrange.[33]

The homoerotic aspect of James's relations with his favorites has often been noted.[34] Elizabeth, in addition to meddling in Scottish domestic affairs, was also insisting that James break off ties charged with passion and affection—in effect playing the heterocentric heavy. In the year preceding James's encounter with witchcraft, this triangular drama of quasi-maternal interference in James's politico-cum-personal relationships played itself out once again. James's favorite of the moment was the earl of Huntly, whose faction was caught red-handed carrying on an intrigue with Philip II of Spain. Elizabeth's intelligence network had intercepted correspondence in which the failure of the Armada was lamented, and Huntly and his friends promised help if Philip should attempt to invade England again. Elizabeth, understandably alarmed, reprimanded James for moving too slowly to punish the conspirators: "Good lord! Methinks

---

33. Bingham, *James VI of Scotland*, pp. 50–66, 71–83; Willson, *King James VI and I*, pp. 32–43, 47–57.

34. For some thoughtful remarks about historians' treatment of this issue, see Bergeron, *Royal Family, Royal Lovers*, pp. 28–31.

I do but dream! No King a week would bear this."[35] Elizabeth's tone, as it so often could be, was condescending, hectoring: she spoke as the seasoned stateswoman, impatient with the naïveté and spinelessness of youth. In her view, perhaps, James had not yet earned the title of king. But James had learned something from his experiences. In the showdown that followed—the Brig o' Dee incident—James moved against the rebels himself, leading his (mostly Protestant) lords against Huntly's faction, imprisoning or scaring off many in a successful military action. Though in the end James let his erstwhile favorite off lightly, he made sure Huntly was removed from power.

In complying with Elizabeth, James set himself in opposition to nobles enacting the will of his other mother, Mary—her ghost still a force to be reckoned with. When the king rode against Huntly, he also rode against the Catholic earls who had been among her most ardent supporters. But more important, he rode against Francis Stewart, fifth earl of Bothwell, nephew and heir to Mary's third husband, the murderer of James's father. In the two years since Mary's death, Bothwell had fashioned himself Mary's champion, the avenger of her death and the national pride she embodied, a more loyal son to mother and mother country than James was himself. At the time of Mary's execution, Bothwell had been especially vocal in his expressions of nationalist outrage, publicly calling on James to take up the sword and avenge his mother's death by invading England.[36] Since then, Bothwell had taken matters into his own hands by carrying out a series of border raids. He had also become a vocal critic of Maitland, James's chancellor, whose policies the aristocracy resented. Bothwell's opposition to Maitland grew out of a private factional quarrel but had acquired a class-based ideological edge, drawing in many other nobles against Maitland. As a result, Bothwell, a Protestant, made an unlikely alliance with Huntly and the Catholic earls at the time their treachery against England was uncovered. In joining with them, he hoped to topple Maitland and end the policies that were eroding the powers of the aristocracy.

Thus, however James responded to Huntly's treachery, he violated the will of a powerful woman and risked humiliation and rebuke from her or her representatives. But James was no longer anyone's pawn. He finessed the situation well, complying with Elizabeth as much to uphold his own

35. Quoted in Willson, *King James VI and I*, p. 101.
36. "Bothwell scoffed at the purple weeds worn by the King as mourning for his mother. The best suit of mourning would be a suit of mail" (Willson, *King James VI and I*, p. 79).

policies and power as to help England. He showed himself capable of decisive leadership and courage on the battlefield, dispelling doubts as to his military competence. He removed Huntly from power but dealt with him leniently and preserved their friendship. He checked Bothwell without risking a full-scale confrontation that might spark further resistance.

There were other signs during this year that James was emerging as a more effective and self-assertive king, willing to risk some defiance of the "grown-ups" but doing so without recklessness. His marriage to Anne of Denmark is a primary example. Elizabeth, along with many of James's nobles, disapproved of his choice, favoring instead Catherine de Bourbon, sister of Henry of Navarre of France. It was rumored, in fact, that Elizabeth would not only discourage James's marriage to Anne, but would stop any marriage he attempted. She wanted his line cut off; she wanted to see him kept from inheriting her crown.[37] Despite this opposition, James recognized that the French connection had unwanted strings attached, and he chose Anne, who was, moreover, younger and reportedly more attractive.[38]

Once the marriage negotiations were settled, James asserted himself further by his unexpected decision to sail to fetch his bride, whose ship en route to Scotland had been forced back to the continent by contrary winds. He left behind an explanation of this seemingly bold and chivalric gesture in a document that Willson has termed a "youthful declaration of independence."[39] He wants it known that he has made the decision on his own both to marry Anne and to go and fetch her. He is taking such action because he knows his countrymen have faulted him for taking so long to marry. Alone, "without father or mother, brother or sister," he is vulnerable, and this "nakednesse" has made him weak and his enemies strong: "one man was as no man," and the want of hope of succession aroused disdain; "yea, my long delay bread in the breastes of mony a great jolousie [suspicion] of inhabilitie as if I were a barron stock." But now, for the good of his country, he will make haste, though "for as to my owne nature, God is my witnesse I could have absteined longer." Some historians have seen in these lines further intimations of James's homoerotic preferences. Patrilineal power, upon which royal power was neces-

37. CSP 10:129; see also Helen Stafford, *James VI of Scotland and the Throne of England* (New York: Appleton-Century, 1940), p. 53.

38. For general treatments of James's marriage and the negotiations that preceded it, see Bingham, *James VI of Scotland*, pp. 112–26; and Willson, *King James VI and I*, pp. 85–95.

39. Willson, *King James VI and I*, p. 89.

sarily grounded, required James to make what he may have indeed felt was an unwelcome sacrifice in submitting to his culture's heterosexual imperative: "one man was as no man" outside of the heterosexual family. For the "weill of my patrie," he would do it, not out of passion but as a result of reasoned judgment.

To the reader, James's haste may also seem a haste to display himself as an adult, a "man," an independent and assertive king. He wants it clear that he has acted alone, that Maitland, for one, has not been involved in his decision. Though some think Maitland has been leading James "by the nose, as it were, to all his appetites, as if I were an unreasonable creature or a bairn that could do nothing of myself," James has made this decision without even consulting with him. Repeatedly he insists that he is capable of making decisions on his own; he is no irresolute "asse who can do nothing of himself." "The place where I resolved this was Craigmillar, not one of the whole Counsell being present their. And as I take this resolution onelie of myself, as I am a true Prince, so advised with my self onelie what way to follow."[40]

There is thus a rather driven quality about James's remarks and the decision to fetch Anne. He is a young man with something to prove. He will not be frustrated by the "contrarious windes," the "notorious tempestes of windes," which have stayed his bride's voyage, just as he will not let the "envious policy" of Queen Elizabeth (as one contemporary termed it) interfere with his marriage plans.[41] Yet he had to pay a price for his self-

---

40. *CSP* 19:174–76.

41. James did not mention Elizabeth in his statement, but at least one historian has seen her opposition as another reason for his haste: "But the envious policy of Queen Elizabeth which stood opposed to his forming any matrimonial alliance,—a policy in which she had succeeded for some years, seems to have inspired him with a resolution to brave every danger rather than endure the apprehension that the consummation of his marriage with the Danish Princess might anywise be frustrated." *Papers relative to the Marriage of King James the Sixth of Scotland*, (Edinburgh: Bannatyne Club, 1828) p. vii. It is certainly true that many of James's countrymen feared Elizabeth would take action to stop the marriage. According to one rumor, England was in more of an uproar over the king's match with Denmark than it had been over the Spanish Armada approaching its shores (*CSP* 10:110); in another, it was "given out here that her majesty has stayed the marriage with Denmark and is not willing he should marry in any place; and that there was 6000 men coming down to the Borders" (*CSP* 10:129). Later, at the time of James's return from Denmark, it was widely "bruted" that Elizabeth had ships of war rigged and ready to "impeach" James as he sailed home (*CSP* 10:284, 293). Elizabeth's true attitude seems to have been much milder, and James knew she would not go to war over the matter. But his counselors, according to one English observer, had long been putting in his head "toyes" of the queen's "intent to kepe him under" (*CSP* 10:110).

assertion, played out as it was in a context of continuing tensions and risk. He was earning the right to be a player within an oligarchy of competing elites—a right, however, that remained precarious, requiring continued vigilance and finesse. His royal powers could still be checked, his prerogatives threatened, his hopes for the future dashed, his royal person humiliated by rebellious nobles in league with his two powerful mothers. James sailed for Norway with at least some of his countrymen still censuring his compliance in Mary's execution—or murder, as some would have it. Put in the worst light, he was complicit in her death after a long history of usurping her power in life. He had defied his second mother, Elizabeth, in his choice of wife and was challenging her control over England's succession in seeking to establish his own line. He had legitimate grievances and much to resent as well as (perhaps) to feel guilty about in his relations with both of them, and yet expressing such feelings could jeopardize his political future as well as create inner conflict. Guilt, anxiety, anger: these would seem to be among the possible by-products of James's new phase of self-assertion.

How might this history of ambivalent relations with women have affected James's response to witchcraft? Exploring this question to an extent depends on determining the order of events as James came to hear about the witchcraft allegations. What did James know and when did he know it? And what emotional resonance might witchcraft have had for him?

James ended up spending about six months in Denmark after going to meet his stranded bride. Witchcraft trials had been taking place in Denmark for fifty years, and in the course of his stay James entertained himself by engaging in philosophical disputations with a number of theologians, among them Nils Hemmingsen (Hemmengius), later cited as an authority in the *Daemonologie*.[42] Witch-hunting was in the air, and James may have been exposed to a broad range of continental thinking on the subject. Allegations that witchcraft had raised the contrary winds that grounded Anne may have come to James's attention while he was still in Denmark; it appears that an admiral had blamed them on the witchcraft of a bailiff's wife whom he had offended. By July 1590, three months after James and Anne had returned to Scotland, reports had reached the Scottish court about the arrests of a half dozen witches in

42. Willson, *King James VI and I*, p. 92.

Copenhagen for raising these winds and possibly also for the storm that struck the king's fleet and sank a ship upon their return.[43] At least by July, then, and more likely even earlier, James had heard about alleged acts of witchcraft with implications for him personally.

James's expedition to fetch Anne was the only major ocean voyage of his life, a storm-tossed separation from the "mother" country which would have aroused fears for personal safety with or without charges of witchcraft accompanying it. It was an act not of erotic passion but of passionate self-assertion, an attempt, through a marriage so daringly undertaken, to demonstrate that he was a fully adult, self-reliant king who could take a wife and produce heirs, thus consolidating his power within Scotland and enhancing his chances of succeeding Elizabeth. Marrying for these reasons may have activated a number of anxieties and unconscious conflicts related to his past history with women. He had crossed Elizabeth's will in choosing Anne to be his wife and perhaps suspected, as did some of his subjects, that she did not wish him to marry at all. He may also have associated the marriage with his own impatient ambition to supplant Elizabeth on the English throne as soon as possible. Was the idea that witches had raised a storm at sea in order to obstruct his marriage and possibly to kill him made credible by the preexisting anxieties aroused by these acts of defiance? Storms are conventionally associated with anger—angry gods, angry heavens, etc.—and in the rumors that reached James the witches seemingly enacted Elizabeth's retaliatory rage at her "son's" transgression. But James, in injuring Elizabeth by turning to another woman, was also repeating a pattern played out with perhaps more serious psychic consequences in his relationship with his real mother, Mary. His decision to marry Anne was embedded in a history in which he had numerous times injured and enraged one woman by abandoning her and turning to another—exemplified in its most extreme form when he abandoned Mary to her execution in exchange for Elizabeth's favor. The witches could be functioning as disguised versions of an angry, reproachful ghost he did not want to acknowledge. James, as mentioned earlier, appears to have viewed his abandonment of his

---

43. *CSP* 10:365. At the same time these reports reached James's court, so did the news that "sundry witches" had been arrested in Edinburgh as well—probably the witches associated with Katherine Roiss Lady Fowlis. Allegedly they had used image magic to kill a young laird, but were not connected with the North Berwick group shortly to come to the king's attention. See *Ancient Criminal Trials*, pp. 192–204, for the dittays against Lady Fowlis and her circle.

mother to her death as a justifiable necessity. But it seems likely that he would also have experienced at least some guilt, however resisted by his conscious ego.

That guilt may ultimately have had roots in his early childhood, when hostile wishes against the mother or other female caretakers would have been confused with acts and experienced as magically dangerous. Was James's sense of the magical destructiveness of his hostile wishes confirmed when Mary decided to flee Scotland and leave him behind at the tender age of one and a half? Did it seem to him he had in some sense "caused" his mother's disappearance? Was he, as an adult, still vulnerable to fears of retaliation for the fantasized injuries to the maternal body inflicted in childhood—fears that might again be activated when he injured other women associated with the mother's role? Such fears, surfacing as guilt, but rejected by the adult ego as unwarranted and too extreme, could be disavowed but not wholly destroyed. Sooner or later, they might return to haunt the ego in the form of fears of persecution from "out there"—fears that were likely to crystallize around figures, such as that of the witch, who resembled the mother in a disguised form. The Danish witches who sought James's death from afar were in a sense both Mary and Elizabeth's "enforcers"; they retaliated as if on their behalf, using hidden powers from the safety of another country, punishing James in unacceptable ways for the many injuries, real and imagined, conscious and unconscious, he had inflicted on them over the years—now subsumed in the injury implicit in his marriage to Anne.

It is of course highly problematic to reconstruct James's early childhood experiences from the limited evidence available; yet it does seem likely that James's childhood conflicts with women—recapitulated in later years—may have predisposed him to take these allegations of witchcraft more seriously than otherwise, especially given their timing. The memory of his mother's death was still fresh as he made this marriage in defiance of Elizabeth's wishes, his position as king was still somewhat insecure, and his identity as an adult had not yet been fully acknowledged by Elizabeth or his countrymen. Acts of self-assertion which crossed the will of maternal figures could still arouse fears of maternal retaliation—fears that would make witch-hunting all the more likely to make emotional sense to the embattled young king.

Four months after the reports of the Danish arrests, state papers indicate that James had become actively involved in the examination of the

North Berwick witches.[44] How had the accused come to his attention? Did the allegations of attempts to use witchcraft against the king surface before or after James's involvement? The letters of Robert Bowes, ambassador from England, are our chief source of information about this phase of the king's involvement, and in his November 28 account Bowes makes no mention of the witches' treasonous intentions. On December 7, however, Bowes wrote that the king "by his owne especiall travell [travail]" had procured a confession from Agnes Sampson about attempts on the king's own life.[45] Were the witches telling the king what he expected to hear? From the first, Bowes questions the veracity of some of the witches' claims and predicts they may damage the reputation of many innocent persons of "good qualities." Soon "evil is spoken of" various noblemen, and by February 23, 1591, Bowes himself has come under suspicion. He concludes: "And many thinges are told to please the examiners—chefelie the King—to wynn grace, and that are farre more strange then trewe, as my self and others touched with a shamelesse and drunken woman can witnesse and prove: wherein my name and place sufficeth to give them matter to rattle at as they list and were—I thinck—suborned."[46]

Bowes's letters suggest that many at the Scottish court responded with skepticism to the "phantastical" claims made by and about the accused. In being brought to court and questioned by the king himself, they were being given special treatment and a celebrity status; it must have been tempting to exaggerate their powers as well as slant their testimony in directions likely to suit the king. It is also clear that the witches' confessions would have been attractive vehicles for carrying out factional vendettas. Given the king's fascination with them, what better way to get back at one's enemy than by persuading an accused witch to name him as an accomplice?

James himself, it appears, reacted with skepticism to much of the witches' testimony. According to *Newes from Scotland*, some of Sampson's responses were "so miraculous and strange, as that his Maiestie saide they were all extreame lyars." Yet he was persuaded to give more credit to Sampson's claims when she accurately described "the verye woordes which passed betweene the Kings Maiestie and his Queene at Upslo in Norway the first night of their mariage, with their answere eache to other: whereat the Kinges Maiestie wondered greatlye, and swore by

44. CSP 10:425
45. Ibid., p. 430.
46. Ibid., p. 463.

the living God, that he beleeved that all the Divels in hell could not have discovered the same."[47]

By what manner Agnes Sampson divined the king's words we will never know. But it is intriguing that James's attention again fixes on an act of witchcraft aimed at his marriage.[48] Did Agnes Sampson's apparent divination offer further confirmation of a fear already emotionally real to James? Did the legacy of his relations with Elizabeth and the dead Mary make him vulnerable to belief in the seemingly omniscient powers of a malevolent female presence, capable of scrutinizing his most private moments and showing a sinister interest in the risk-filled first night of his union with his new wife? Agnes Sampson's divinatory power is suggestive not only of the powers attributed to the childhood mother but also of Elizabeth's and Mary's surveillance of the young king; from afar they "watched" James unawares through their elaborate intelligence networks, using spies as their eyes and ears, their "familiars," subjecting him to a sometimes unfriendly if not altogether malevolent female gaze. Such knowledge can give power over life and death, just as knowing the king's private words or possessing a piece of his linen can give the witch power over his person.

In the days and months that followed, James had the opportunity to reverse the direction of this surveillance, to replace magical modes of information gathering with juridical ones, and to make women the object of a distinctively male gaze. The control he was not able to exercise over Elizabeth or his mother he was able to exert over the North Berwick witches. In the process, power itself could be redefined as male and the subordinate status of women could be reasserted. Witchcraft associates women with powers like those the child attributes to its mother, powers that can threaten the emergent identity of sons until they more fully recognize the different (not to mention culturally privileged) powers conferred upon the male bodies of their fathers. Even then, the son's sense of a separate identity capable of coping with the challenging environment around him may remain precarious for a variety of reasons. Was James's own faith in masculine autonomy subtly undermined by his dependence on the favor of two exceptionally powerful women? Did his encounter with Agnes Sampson further undermine this faith by reviving the child's linkage of omni-

---

47. *Newes from Scotland*, p. 15.
48. And again on an act of divinatory magic. Back in July, at the time of the reports of the Danish arrests, James's interest had been sparked by a woman from Lubeck: "The King sent Mr. George Yonge to understand the divination of the gentlewoman of Lubeck as to the great honours destined to him," reported Bowes, *CSP* 10:365.

science with the female body, rendering the male body he inhabited deficient by comparison? As we have seen, there is a good deal of evidence to suggest that James at the time of his involvement in the witch trials felt that his "manhood" was not fully recognized either by Elizabeth or by the nobles of his court and council; did he also doubt himself? If so, the witch trials as they evolved in the coming months allowed him to reassert not merely male autonomy but male superiority, and to do so in terms particularly favorable to himself.

James's reassertion of masculine power would have been facilitated both by continental notions of the demonic pact and by the allegations of aristocratic involvement that the investigations elicited. The theory of the demonic pact—in contrast to popular beliefs about maleficium—made it clear that the witch's power was subordinate to the masculine power of the devil, whose power in turn was contained by God's. The preoedipal, dyadic fantasies of mother and child which seem to inform popular belief gave way to triangular relations: a bad "mother" now supporting a diabolic rival against a father-god. The witch's divinatory skill, her occult ability to raise a tempest and literally engulf her victims in her wrath, these were no longer under her personal control but were conferred by the devil; what was supernatural in her acts of magic was also masculine. The devil deluded her into thinking she had power, the better to ensnare her soul; in reality he controlled the show. The allegations that noblemen had instigated the treasonous activities of the witches further masculinized the crime and subordinated the role of women by shifting agency as well as power from female to male. The witches became mere vessels of an exclusively masculine malevolence, not the devil's dam but his minion.

Certain features of the witches' own testimony may have helped to make this shift of emphasis possible. Christina Larner, it has already been mentioned, credits James alone with importing the idea of the demonic pact to Scotland. Her argument elides the possibility that popular practices in Scotland may also have supported the theory, at least in part.[49] The surviving documents that record the charges against the North Berwick witches are fragmentary and contain discrepancies, and their "confessions" undoubtedly were subtly shaped by the beliefs and expectations of their examiners;

---

49. Nor does she explore the possibility that other members of the ruling elites were interested in demonological theory. Adam Bothwell, bishop of Orkney, for one, had the *Malleus Maleficarum* and Bodin's *De la Demonomanie des Sorciers* in his library (Cowan, "Darker Vision," p. 139). Nevertheless, as king, James's energetic interest in promoting his demonological views would have had by far the greatest impact.

testimony may also have been suborned, as Bowes believed. Nevertheless, a careful reading of the documents supports the idea that popular practice, and not just the views of authorities, may have contained some features that converged with the theories of continental demonologists.

The investigations sparked by the examination of Jill Duncan led to the arrest of some thirty people—women and men who knew each other, exchanged information about magical practices, and may have met in a semiorganized fashion to engage in witchcraft and necromancy.[50] Two or three of the more important witches were male; one of these, Dr. Fian, was described as the "clarke" or register who kept track of those sworn to the devil's service.[51] Richard Graham was described as another of the principals, who had wrought "mekle mischeif."[52] Most, however, were female. Sampson was described as the "eldest Witch of them al."[53] Barbara Napier and Eufame Makcalzane emerged later as prominent in their powers also. Many of the items listed against them contain descriptions of conventional village-level maleficium—using incantations, charms, and familiar spirits to cause sickness or harm their neighbors. Much of which they were accused could also be described as white magic—using their skills to heal and to predict the future as well as to harm. The devil, when mentioned at all, is variously represented. In the items charged against Agnes Sampson (one of the first to be convicted), he appears at times in the likeness of a dog and serves her as any English familiar might, coming and going at her orders, but he also appears to her "in mannis liknes."[54] Descriptions of the "conventions" led by the devil on All Hallows' Eve and at other times appear in all the dittays; during these, he presided over necromantic activities that had mundane as well as treasonous objectives. It is their accounts of the devil's address from the pulpit on these occasions, the formal oaths of service made to him, sealed by the kissing of his "erse" (figures 10, 11, and 12)—all clearly in mocking inversion of the mass—which have been assumed to be the most "contaminated" by the authorities' demonologically influenced preconceptions. Perhaps so. Yet James could have been influenced by many details in other segments of their testimony which prefigured the notion of the demonic pact, finding

50. Larner implies that the "coven" idea is a figment of the demonologist's imagination; yet there really is no reason to assume magical practitioners always worked alone.

51. In *Newes from Scotland*, pp. 18–19. In the dittays, he is described as "ewer nerrest to the Devill, att his left elbok [elbow]" (*Ancient Criminal Trials*, p. 240).

52. Ibid., p. 235.

53. *Newes from Scotland*, p. 10.

54. *Ancient Criminal Trials*, pp. 235–36, 239. See items 34, 38, 50.

Figure 10. The devil instructs his followers, from Francesco Guazzo, *Compendium Maleficarum* (1608). Courtesy of Special Collections, The Library and Center for Knowledge Management, University of California, San Francisco.

apparent support for his own preconceptions. A loose network of (mostly female) witches, with a few males in prominent positions, engaged in magical practices that involved following the instructions of a devil in the likeness of an adult male—such were some of the details that may have enabled James to find support for his preconceptions, then to push their testimony further in the direction of a full-fledged witches' sabbath.

"I call them witches which doe renounce God and yeld them selves wholely to the devill," James was to say at a somewhat later stage of the investigations, in a terse statement of the essence of the demonic pact.[55] In giving so much emphasis to the devil's role in the work of witchcraft, James was also emphasizing the hierarchy of male over female. The pamphlet *Newes from Scotland*, probably written under the king's guidance, and certainly written to make him look good to an English audience, fur-

55. *CSP* 10:525.

Figure 11. Witches pay homage to the devil by kissing his buttocks, from Francesco Guazzo, *Compendium Maleficarum* (1608). Courtesy of Special Collections, The Library and Center for Knowledge Management, University of California, San Francisco.

ther suggests a shift in the direction of masculinizing supernatural power. Despite the fact that most of the accused were women, the pamphlet foregrounds the case of Dr. Fian in its title and in its text makes much of his role as the devil's right-hand man. Very little mention is made of the acts of conventional maleficium which form the bulk of the charges in the dittays (acts in which the figure of an adult devil giving orders is conspicuously absent). There are no familiars. The leadership role of the devil is accentuated; he presides over the witches' activities, requires signs of duty, and expects "good and true service" from them. He is the chief agitator against the king of Scotland; after "he did greatly inveighe against the King of Scotland," the witches asked him why he so hated the king, "who answered, by reason the King is the greatest enemy he hath in the worlde." They attempted the king's death "by the Divels perswasion."[56]

56. *Newes from Scotland*, pp. 14–15.

Figure 12. Witches and devils dance to music, from Francesco Guazzo, *Compendium Maleficarum* (1608). Courtesy of Special Collections, The Library and Center for Knowledge Management, University of California, San Francisco.

By contrast, in the dittays that describe the All Hallows' convention and others like it, there is more give and take between witches and devil. Indeed, it is the witches who are impatient to take action against the king, and the devil who drags his heels. In one, for example, Agnes Sampson proposes the "distructioune of his hienes persoun, saying to the Devill, 'We haif ane turne to do, and we wald fayne be att itt gif we could, and thairfore help us to itt.'" In response, the devil indicates the difficulty of the task: "He soud do quhat he could, bott it wald be lang to." When they next meet, he does not have the wax image of the king properly enchanted yet, and their project cannot go forward.[57] In the transition from dittay into pamphlet, then, the devil's role becomes discernibly more central; his active intervention and dominance over a dutiful legion of primarily female followers is emphasized, and the gender hierarchy within

57. *Ancient Criminal Trials*, p. 245.

his chain of command is displayed. In the dittays, the devil is a helper, a go-between, a servant of the witch, whose assistance is sometimes required and sometimes not; the witch herself is represented as a skilled and often autonomous practitioner of magic. In the pamphlet, the devil is the central player, necessarily involved in every magical act.

This shift of emphasis is likely to reflect James's own preoccupations, at least in part. James may have seized upon those aspects of the witch's testimony which best supported the theory of the demonic pact, while downplaying or ignoring the rest. In doing so, he converted a female threat into one both female and male: the threat of magical retaliation came not from women acting autonomously against him but from women complicit with a castrating male rival, women who aided and abetted the foremost enemy of God and godly rule. The witches, in seeking to harm James, betrayed him in an ultimate act of disloyalty. If they were now subordinate figures, they were no less guilty; arguably they were more so. As their powers diminished, the severity of their crime increased: treasonous maleficium was compounded by the sting of personal betrayal, as they rejected James and the God he served and turned to his rival.

For James, this supernatural rival also had an earthly counterpart: the earl of Bothwell. James had not pursued earlier allegations of aristocratic involvement. The "evil" spoken of Lord Claud and other unnamed persons (mentioned in Bowes's December 7, 1590, letter) apparently came to nothing, and in February, Bowes was cleared when it turned out the witch alleging his involvement could not accurately describe what he looked like.[58] But the charges made against Bothwell in April appeared more credible to the king, especially when Bothwell conceded that he had in fact consulted Richard Graham, one of the "principal" witches in the North Berwick group. Bothwell insisted it had not been for treasonous purposes. Instead, Graham had offered Bothwell "a ring of sundry colours, showing him that there was a spirit enclosed in it whereby he might know what should betide himself, and whether his servants dealt truly with him, which ring he scorned."[59] Bothwell had, at the very least, a history of "consulting with witches."

Bothwell also had a long history of flirting with treason. Thus, the clear revelation of his consultations with witches must have made it almost impossible for James to disbelieve the allegations against him. Graham stuck

---

58. *CSP* 10:430; Bothwell himself had been named earlier by Jill Duncan and others, but they subsequently denied their testimony. *CSP* 10:502.
59. *CSP* 10:504.

to his story, despite the insistence of Bothwell and his supporters that he must have been suborned by one of Bothwell's many enemies. The king had Bothwell imprisoned and set about preparing for a trial.

In one account of the witches' Lammas Eve convention, the devil made his purpose unusually clear: he sought "his hienes distructioune, that ane uther mycht haif rewlit in his Maiesties place, and the ward [realm] mycht haif gane to the Dewill."[60] To James, Bothwell must have seemed especially likely to be the devil's choice to replace him. Bothwell summed up those aspects of the aristocratic mind-set which gave James most trouble. The Brig o' Dee incident had been only the most recent demonstration of Bothwell's tendency toward insubordination and contempt for the royal prerogative. He had feuded with James's chancellor and his centralizing policies; he had made James look bad in front of Elizabeth; he had been disrespectful of the king's royal presence; he was popular with the commons and had a reputation for military boldness James lacked. He may have been a seductive sexual presence as well; later it would be rumored that the young queen favored him.[61]

Moreover, he carried unavoidable associations with his uncle, the fourth earl of Bothwell—the man for whom James's mother had abandoned her son, the husband who had murdered James's father.[62] Bothwell was a tormenting reminder of the type of male James's mother had preferred—seductive, murderous, treacherous. Later, as James grew up, Mary and Elizabeth had used nobles of a similar type against him to advance their various causes. Now the witches, in serving Bothwell and his apparently murderous intent, repeated the narcissistic wound inflicted on him and his father in the past. Like the theory of the demonic pact, the allegations of aristocratic involvement transform the witches' crime; witches betray as well as malevolently injure, humiliate as well as kill. They aid and abet an earthly rival as well as a spiritual one. In so doing, they also punish James's "betrayal" of his mother(s) (as symbolized by his marriage to Anne) with a betrayal of their own.

Perhaps this psychic plot explains the vehemence of the king's response to the acquittal of Barbara Napier, who had sent a letter to her friend

---

60. *Ancient Criminal Trials*, p. 245.

61. On Bothwell's character and beliefs, see Lee, *Great Britain's Solomon*, p. 73; Willson, *King James VI and I*, pp. 100–101.

62. According to Willson, "it was this uncle . . . whom the younger Bothwell resembled in conduct and character. He was fierce, profligate and lawless, spending his time in carousals, feuds, and rebellions" (*King James VI and I*, p. 100).

Bothwell while he was in prison, telling him to "stand fast" against his enemies.[63] Napier came to trial in May, a few weeks after Graham first made his allegations against Bothwell (who was still in prison awaiting trial). She was charged with participating in the attempts against the king's life during the Lammas Eve and All Hallows' Eve conventicles, now believed to be undertaken at the behest of Bothwell. She was further accused of being responsible for the death by witchcraft of the earl of Angus, as well as other "sorceries, witchcrafts, and consulting with witches." Unexpectedly, the jury acquitted her of witchcraft against both the king and the earl, convicting her merely of the lesser charge of "consulting with witches" (which nevertheless also carried a penalty of death). "This is not fallen out as was looked for," reported Bowes back to England, "and further consideration will be had of these matters, which daily slide into great dangers."[64]

Barbara Napier, like some of the others accused as witches, was of fairly high social status—a burgess's wife, apparently well regarded in North Berwick.[65] She had many kinsfolk and friends in the area from which some of the jurors came, and according to Bowes, her connections had much to do with her acquittal. The king was "greatly . . . disquieted" and had the jury arraigned to "answer for their errors."[66] He came to the trial in person and had a speech read by his advocate to the jurors.

A number of issues preoccupied the king in this speech.[67] Juries, he felt, had inconsistent consciences. They tried too hard to avoid punishing the innocent and thus too often failed to convict the guilty. Juries must make sure they condemned the guilty as well as cleared the innocent. He hoped his action against this jury would serve as a warning "to make men more wary how they gyve false verdictes." Crime was rife in Scotland, and the reason was "that all men set themselves more for freendes then for justice and obedience to the lawe. This corrupcion heere bearnes sucke at the pap. And let a man commyt the most filthie crymes that can be, yet his freendes take his parte, and first keepe him from apprehencion, and after by feade or favour, by fals assisse or some waie or other, they fynde

63. CSP 10:506.
64. Ibid., p. 514, 515.
65. In Newes from Scotland, she and Eufame MakCalzane are said to have been "reputed for as civill honest women as any that dwelled within the Citie of Edenbrough, before they were apprehended" (p. 11).
66. CSP 10:518.
67. The full text is reprinted in CSP 10:522–25. I paraphrase and quote from it in the paragraphs that follow.

moyne [means] of his escape from punishment." He himself, he told them, had been accused of this very fault "in courte and quyre, from prynce and pulpet." But he was innocent of all such injustice and partiality to friends; he had acted justly even when matters had gone against his will. He had a clear conscience and asked the people to be his judge. He would continue his rule as he had begun, not because he had the power to do so but because God had appointed him king with power "to judge righteouse judgmente."

Witchcraft was an abominable sin, odious to both man and God, and was growing all too common in Scotland. By maleficium and veneficium, as man's law described the crime, witches sought to murder the people. Rather plaintively, James reminded them that if it was death that witches practiced against the common people, it was death when against the king: surely the king's life was worth as much as a subject's. If some still believed witchcraft was but fantasy, they should "be catechized and instructed."

James stopped short, however, of accusing the jury of "setting themselves more for friends than for justice." He did not doubt their loyalty, he told them; he assured himself that they "in no sort would for favour lean rather to a woman then to their prynce." Ignorance of legal custom must have caused their error. Apparently, the jurors had been reluctant to convict on the basis of testimony that came only from other accused witches. Though even judges at this time were divided on this point, James based his approach on the civil law: witchcraft was to be likened to cases of heresy and lese majesty, in which the testimony of women, children, and infamous persons could be used.[68] Moreover, witches who had repented were no longer to be accounted witches; their testimony was thus as acceptable as anyone else's. He absolved the jury of their error, his purpose being to instruct rather than to punish.

Several things are noteworthy here. James's frustration with this jury had roots in a much wider problem: his government was engaged in a protracted struggle to diminish the influence of kinship ties and to decrease the control of local lords over the justice system.[69] But the immediate context of this particular case also intensified that frustration; the acquittal came at a time when James was having trouble gathering enough support among his nobles to bring Bothwell to trial. Bothwell's

68. *CSP* 10:522.
69. See especially Williamson, "The Failure of Antichrist," and Wormald, *Court, Kirk, and Community*, on this point.

"freendes" were busy on his behalf, and even in the event that a jury of Bothwell's peers could be summoned, it appeared they would be reluctant to convict—especially when the only evidence against him came from an admitted witch. It is to Bothwell's "freendes" the king is addressing himself as well as to Napier's.

Subtly, James constructs the problem in gendered terms: setting oneself more for friends than for justice is a "corruption bearnes suck at the pap." Implicitly, the partiality of friends and kin for their own is likened to the partiality mothers feel for their infants. It is a fault "learned at the mother's breast," we might gloss it today—but that would be to lose some of the historically specific resonance of James's phrasing. Such partiality is figured as a corruption "in" the mother's milk, physically passed from mother to child. As sins could be passed "in" the blood, so the mother's (or wet nurse's) faults could be passed to her infant through her milk, contaminating from within.

James denigrated his opponents by associating them with this tainted mother's milk. At the same time, he sharply differentiated his own actions from theirs. He was well aware of an audience that criticized him for being too partial and letting his own "friends" off too lightly—as in the case of Huntly and the other Brig o' Dee conspirators. Now some—including Elizabeth and the Kirk—saw him as dragging his heels with Bothwell.[70] His action against Napier's jury gave him the opportunity to display his will to convict, his "law and order" rigor, when he was powerless to do so elsewhere. In so doing, he purged himself of the corrupting influence of the maternal breast. His figure of speech seems of a piece with other attempts in his address to the jury to distinguish a (good) maleness from a guilty and punishable femaleness—guilty and punishable because too partial to a "bad" male rival. He is sure, he tells the (male) jurors somewhat facetiously, that they would not favor "a woman" over their king: he knows they are loyal subjects. That woman, James believed, was partial not only to Bothwell but to the devil himself, helping the devil enlarge his kingdom at the expense of James's own, enlisting the devil's assistance in seeking James's death, hoping (presumably) to replace him

---

70. Bowes met with the king a few weeks before his speech to the jury and gave him advice "in her majesty's name." After reminding him of the faults Bothwell had already displayed, bringing danger to "the peace of both crowns," he urged the king take action to protect the innocent and punish the guilty, "to dandle no longer offenders to the perill of himself and [their] common causes" (*CSP* 10:511). Bowes's general point is much the same as the one made by the king in his speech.

with a king more to her liking. Aristocratic faction on earth thus was paralleled by and yet intertwined with a diabolic faction in the supernatural realm. As in many such uprisings, the underlings and minions were easier to suppress than the leaders; Barbara Napier became to an extent a scapegoat for Bothwell, who remained too powerful for James to bring under his sway.[71] But more important, she and the other witches who continued to be prosecuted became examples of the long shadow cast by James's own mother, Mary Queen of Scots, herself too partial to an earlier lawless and murdering Bothwell. Mary had seemingly betrayed son, father, and country by her compliance with Bothwell, in the process becoming the corrupting maternal breast that James was anxious to disavow and punish in many ways. But while his mother (and her successors) necessarily eluded him, the witches of North Berwick provided a target James could "discover," control, and finally destroy.

If James's confrontation with witchcraft began in the alarming possibility of a special female access to supernatural power—a power that recalled the preoedipal mother's apparent powers over her comparatively helpless child—it evolved into a discovery that, while more reassuring for male gender identity in a patriarchal culture, also reconfigured and in some ways intensified the threat the witch could carry with her. James's investigations subjected the powers attributed to the witch in popular belief—to raise storms in angry retaliation, to control other bodies through symbolic representations, to detect the hidden and the private—to his intense scrutiny and interrogation, testing them against demonological theory. In so doing, he appropriated the mother's seeming powers and omniscience for his own and turned them against her substitutes, exposing the witch's vulnerabilities and limits, making the witch the object of his surveillance and control, relegating the witch to a subordinate role, making her powers purely derivative. In constructing the witch as a be-

---

71. What exactly happened to Napier is somewhat unclear. Even though convicted only on the lesser charge of "consulting with witches," she was sentenced to death, but she claimed to be pregnant and was to be released until she had her child. In *Ancient Criminal Trials*, Pitcairn includes a note that says "nobody insisting in the persute of her, she was set at libertie" (p. 244). Yet it seems hard to believe that the king would allow her to slip through his fingers. In a letter to Maitland (date unknown but presumed by the editors to be late April), the king wrote, "Trye by the medicinairis aithis gif Barbara Nepair be uith bairne or not. Tak na delaying ansour. Gif ye find sho be not, to the fyre uith her presesentlie, and cause bowell her publicclie" (*CSP* 10:510). From Bowes after the trial we hear "no judgement is given, but she [Napier] is at the King's pleasure" (515).

traying servant, James could sidestep if not fully forget her connections to unsettling memories of the childhood mother, and male superiority could be reasserted. Yet in shifting her loyalties elsewhere, in taking the devil's part, the witch in her very submission to male power became a producer of a different sort of injury, an associate of a new source of threat. She inflicted a painful wound to the self-esteem; she refused to acknowledge the value of the young king; she slighted him, constructed her own hierarchy, and chose her own masters, in the process implying some deficiency in the one she had rejected. She endorsed alternative modes of male identity and aided a formidable rival, one who could not be defeated by human power.

Thus, male mastery was thwarted in the moment of its assertion. Although James could easily procure the prosecution of a long procession of lower-class witches, it was not so easy for him to control factious aristocrats such as Bothwell—or the many Jesuits and Presbyterians whom James later saw enlisted in the devil's ranks. In 1596 James took steps to protect his mother's memory through an act of Parliament.[72] In the following year his zeal for witch-hunting began to ebb.[73] By 1603, it had all but ceased. When Elizabeth finally died, so, perhaps, did his need for the witch. But not for the devil: when James inherited the long-coveted English crown, he inherited along with it a power elite now almost uniformly male—and no less treason-minded, malevolent, and murderous for being so.

72. This act—part of James's persistent attempts to secure the English succession—made it treasonable to slander either Mary or Darnley. Two persons were executed under its provisions. According to Willson, he "venerated Mary's memory in order to defend himself against the accusation of bastardy" (*King James VI and I*, p. 139). In the same year, he protested Edmund Spenser's portrayal of Mary in *The Faerie Queene*; this episode is suggestively discussed in Goldberg, *James I and the Politics of Literature*, pp. 1–17.

73. In this year, he revoked the standing commission for examining witches set up in 1591, probably as a result of complaints about the growing number of innocent persons being accused (the Order of Council that ended the commission itself refers to this problem). James personally intervened that summer in several trials to mitigate punishment or drop charges. This order did not, of course, end the witch-hunts in Scotland; it left an opening for local authorities to apply to the central government to set up their own commissions after that. But the rate of prosecutions dropped significantly; according to Larner, only two or three witches were tried per year during the period 1597–1621. See her *Enemies of God*, pp. 69–72; and Clark, "King James's *Daemonologie*," pp. 162–63.

CHAPTER FIVE

PERFORMING PERSECUTION

From the first, the Renaissance stage was fascinated with witch-craft and magic, as the medieval stage had been with the devil and the Vice. But this fascination did not on the whole manifest itself through the witch: rather, the male conjurer or magus oc-cupied center stage. His magic circle, his raising of "spirits" who might tell of hidden things or past or future events to a rapt audience, had obvi-ous parallels with the stage and its actors, who enacted a playwright's fancies. The magus, in fact, *was* an actor-stagemanager of sorts; as court entertainer and illusionist he might offer theatrical spectacle as part of his "act."[1] (Faustus becomes just such an entertainer in act 4 of Marlowe's play.) While suggestive of many other meanings as well, the magus could function as the playwright's double, taking his art one step farther. Aspi-ration, curiosity, and invention, freed from everyday constraints, might lead the magus to an overreacher's end, but not before he had tested the limits of theatrical power.

In the documents about her case, Mrs. Dewse's magical aspirations ac-quire a subtly theatrical aspect when she plans to use image magic to make her husband's enemies fall ill, "that they might think it was God's doing."[2] Much like Prospero, she hoped her sorcery would simulate the

---

1. On the magician as court entertainer, see Kieckhefer, *Magic in the Middle Ages*, pp. 96–100ff.

2. Birche reported that Mrs. Dewse "was mynded she would make all their pictures & pricke thme with pynnes, that they mighte thinke it was Gods doinge because they would suffer theeves to overthrowe her husband without any cause." In response, Birche piously reminds her that the "best meanes" of achieving her goal is through prayer, not sorcery. Hart, "Observations," p. 396.

illusion of divine judgment, prompting her victims to repentance. But on stage there are no female Prosperos, no female Faustuses, not even a female fraud of the skill and stature of Jonson's Alchemist. The witch appears in generally marginal roles. She is seldom a "pure" version of either village-level or elite beliefs. Instead, she is almost always a hybrid, "contaminated" by multiple traditions, a composite not only of the village witch, the pamphlet witch, the witch of religious tracts, but also of the fairy-tale witch, the witch of ballads, medieval romance, continental demonological texts, the Bible, and the Greek and Roman classics; Hecate, Medea, and the Witch of Endor shape the stage witch as much as if not more than the real women being tried for witchcraft. The magical practices of stage witches are also influenced by the conjurer's or necromancer's tradition; while associated with cursing and the use of familiars, they also perform incantations and magic rites.[3] Yet despite the complex intertextuality of many stage witches, their "foreign" influences ultimately seem to be read through "native" village and elite stereotypes. Powerfully organizing these play texts at a deeper level are the figures of the malevolent mother and the betraying servant in league with a transgressive male rival.

The hybridity of stage witches befits the hybrid class position of many of their makers. Playwrights tended to be "middling sorts" who straddled the shifting boundary between "gentle" and "common" and who wrote for an audience that mixed "high" and "low."[4] In Shakespeare's case, the impetus for hybridization might have been intensified by his straddling of regional as well as class boundaries. His childhood and youth in Stratford undoubtedly brought him into close contact with village-level beliefs. As a sophisticated urban playwright based in London, however, he also was

---

3. Of course the village-level witch is not always "pure" to begin with; conjuration may be one way she first acquires her familiar, as seems to be the case with Joan Cunny. Rosen, *Witchcraft*, pp. 183–84. Some informants believe they have witnessed the ritual use of a magic circle, as in the case of Mother Staunton (p. 97). In Scotland, the North Berwick witches allegedly practiced necromancy and were so represented in the pamphlet *Newes from Scotland*.

4. On the class situation of playwrights, see David Riggs, *Ben Jonson: A Life* (Cambridge: Harvard University Press, 1989), pp. 22–28; Gerald Bentley, *The Profession of Dramatist in Shakespeare's Time* (Princeton: Princeton University Press, 1971); on audiences, see Andrew Gurr, *Playgoing in Shakespeare's London, 1576–1642* (Cambridge: Cambridge University Press, 1987). Just how "low" London audiences got has been a matter of debate: see also Ann Jennalie Cook, *The Privileged Playgoers of Shakespeare's London, 1576–1642* (Princeton: Princeton University Press, 1981); and Martin Butler, *Theater and Crisis, 1632–1642* (Cambridge: Cambridge University Press, 1984), pp. 293–306.

exposed to gentry-level and aristocratic views of the witch: Reginald Scot's *Discoverie of Witchcraft*, James I's *Daemonologie*, the pamphlet *Newes from Scotland*, and other such texts have all been cited as sources for his plays.[5]

Despite their hybrid features, as characters stage witches tend to be one-dimensional. They are caricatures of evil, embodiments of monstrous sexual appetite, part of a transgressive "world turned upside down" which contrasts with and in turn is overthrown by "good order." "Good order" is typically a matter of gender order. Stage witches are regularly absorbed into an antithetical structure that splits "woman" into good and bad; they are used in many plays to endorse a normalizing set of beliefs about women's "proper" role, including in particular female chastity, modesty, and subordination. Such an antithetical structure is especially obvious in Jonson's *Masque of Queenes*, but it is also apparent in such plays as John Marston's *Sophonisba* and Thomas Middleton's *Witch*. Even *The Witch of Edmonton*, which contains a more sympathetic and complex treatment of the "historical" witch Elizabeth Sawyer, to an extent constructing her as a subject in her own right, gets around to using her as a mouthpiece to condemn the "painted things in princes' courts, / Upon whose eyelids lust sits, blowing fires / To burn men's souls in sensual hot desires" (4.1.105–7) and the "city witches" who "turn / Their husband's wares" to "garden's of stol'n sin / In one year wasting what scarce twenty win" (115–18)—though to be sure, Elizabeth also criticizes "men-witches" (144)—lawyers, seducers of virgins.[6]

Such representations display many attributes of the village witch. Middleton's Hecate, for example, is a malevolent mother who controls familiars with names straight out of the trial records: "Titty and Tiffin, Suckin and Pidgen, Liard and Robin"; they serve her as an autonomous power, and she indulges in magic against neighbors who

5. For Shakespeare's life, see Samuel Schoenbaum, *William Shakespeare: A Compact Documentary Life* (Oxford: Oxford University Press, 1977); C. L. Barber and Richard P. Wheeler, *The Whole Journey: Shakespeare's Power of Development* (Berkeley: University of California Press, 1986), pp. 39–66. For an overview of the sources for Shakespeare's witchcraft plays, see Anthony Harris, *Night's Black Agents: Witchcraft and Magic in Seventeenth-Century English Drama* (Manchester: Manchester University Press, 1980).

6. William Rowley, Thomas Dekker, and John Ford, *The Witch of Edmonton* (1621), reprinted in *Three Jacobean Witchcraft Plays*, ed. Peter Corbin and Douglas Sedge (Manchester: Manchester University Press, 1986), along with John Marston, *Sophonisba*, and Thomas Middleton, *The Witch*. A pamphlet about the actual Elizabeth Sawyer's trial, to which the play is believed to be indebted, appeared the same year: Goodcole, *The wonderfull discoverie of Elizabeth Sawyer*.

denied me often flour, barm and milk,
Goose-grease and tar, when I ne'er hurt their charmings,
Their brew-locks, nor their batches, nor forspoke
Any of their breedings. Now I'll be meet with 'em.
Seven of their young pigs I have bewitched already
Of the last litter, nine ducklings, thirteen goslings,
And a hog fell lame last Sunday, after evensong too;
And mark how their sheep prosper, or what sop
Each milch-kine gives to th' pail
Those snakes shall milk 'em all beforehand.
The dewed-skirted dairy wenches shall stroke
Dry dugs for this and go home cursing. (1.2.53–64)

With the possible exception of sending "snakes" to drain the cows of
their milk, Hecate's activities here are entirely consistent with those of the
village-level witch. Yet elite discourse also shapes the play. Hecate's magic
draws upon necromancy and Latin incantations, her name locates her
within classical tradition, and unlike the village witch, she is associated
with a monstrous female sexuality that has roots in continental demonology: "What young man can we wish to pleasure us / But we enjoy
him in an incubus?" (1.2.30–31).[7] Yet oddly, though "the" devil is in theory the source of Hecate's power, he is not evoked as an important presence on stage; the figure of a transgressive male rival instead enters the
play in the character of Sebastian, who wants Hecate to disrupt the marriage of Antonio to his former girlfriend by rendering Antonio impotent.[8]
In an important sense village-level discourse remains in control of Middleton's construction of the witch: she is no betraying "drudge" of a diabolic master but a dominatrix in her own right. Middleton uses other
traditions to build on the malevolent mother *topos*: not only does
Hecate's spell involve the use of the dead body of a baby—an "unbap-
tized brat (18)"—she is also the mother of a son whom she has coerced
into an incestuous relationship. The son's asides to the audience reveal his
resentment of his mother, and he seeks a night off from sleeping with her
to "ramble abroad . . . with the Nightmare, for I have a great mind to

7. The incubus is described at length in Kramer and Sprenger's *Malleus Maleficarum*
but never (to my knowledge) appears in English trial documents.
8. To be sure, just who the transgressive rival is here remains fundamentally ambiguous, as a fuller analysis of the play would need to take into account. The audience, at least
at first, is encouraged to feel sympathy for Sebastian, who was earlier betrothed to Isabella,
then parted from her. In the last act, Antonio is revealed to have deceived Isabella into thinking Sebastian dead in order to win her hand in marriage.

overlay a fat parson's daughter" (94–95). Hecate as a fussy, domineering mother comically reproaches him: "And who shall lie with me then? . . . You're a kind son! / But 'tis the nature of you all, I see that. You had rather hunt after strange women still / Than lie with your own mothers" (99–101). A monstrous sexual appetite becomes merely another aspect of a malevolent maternal power; Middleton has absorbed the eroticizing tendencies of continental representation into a primarily village-level conception of the witch.

At the same time, in keeping with elite texts about the witch, the play's plot and style work to dissolve the threat of the malevolent mother and to devalue the maternal body: "real" power remains with the male. The play preserves the sanctity of marriage against the threat posed by Sebastian's recourse to the malevolent mother's power: her potions cannot "disjoin wedlock," which is "of heaven's fastening" (1.2.172–73). The scenes with Hecate are spectacular but not frightening. Primarily comic in effect, they travesty more than demonize her. Other plays of the period also participated in this comic hybridization. It is possible such plays served as a skeptical critique of the witch-hunts: in caricaturing the witch, the theater also trivialized her and foregrounded her magic as theatrical construct. Such entertainments demystified the witch much as George Gifford did in exposing her supposed powers as the devil's theatrical deceptions. Staged for an urban, sophisticated audience, they may have reinforced a tendency to see the rural witch as a figure of ridicule or an embodiment of ignorant superstition rather than in any sense a serious threat to the commonweal. In so doing, they also reassured a male audience that there was really nothing "special" about the female body which gave it access to supernatural power—a lesson possibly reinforced by the use of boy actors in female roles.[9]

The theater was also a workshop for the generation of new metaphorical meanings for witchcraft, in the long run perhaps destabilizing the definitions of legal discourse. Witchcraft metaphors make their appearance in many plays where no literal witches are characters. Theater, rhetoric, even language itself became coded as "bewitching" in many contexts. In working the changes on such tropes, stage plays suggested a parallel between the-

9. On the (multiple) implications of the use of boy actors in female roles, see, among others, Peter Stallybrass, "Transvestism and the 'Body Beneath': Speculating on the Boy Actor," in *Erotic Politics: Desire on the Renaissance Stage*, ed. Susan Zimmerman (New York: Routledge, 1992), pp. 64–83; Steven Orgel, "Nobody's Perfect; or, Why Did the English Stage Take Boys for Women?" *South Atlantic Quarterly* 88 (Winter 1989): 7–29.

atrical manipulation and literal witchcraft which worked to blur the boundaries between them, creating an opening for a rationalistic defense against witchcraft accusation of the sort that Othello makes when charged with using witchcraft on Desdemona. The Duke's reaction to Brabantio's initial accusation of Othello, in fact, contains what may be a glancing criticism of contemporary legal practice, indicting the increasing willingness to accept highly circumstantial evidence in witchcraft trials. (The Duke requires a "wider and more overt test / Than these thin habits and poor likelihoods / Of modern seeming do prefer against" Othello [1.3.109–11]).[10] Othello goes on to convince the Duke and other senators (who are acting as jury) that narrating the "story" of his life has been his method of bewitchment: "She loved me for the dangers I had passed / And I loved her that she did pity them. / This is the only witchcraft I have used" (1.3.169–71). Similarly, George Gifford, Reginald Scot, and other critics of the evidence used in witchcraft trials could draw upon such analogies in offering alternative explanations for accusers' testimony.[11]

Drawing such a parallel also opened a space for situating witchcraft *within* rhetoric or theater—that is, for ascribing to words, spectacle, or manipulation of appearances a dangerous, quasi- or even fully demonic power, the capability of acting on an audience's mind as invasively and destructively as the most fearful witch's spell. In *Othello*, Iago explicitly differentiates his strategies from those of the witch. Reassuring the impatient Roderigo, Iago says, "Thou know'st we work by wit, and not by witchcraft, / And wit depends on dilatory time" (2.3.366–67). Yet by the end of the play, his "wit" has displayed a destructive power that has in effect resituated witchcraft within words.[12] The fear of a "real" witchcraft is also revived before the play's end. Despite the skepticism about witchcraft charges seemingly endorsed at the beginning of the play, Iago's use of his "wit" unnervingly reawakens belief in the possibility of a genuine threat in witchcraft when we learn from Othello that Desdemona's lost handkerchief was the gift of an Egyptian charmer: "There's magic in the web of it" (3.4.71). Othello's account arouses uncertainties never fully

10. *Othello*, ed. David Bevington (Toronto: Bantam, 1988).

11. Thus for Gifford the belief that the witch has real magical powers is part of a "play" staged by the devil; he is a "Juglar" who tricks the witch through a combination of clever timing and persuasive art into believing she can send spirits to cause sickness or death. *Dialogue*, p. E.

12. The play toys with the possibility that this malevolent "wit" might have genuinely diabolic origins when Othello says to Iago, "If thou be'st a devil, I cannot kill thee," and then succeeds only in wounding him (5.2.295–96).

resolved by the play. Has Othello, having succumbed to Iago's diabolic wit, made up a history for the handkerchief purely to intimidate Desdemona? Has Iago persuaded Othello to believe in his own story? Or has a literal magic in its web indeed been activated when Desdemona loses it, making her terrible fate inevitable? In this play, at any rate, unbelief is no more certain than belief in the witch, rhetoric no less demonically dangerous than the witch's craft.

The tropes of witchcraft are not only linked to theater and rhetoric, of course. Like the stage witches themselves, witchcraft tropes are frequently associated with women's dangerous seductive powers or outright violations of gender hierarchy, both often manifesting themselves in unruly speech. In many plays the vocabulary of witchcraft is commonly used to describe the erotic power of women; the first citations for such figurative uses in the *Oxford English Dictionary*, in fact, come from the 1590s and early 1600s, often from stage plays. Such metaphors do not, of course, merely demonize female sexuality or unruly behavior; they may more complexly suggest the ambivalence a Cleopatra or a Duchess of Malfi may evoke, as well as express a compliment. But most frequently they were used, by characters if not by playwrights, to foster a conservative gender ideology; the witch as role and as metaphor became an important marker in a discourse that policed "proper" female behavior and sought to limit female speech.

Kathleen McLuskie has made the point succinctly: "When witches cease to be hunted as witches, the traditions of their theatrical representation give greater scope for them to be hunted as women."[13] "Hunted" here can be misleading: a discourse that registers social disapproval does not "hunt" women in the same sense that legal discourse was used to hunt witches; the "violence of representation" is not identical to the violence of the state. But such discourse did contribute to a normalizing, male-centered apparatus of social control which subordinated women to men and interpellated them into "proper" female roles. In the courtroom, the witch's gender transgression was rarely an explicit feature of the case against her; in the theater, it is almost always so. Playwrights made the subtext of legal prosecution their main text on stage.

Ultimately it is dangerous to generalize about the relation of the theater to the witch-hunts, as if "theater" were a unitary phenomenon. Different

---

13. Kathleen McLuskie, *Renaissance Dramatists* (Atlantic Highlands, N.J.: Humanities Press International, 1989), p. 72.

plays intervened in the discourse of witchcraft and witch-hunting in different ways: the marketplace economy governing most theatrical production meant a measure of diversity was inevitable. The theater was a site of contestation, spurred on by the rivalries and quarrelsome concern for reputation which infused the whole culture.[14] I turn, therefore, to a focused study of the works of a single playwright—Shakespeare—to investigate how a man of the "middling sort" constructed the witch.

Shakespeare's plays share with others of the period a tendency to privilege the male magus (generally represented as learned and benevolent) over the female witch (generally represented as lower class and malignant); Prospero has no female counterpart.[15] They regularly link witch figures and witchcraft metaphors with transgressive forms of female desire. Nevertheless, such linkages tend not to function in any simple way to demonize female desire or to fix "disorderly" women on one side of a rigidly dichotomizing structure that would mark them as the antithesis of "good order." While ostensibly sharing the antithetical structure found in the witchcraft plays of his contemporaries, Shakespeare's plays instead offer a particularly compelling reading of the psychodynamics of witch-hunting which deeply complicates the demonizing mode. Shakespeare's plays regularly call into question "order" as well as "disorder"; his use of the tropes of witchcraft register ambivalence about the women with which they are associated rather than simplistically scapegoating them.

In the following chapters, I focus on the Shakespeare plays most centrally concerned with witchcraft and witch-hunting: the *Henry VI* plays, *Richard III*, and *Macbeth*. Although literal witches do not appear in *Henry VI, Part 3* or *Richard III*, witchcraft metaphors and accusations do, continuing a trajectory begun in *Henry VI, Parts 1 and 2*. The resonance of witch tropes throughout these four plays, in fact, is one of the compelling reasons for considering them in some sense a "cycle." *Henry*

14. Playwrights were as apt as village men and women (or aristocrats) to find themselves in quarrels, brawls, feuds, and litigation. Ben Jonson's career offers a particularly good example. See Riggs, *Ben Jonson: A Life.*

15. Other benign male magicians include Cerimon in *Pericles*, the soothsayers in *Julius Caesar* and *Antony and Cleopatra*, and arguably, Cornelius in *Cymbeline* and Doctor Pinch in *Comedy of Errors*. Edward III's magical healing touch is described at length by the Doctor in *Macbeth*. Owen Glendower is not so benign, but neither is he clearly demonized. Roger Bolingbroke in *2 Henry VI*, glimpsed only briefly, would appear to be the only truly malevolent male magician. In contrast, Shakespeare's female witches—Joan la Pucelle, Margery Jourdain, the Weird Sisters, Sycorax—all have unmistakable links to the demonic. Some women, however, come to function metaphorically as white witches—Paulina most notably, but also, as I shall argue, the women of *Richard III*.

VI, Parts 1 and 2, and *Macbeth* include literal witches among their cast of characters: Joan la Pucelle, Margery Jourdain, her partner Roger Bolingbroke,[16] and (of course) the Weird Sisters; in addition, Eleanor, Duchess of Gloucester "consults" with witches in a legally culpable manner.[17] Moreover, all five plays include wives and mothers who are associated with witchlike powers: Margaret and Lady Macbeth are the most prominent examples. Arguably, they are the "real" witches in these plays. The Countess of Auvernge (in *1 Henry VI*) and Queen Elizabeth, Jane Shore, and the Duchess of York (in *Richard III*) are also at times inscribed with witchlike features.

Like the witchcraft plays already discussed, Shakespeare's plays incorporate elements of both village-level and elite constructions. His witches are richly associated with the figure of the malevolent mother; they practice maleficium, utter curses, employ familiars, and there are references to the witch's teat and other aspects of village belief. At the same time they are regularly involved in rebellious plots against the state and their magic is at least glancingly attributed to a Satanic male power, their crime betrayal as well as maleficium. In a manner reminiscent of Gifford's and Perkins's tracts, the trajectory of the first tetralogy works to expose the underlying weakness of the witch. Joan la Pucelle's ascendancy, for example, proves to be only temporary, her supernatural strength bestowed upon her by diabolic male "masters" who eventually abandon her. Her body is then revealed to be the site of an essential powerlessness; breast and womb have no lasting hold over the supernatural. The female reproductive body need not excite male envy but may be subjected to male control. As in many elite texts, demystifying the witch means degrading the maternal body.

Shakespeare's plays, however, also endow the witch with some attributes not featured in any of the texts discussed earlier; she possesses a masculine "part" and attempts to invert gender hierarchy. Joan cross-dresses and acquires a male warrior's fighting skill; the Countess of Auvergne, Margaret, Eleanor, and Lady Macbeth have a masculine "spirit" and usurp the male role; the witches in *Macbeth* have beards that cause Banquo to question their sex; even Margery Jourdain becomes a mouthpiece for a male demon in her trance state. Yet, while often repudiating the fem-

16. Termed a conjurer in the dramatis personae, he describes himself as a wizard.
17. She would also be subject to the 1581 "Act against Seditious Words and Rumors," which specifically prohibited divination or conjuration for the purpose of predicting the queen's death. See Ewen, *Witch Hunting and Witch Trials*, p. 18.

inine, Shakespeare's witches nevertheless embrace the maternal: they are masculine mothers who in effect pursue completeness through a form of hermaphroditism, associating power with breast and phallus but shunning the vulnerability of the vagina. They have affinities with the figure of the phallic mother in psychoanalysis.[18] But whereas in traditional psycho-analysis fantasies about the phallic mother typically function as a defense against the son's castration fears, Shakespeare's witch-mothers function more obviously to intensify those fears (which in any case involve more than castration). On the one hand, witch-mothers threaten through their ability to arouse in some males (Charles the Dauphin, Suffolk, the Macbeth of acts 1 and 2) a "regressive" desire to return to a state of dependence on a figure who seems to "have it all"; such males in effect seek to recover the preoedipal mother through the witch. On the other hand, as masculinized women they may also appear as rivals to the male, threatening to defeat men on their own terms (Joan vs. Talbot, Margaret vs. York and Richard III). Either way they are portrayed as dangerous, using males instrumentally to extend their own phallic identities; in doing so, they regularly humiliate or attack these males for their "defective" masculinity.

Like the play of Middleton discussed earlier, Shakespeare's plays invoke the notion of a Satanic overlord who rules the witch; yet ultimately the figure of the malevolent mother, experienced as an autonomous center of power, informs them more centrally. Rather than trivialize this figure as Middleton does, however, Shakespeare constructs maternal malevolence as a force to be reckoned with. The strategies employed to

18. On the concept of the phallic mother, see Irene Fast, *Gender Identity: A Differentiation Model* (Hillsdale, N.J.: Analytic Press, 1984), pp. 65–67ff. In Freud's view, fantasies that attribute a penis to the mother may also involve a denial of "breast envy"; the traits valued in the breast are transferred to the penis. Fast offers a modification to the traditional Freudian view in claiming that the son may attribute both male and female characteristics to his representations of self and mother, and that once sexual difference is acknowledged, children of both sexes may envy the other sex out of longing for "bisexual completeness"—that is, they wish to possess the valued attributes of both sexes. Insofar as fantasies of the phallic mother are used to reduce anxiety about sexual difference, they would not seem directly relevant to the masculine mothers in these plays, who are envied, feared, and erotically desired. Klein's notion of the "combined parent figure" may be more relevant. For Klein, the young child at first represents the mother as a collection of body parts, among which the father's penis may be included. This representation may become caught up in persecutory anxieties, like any other representation of the mother. Once the mother who possesses both breast and penis becomes the object of envious, hostile fantasies, she will also become feared as a retaliator. See Hinshelwood, *Dictionary of Kleinian Thought*, pp. 242–43. Just how these psychoanalytic notions might be integrated with early modern theories of the "one-sex body," as described by Thomas Laqueur and others, is still another question.

restore male dominance regularly fail and a witchlike maternal power keeps resurfacing. His plays are significantly shaped by what I call the persecutory mode and invite their audiences to escape the fearful attractions of the witch-mother through retaliatory violence and the construction of "all-male" identities (exemplified most fully by York, Richard III, and the later Macbeth). Yet the plays go on to stage the failure of these attempts: such identities have their own special perils. To disavow the maternal entirely proves impossible; the attempt entails tragic loss. The plays grope toward other solutions and alternatives for male identity.

At the same time, they move away from demonizing the witch and provide a critique of witch-hunting. Witchcraft is displayed as one means among others for women to empower themselves in a cultural system that drives men as well as women at all social levels into rivalries, feuds, civil war. The threat of women's access to supernatural power gives way to the threat of maternal ambition enacted in and through patrilineal values. The plays ultimately locate the impulse to blame the witch (and the witchlike woman) in the son's early dependence on a mother experienced as the "originary" voice of patriarchal values. This mother is typically an aristocrat shaped by the feudal honor culture and its military ambitions (Margaret, the Duchess of York, the "mother" summoned up by Lady Macbeth); she thus gives voice to a historically specific form of patriarchal ideology. It is her discourse that begins the son's interpellation into its hierarchizing binarisms—not only of male/female difference but also male/male, first son/second son, manliness/effeminacy, whole body/deformed body. Through the characters of Richard III and Macbeth in particular, Shakespeare calls attention to the son's vulnerable relation to such a mother and to the painful effects of a female discourse about male inadequacy which reenacts the mother's early, often violent rejections of him.

Thus, Shakespeare's plays make it possible to interpret witch-hunting in terms of displacement. Though the plays also suggest that "real" witches exist, the woman hunted as a witch may be falsely accused when she is confused with the childhood mother. In the most explicit example, Richard accuses Jane Shore and Queen Elizabeth of deforming him through witchcraft, clearly displacing onto them his rage at the deforming power he associates with his own mother's womb and maternal discourse; his politically expedient, self-consciously deceptive charge of witchcraft nevertheless serves deeply felt emotional needs. But rather than merely substitute "blaming the mother" for hunting the witch, Shakespeare makes any certainty about the mother's culpability problematic.

The plays ultimately hold the sons of the witch-mothers—Richard, Macbeth—accountable for their own misdeeds as a more positive assessment of maternal power becomes possible. Neither the persecutory project of witch-hunting nor that of mother-hunting can be completed; their object(s) become complex, shifting, ultimately elusive. In these Shakespearean plays, there are no unequivocal victories.

Gender and Political Crisis in the Henry VI Plays

Recent work on the *Henry VI* plays has focused especially on the unruly female characters who, from early in Part 1, rise up in quick succession and assume their right to act as players in the normally all-male realms of military and political struggle. Joan la Pucelle, the Countess of Auvergne, Queen Margaret, and Eleanor, Duchess of Gloucester—all to one extent or another appropriate masculine modes of action in their quests for autonomy, power, or social prestige; they defy established hierarchies of gender as well as "degree." In so doing, as David Bevington claimed as long ago as 1966, they become both "source and symbol" of the disorder associated with civil war.[19] More recently, a number of feminists have stressed that the subversiveness of these characters, while sometimes carrying more complex implications, functions primarily to endorse the need for a return to patriarchal order.[20] The female charac-

19. David Bevington, "The Domineering Female in *1 Henry VI*," *Shakespeare Studies* 2 (1966): 51–58.

20. Such arguments have especially focused on *1 Henry VI*. See, for example, Phyllis Rackin, "Anti-historians: Women's Roles in Shakespeare's Histories," *Theatre Journal* 37 (October 1985): 329–44, now incorporated with additions into *Stages of History* (Ithaca: Cornell University Press, 1990). A similar argument is made by Nancy A. Gutierrez in "Gender and Value in *1 Henry VI*: The Role of Joan de Pucelle," *Theatre Journal* 42 (May 1990): 183–93. Marilyn L. Williamson, discussing the tetralogy as a whole, argues that Shakespeare attempts to mitigate the horror of civil war "by displacing much of the opprobrium for the conflicts on a series of women," shifting blame away from the male feudal nobility. See " 'When Men Are Rul'd by Women': Shakespeare's First Tetralogy," *Shakespeare Studies*, (1986): 41–59. See also Gabriele Bernhard Jackson, "Topical Ideology: Witches, Amazons, and Shakespeare's Joan of Arc," *ELR* 18 (1988): 40–65; and Marcus, *Puzzling Shakespeare*, pp. 67–83. In discussions that focus on Joan la Pucelle, both of these critics foreground a subversiveness that to an extent escapes containment, made visible by reading the play in relation to topical issues. Other feminist treatments of the sequence include Kahn, *Man's Estate*, pp. 47–66; Patricia-Ann Lee, "Reflections of Power: Margaret of Anjou and the Dark Side of Queenship," *Renaissance Quarterly* 34 (1986): 183–217; Woodbridge, *Women and the English Renaissance*, pp. 160–61, 194; and Irene Dash, *Wooing, Wedding, and Power: Women in Shakespeare's Plays* (New York: Columbia University Press, 1981), pp. 155–207.

ters, villified especially as witches or witchlike women (but also as Amazons and whores), confirm the order they rebel against, attaining only temporary ascendancy. They end shamed, subdued, or burned at the stake.

Important as these arguments are, many of them imply that the male order represented in the *Henry VI* plays—variously characterized as "male narrative," the "male prerogative," the "patriarchal historiographic enterprise"—would be untroubled and harmonious were it not for the disruptive presence of the female characters. Once the threat associated with witches and unruly women is contained, the male order is "reinforced" or "ratified," as if returning to a uniform and stable whole.[21] But in fact disorder enters these plays from multiple sources; division and contestation are there from the start, even in domains that would seem to be free from women's destabilizing presence. At times in Parts 1 and 2 Shakespeare indeed scapegoats women in what appears to be an attempt to consolidate male identity. But each apparent triumph over the witch or the unruly woman is at the same time an enactment of continuing crisis; the male figures who help defuse or destroy her power are not heroes but hero-villains, counterparts of the witch that attracts yet endangers, subject to a richly ironic mechanism at work in history, language, and patrilineality which exposes their limits and illusions. And as the sequence unfolds, women linked to witchcraft are represented in increasingly complex and ambivalent ways: male investments in their powers—especially their powers as mothers—prove too strong to do without them. Though by the tetralogy's end women's powers are no longer literally magical, witchlike women are represented in more positive terms, proving instru-

21. Thus Phyllis Rackin sets "female subversion" against "patriarchal history" in her important study of Shakespeare's English history plays, *Stages of History*. While praising Shakespeare for at least giving women a voice, enabling their challenge to the "logocentric, masculine historical record" to be heard, these voices are ultimately contained: "Shakespeare contrives his action to subvert the subversive female voices and ratify the masculine visions of the past" (pp. 148–49). Elsewhere in her book the fissures in male historiographic traditions are apparent (as, for example, in her discussion of the tensions between Machiavellian discourse and providential history), but when gender is the topic these discontinuities are reconstituted in terms of a "clear, univocal" voice; the "masculinity" of the "masculine historical project" is represented as a singular, uncontested entity. Similarly, Nancy Gutierrez speaks in her essay about "the patriarchy" as a monolithic entity. Shakespeare's representation of Joan "demonstrates the patriarchy's need to defuse and neutralize any female threat by transforming it into a reinforcement of the male prerogative" (p. 183). As I hope to show, the efforts to contain subversive females in these plays are regularly related to a "masculine project" divided against itself, exposing its contradictions rather than reinforcing order.

mental in the founding of the Tudor regime even as they cast a shadow over its new order.

Shakespeare's exploration of gender disorder, I believe, is closely intertwined with his reading of a feudal past of civil war. He interprets this past in the light of a conflict between what I call the "state-centered" values of emergent Tudor elites and the military values of the late feudal nobility. As the tetralogy progresses, the state-centered values the plays tacitly endorse become increasingly linked to the "problem" of male effeminacy, while the values of aristocratic faction which the plays largely criticize are linked to a "manly" excess and misogyny presented, for much of the sequence, in attractive terms. Male identity, in other words, is a site of contestation: the tetralogy as a whole may be viewed as an attempt to negotiate between rival models of masculinity as well as of political belief. Witches and witchlike women become a particular crux in this process, exposing its conflicts and contradictions.

Thus, in my view, disorder is invited into the world of the tetralogy by the male order itself, and analyses of unruly women need to take that paradox into account. The plays may be thought of as an extended meditation on the patrilineal inheritance system—that is, on the body of custom and law which governed the transmission of titles, property, and privilege from one generation to the next—a system that Shakespeare represents as a necessary and emotionally compelling source of social order sanctioned by God and nature and, simultaneously, as a dangerous source of instability. As the first scene of *1 Henry VI* highlights, the state is vulnerable in part because of the rules that govern royal succession, which may at any time leave the crown in the hands of a child, a woman, an incompetent, or even no one at all. Here, the premature death of a heroic father, Henry V, has brought a child-king to the throne, opening a space for the wrangling of rival uncles and brothers as well as for the intrigues of ambitious, witchlike wives.[22]

The vulnerability of the state is further increased by the propensity for factional conflict among the late feudal nobility—conflict made possible by ambiguities inherent in the inheritance system and encouraged by the resentments that system could arouse. The "line" of the patrilineage ideally passed from father to first son, excising not only all daughters but

---

22. Shakespeare was dealing with an issue with resonance for a sizable segment of his audience. According to Lawrence Stone, one out of three children in the early modern period experienced the death of a parent before reaching the age of fourteen. See *The Family, Sex, and Marriage*, p. 74.

also the younger brothers and uncles of that son. In Part 1, the first significant conflict breaks out between the brothers Winchester and Gloucester, great-uncles to the young king, each accusing the other of usurping more than his rightful share of power as each attempts to expand his own sphere of influence. Linked to Cain and Abel (1.3.39–40), the brothers carry on a conflict whose origins precede the play, having no clear cause save envy. Similarly, the factional conflict between York (here still Plantagenet) and Somerset begins obscurely, in the famous Temple Garden scene, in a quarrel over an unstated point of law, a quarrel that quickly segues into another over York's inheritance. Is York a mere "crestless yeoman . . . exempt from ancient gentry," in Somerset's contemptuous phrase, "attainted" because his father was executed as a traitor? Or was his father merely "attached . . . / Condemned to die for treason but no traitor," therefore leaving the nobility of York's blood unaffected? (2.4.90–99).[23] This seminal quarrel of the War of the Roses will, as York continues to press and broaden his lineal claim, eventually call legitimacy itself into question, as the ambiguities of succession come to make York, Henry VI, and even Jack Cade seem equally valid—or invalid—as kings.

In Part 1, aristocratic faction is an object of explicit critique, as a series of characters who stand outside the main action declaim prophetically about its disastrous consequences (1.1.44, 48–54, 2.4.124–27, 3.1.190–202, 4.1.111–13, 4.1.182–94, 4.4.20–25). Through these uncanny, anachronistic moments, Shakespeare participates in the sixteenth- century reconfiguration of the honor code, viewing the late feudal honor violence from a state-centered Tudor perspective. Historians have traced shifting emphases in the aristocratic honor code as it moved away from the "culture of violence" associated with the late feudal nobility, which stressed military achievement, competitive assertiveness, local loyalties, and clan ties over loyalty to the king.[24] By the mid-sixteenth century, the efforts of Tudor

---

23. All citations of the first tetralogy are to *Henry VI, Parts One, Two, and Three and Richard III*, ed. David Bevington (Toronto: Bantam, 1988).

24. "Culture of violence" is the phrase of Mervyn James; see "English Politics and the Concept of Honour, 1485–1642," in *Society, Politics, and Culture*, pp. 308–415. For the late feudal aristocracy, says Lawrence Stone, "personalized loyalty and lordship was the highest and most prized of qualities, taking precedence over those of obedience to the Ten Commandments, of submission to the impersonal dictates of the law, and of deference to the personal authority of the King. It was a bounded, localized, highly personal world, which had yet to be affected by wider notions of loyalty to more universalistic codes and ideals" (*Family*, p. 73).

monarchs to strengthen their control over the nobility and the impact of Reformation and Renaissance ideas transformed the honor code and the aristocratic culture in which it was embedded, pushing it in a "state-centered" direction that stressed a primary loyalty to king and to nation (as distinct from clan and county), submission to a centralized legal system, and recognition of achievement in law, letters, adminstration, and courtiership as well as in military areas. "Honor" now included dutifully keeping one's oath of office within the expanding state bureaucracy as well as serving loyally on the battlefield. Morever, honor values needed to be reconciled with the moral values promoted by humanists and religious reformers. The goal of accumulating as many honors as possible, the impulse to retaliate violently for any slight, no matter how trivial, was at odds with the new "godliness" that stressed moderation, restraint, magnanimity, and Christian forgiveness—as well as with the stability of the nation-state. Hence Tudor kings and queens had presided over a series of initiatives designed to end "private" quarrels of factious aristocrats and their retainers. By the end of the sixteenth century, these efforts had led not to an end of faction itself but to an impressive reduction in bloodshed from vendettas, blood feuds, and brawling.[25]

25. Some of the structural changes made under Tudor kings and queens included the establishment of an office of heraldry under the control of the king, which centralized record keeping of ancestry and family honors; the imposition of limits on retainers kept by local lords as "factions" (origin of the term); the elimination of the nobility's right to confer knighthoods, which then became the sole prerogative of the king; the centralizing of the court system, formerly under the control of local lords and often highly nepotistic; the centralizing of patronage, as the royal court became the main point of entry for advancement. Broadly speaking, Tudor monarchs imposed limits on the autonomy and powers of the feudal barons, but were far less successful in suppressing them; Elizabeth sought to contain and channel their energies rather than enforce submission. See James, "English Politics"; Lawrence Stone, Crisis of the Aristocracy, 1558-1641 (Abridged edition; London: Oxford University Press, 1965); Christopher Haigh, Elizabeth I (London: Longman, 1988). Historians seem to agree that the violence associated with blood feuds and factional rivalries decreased in England throughout the sixteenth century, partly as a result of the efforts of state authorities; but the exact extent to which a "culture of violence" continued into the Elizabethan and early Stuart periods has been a matter of debate. See Alan Macfarlane, The Justice and the Mare's Ale: Law and Disorder in Seventeenth-Century England (London: Oxford, 1981); Lawrence Stone, "Interpersonal Violence in English Society, 1300-1980," Past and Present 101 (November 1983): 22-33; and J. A. Sharpe, "Debate: The History of Violence in England: Some Observations," and Lawrence Stone, "A Rejoinder," both in Past and Present 108 (August 1985): 206-24.

It would be misleading, however, to suggest that the reconfiguration of the honor code was accomplished solely by monarchic absolutism. A variety of sources converged in its reshaping. Most religious reformers, for example, did not promote a more godly moral code for its utility to a growing state bureaucracy or in order to enhance the power of the king.

As Shakespeare represents it in the first tetralogy, aristocratic honor violence is arbitrary, individualistic, destabilizing, destructive. It escalates by its own inherent logic from verbal abuse into open violence, from a quarrel between individuals to a cycle of revenge that draws families, clans, allies, eventually whole countries into civil war. It illustrates the danger posed by a class whose primary loyalty is to the father's "name" and clan rather than to king or rule of law. Insofar as the plays offer characters up for the audience's admiration, they are at first those associated with a state-centered point of view. Talbot serves his king unwaveringly when other nobles refuse to send their troops to fight in France; his "submissive loyalty of heart" to God and sovereign is foregrounded in act 3, scene 4, where Henry VI rewards him for his honorable service by making him Earl of Shrewsbury. Gloucester emerges as another state-centered voice; despite his role in Part 1 as just another wrangling peer, in Part 2 he demonstrates his loyalty to the office of protector and to the king in the scenes in which he resists the ambitious desires of his wife, Eleanor (scenes with obvious parallels in Macbeth). Eleanor gives voice to the competitive assertiveness associated with the late feudal honor culture; Gloucester resists it in his Renaissance submission to king and office.

Henry VI himself can be considered another state-centered voice, if also a problematic one. Book learned, religious, he plays the role of mediator between Winchester and Gloucester, Somerset and York, denouncing the civil dissension that results from aristocratic faction. "Good Lord, what madness rules in brainsick men, / When for so slight and frivolous a cause / Such factious emulations shall arise!" the

---

Nevertheless, in encouraging both king and aristocracy to submit to a "higher" law, reformers tended to benefit the king more than the nobles who were trying to uphold their ancestral prerogatives. (The Elizabethan Book of Homilies is one notable product of this intersection of religious and state-centered interests; see especially the "Homily against Disobedience and Willful Rebellion" and the "Homily against Contention and Brawling"). Tudor kings/queens did their best to seize the moral high ground from the aristocracy, claiming their state-centered initiatives served a *national* interest, an *impartial* justice, a *transcendent* moral code, and *true* religious doctrine, as against the supposedly *private* and *partial* interests of the aristocracy. In so doing, they in effect replaced one type of partiality with another. The Tudors' state-centered policies represented a new set of alliances, serving not only the king but also the growing ranks of lawyers, magistrates, clergymen, merchants, courtiers, educators, playwrights, and other cultural workers whose occupations tied them to the court or to the central bureaucracy. Insofar as the crown succeeded in curtailing aristocratic power in its feudal configurations, it did so largely in alliance with gentry and middle-class elements. The sixteenth-century reconfiguration of the honor code thus gave "honor" a gentrified, middle-class, Protestant twist at the same time as it served monarchic absolutism.

king exclaims as he attempts to settle one quarrel (4.1.111–13). He is above all a peacemaker. But we are brought to see his rule as deeply flawed: he is too much the peacemaker, too easily persuaded to make ignoble concessions to France. To York in particular, Henry seems the architect of an "effeminate" peace (5.4.105); he holds the scepter in a "childish fist"; his "churchlike humors" do not fit the crown; his "bookish rule" has "pulled fair England down" (2H6, 1.1.243, 245, 257.) And in most respects the plays bear out York's negative evaluation of Henry as a leader.

In fact all the characters with a state-centered orientation are doomed in this world; they are too isolated and, in any case, embody state-centered values only fragmentarily. Gloucester, like Henry, is haunted by the charge of effeminacy, even as he upholds the honor of his office. He is placed in a double bind: his wife clearly thinks him unmanly for refusing of her plot ("Were I a man, a duke, and next of blood, / I would remove these tedious stumbling blocks / And smooth my way upon their headless necks" [2H6. 1.2.63–65]); yet had he succumbed to her suasion, he would have looked like a henpecked husband, confirming his brother's smear ("Thy wife is proud. She holdeth thee in awe" [1H6 1.1.39]). As things turn out, Gloucester looks bad anyway for his failure to control his wife; his fall from power and eventual murder proceed directly from the exposure of her plot against the king.

Thus, the state-centered figures that Parts 1 and 2 explore as alternatives to the restless, factional energies of nobles such as Somerset or York sooner or later prove weak, vulnerable, "effeminate." It is as if in giving up the individualistic pursuit of honor as an end in itself—an honor that can be achieved only through violence and the competitive shaming of one's enemies—one is also giving up one's hold upon masculine identity. Without military skill or unrestrained ambition, these characters are left unprotected and vulnerable, prey to the strong and the wicked. With the death of Gloucester at the beginning of Part 2 until the end of *Richard III*, we hear no more state-centered voices, other than that of Henry VI as he moves from weakness through deposition to death. In the place of this son who never quite grows up to be a father rules instead a witch-mother, as the plays turn back and surrender to a fascination with the compulsively bloody and ambitious strategies of the wrangling peers and those who imitate them, the Yorks and the Suffolks, the Jack Cades, the Cliffords—a fascination most fully realized, of course, in the character of York's son, Richard III.

Ultimately the sets of values I have demarcated by the terms "Tudor" and "late feudal," "state-centered" and "military" cannot be fully separated: they overlap as much as they differ. The sixteenth-century reconfiguration of the honor code decentered such things as military achievement and clan ties but did not fully erase the value placed on them. Rather, they were repositioned within a larger whole. Patriarchal formations within family and state crucially structured both feudal and Renaissance honor cultures. Underwriting "faction" in particular was patrilineality—erratically bringing to power the weak as well as the strong, its line of exclusions encouraging envy and unanticipated alliances between women and "second sons."[26] Particularly in *1 Henry VI*, Shakespeare's attempt to renegotiate honor-based male identities is enacted in terms of crudely partitioned oppositions, by means of "English" scenes that oppose faction to obedience and "French" scenes that oppose "manhood" to witchcraft and effeminacy. But this reductive analysis begins to break down even before Part 1 is over. English fighting men, including Talbot, falter before Joan la Pucelle; even more decisive, Suffolk determines to bring Margaret home to England to marry his king. What is "French" becomes "English," and the desires of both "state-centered" and "factional" characters, it would appear, converge and prove vulnerable to the witch. The witch helps to make visible problems that Shakespeare's renegotiation of male identities cannot seem to resolve—problems linked to contestations aroused by patrilineality.

Joan la Pucelle

Although tropes of witchcraft run throughout these plays, the only extended literal witch to whom the tetralogy gives attention is Joan. She is, of course, not merely a witch. Variously represented as an Amazon "who fightest with the sword of Deborah," "Astrea's daughter," "bright star of Venus," adulteress, and unruly woman, Joan is a relatively complex fig-

---

26. The "three P's" summarized by Lawrence Stone are relevant here: "The sixteenth-century aristocratic family was patrilinear, primogenitural, and patriarchal: patrilinear in that it was the male line whose ancestry was traced so diligently by the genealogists and heralds, and in almost all cases via the male line that titles were inherited; primogenitural in that most of the property went to the eldest son, the younger brothers being dispatched into the world with little more than a modest annuity or life interest in a small estate to keep them afloat; and patriarchal in that the husband and father lorded it over his wife and children with the quasi-absolute authority of a despot" (*Crisis of the Aristocracy*, p. 271; quoted and discussed in Kahn, *Man's Estate*, p. 13).

ure in the context of *1 Henry VI*. Despite the English chauvinism and misogyny that clearly influence her character, critics have found Joan to be a lively stage presence, arousing fascination as well as censure, a precursor of hero-villains more fully realized in later plays. Her multiple identites are rich in topical associations, linking her especially to Queen Elizabeth, another "woman on top," whose carefully controlled self-representations took advantage of many of these same tropes. In Leah Marcus's rich analysis of the unsettling "chains of local associations" the play could have aroused, for example, Joan is Elizabeth's demonized French opposite—"empty and demonic because [she] lacks an essential element of the queen's self-presentation, the sacred 'immortal body' of kingship." But Joan, Marcus goes on to suggest, may also more covertly function as Elizabeth's double, becoming a locus of English male anxieties about female rule and its potentially effeminizing effects.[27]

Marcus's point here parallels one I have made elsewhere in this book: anxieties about female power readily translate into witch-hunting. Yet her analysis, in emphasizing the fear and contempt Joan evokes, tends to downplay the attraction she exerts as witch and "unruly woman." And though Marcus discusses Joan as witch, she does not primarily focus on the witch as represented in popular belief. The two issues are related: Joan's power to arouse desire as well as condemnation has much to do with her affinities with village-level representations of the witch as malevolent mother. Joan is a medieval figure, and Shakespeare draws upon chronicle histories and continental traditions to fashion her as a demonically empowered sorceress. But he reads these traditions, I suggest, through "native" village-level beliefs. The trope of the witch as malevolent mother informs his representation of Joan—and also of the witches and witchlike women who appear later in the tetralogy.

As Amazon and warrior, Joan would at first glance seem to have little connection to the mother. It is clear, however, that she is an object of desire as well as a threat, invited into being, as it were, by a son's youth and need. Desperate until Joan arrives with her promise of "assured success," the Dauphin Charles finds she provides erotic as well as military oppor-

27. Marcus, *Puzzling Shakespeare*, pp. 70, 76. "The furthest limit of our speculations about Joan of Arc and Elizabeth is to suggest that Joan's demonism in the play evokes contemporary fears about Elizabeth's 'strange' and unfathomable powers—in particular, a fear that the queen's anomalous self-display as a male warrior [at Tilbury] had in some mysterious fashion drained away the efficacy of the English forces" (p. 82).

tunity. He invites her to duel with him to demonstrate her skill, and her victory sparks his sexual interest:

> Impatiently I burn with thy desire;
> My heart and hands thou hast at once subdued.
> Excellent Pucelle, if thy name be so,
> Let me thy servant and not sovereign be.
> 'Tis the French Dauphin sueth to thee thus. (1.2.108–12)

Here, Joan turns normative sexual relations upside down, transforming a prince into her servant and a male into her "prostrate thrall" (117). It is specifically the victory that places her "on top" which awakens Charles's desire. As dominatrix, she is a strange combination of contradictory images: warrior, virgin, beautiful female, boy Adonis, "Astrea's daughter," greater than "Helen, the mother of great Constantine" (142), her attractions are variously defined, crossing gender and generational lines. Above them all hovers the image of "God's mother," who Joan tells us has given her both miraculous strength and Venus-like beauty. Through Joan it seems as if the Dauphin gains access to the supernatural help and protection of a seemingly omnipotent mother, one who acts as an autonomous center of power, God's equal if not his superior. Her references to "God's mother" (78), "Christ's mother" (106), seem to reduce divinity to the position of a child: paternal power itself is under a Great Mother's control.

Thus Joan is linked not only with a male warrior's strength but also with maternal power. As the play progresses, however, that power comes increasingly to seem staged, a function of Joan's ability, through rhetoric, to manipulate male desires. Thus Joan "turns" Burgundy, the French duke initially loyal to the English, back into a loyal Frenchman by playing on his emotional ties to the mother, who becomes associated with his native land. In her appeal, she at first positions Burgundy as himself a mother:

> Look on thy country, look on fertile France,
> And see the cities and the towns defaced
> By wasting ruin of the cruel foe.
> As looks the mother on her lowly babe
> When death doth close his tender-dying eyes,
> See, see the pining malady of France! (3.3.44–49)

After appealing to Burgundy's identification with the mother, Joan uses that identification to arouse guilt, as France the country becomes the mother—more specifically, the mother's breast—which Burgundy has wounded with his sword:

> Behold the wounds, the most unnatural wounds,
> Which thou thyself hast given her woeful breast.
> O, turn thy edged sword another way!
> Strike those that hurt, and hurt not those that help!
> One drop of blood drawn from thy country's bosom
> Should grieve thee more than streams of foreign gore. (50–55)

"Either she hath bewitched me with her words, / Or nature makes me suddenly relent," Burgundy comments as her words begin to take effect (58–59). In a sense, Burgundy misses the point, for bewitchment here is not separate from nature but works by means of it. It is by manipulating the supposedly "natural" tie between mother and child that Joan's words become bewitching, the play suggests. Men are vulnerable precisely because of this buried tie to the mother, which leaves them at the mercy of those who can activate the longing for a return to her, potentially subjecting them to a humiliating loss of manhood. The language of defeat echoes in Burgundy's change of heart; he ends "almost" on his knees before Joan just like Charles: "I am vanquished. These haughty words of hers / Have battered me like roaring cannon-shot / And made me almost yield upon my knees" (78–80). Joan's linkage of "native land" with "mother" is part of the conventional rhetoric of nationalism (elsewhere in the tetralogy, England is linked to the maternal body); here that rhetoric is presented as capable of compelling a man into a humiliating subordination. At the same time as a woman assumes a position "on top," the subordinated male is feminized. "Done like a Frenchman—turn and turn again!" gloats Joan in an aside; to capitulate to her argument is to become the equivalent of a fickle, changeable woman.[28]

If the French males enact the hope that submission to or identification with a powerful maternal figure will be gratifying, the English scenes, by and large, tell us this is a dangerous delusion: the "mother" is a malevolent one, a witch or "devil's dam" (1.5.5), who uses earthly sons purely as instruments in her own individualist quest for glory and power. It is on the battlefield, of course, that Joan's witchcraft displays itself most spectacularly. The language of "turning," "whirling," and shape changing is

---

28. This is just the sort of comment that Richard III will make later on, when he "turns" Lady Anne and (so he thinks) Elizabeth.

frequently used in connection with Joan's military conquests, and Talbot, the English hero, is reduced to utter confusion in his first encounter with her. His sense of identity is called into question when the subordinate becomes dominant: "My thoughts are whirled like a potter's wheel; / I know not where I am nor what I do" (1.5.19–20). His soldiers are also transformed: "They called us, for our fierceness, English dogs; / Now like to whelps, we crying run away" (25–26). Even at her most "masculine," then, Joan's associations with maternal power can be glimpsed: these English fighting men have been turned back into fearful children.

By act 5, however, maternal power is revealed as pure illusion. Shakespeare draws upon village-level beliefs about the witch as mother most overtly at the moment he is undoing them. As Joan begs her familiar spirits to continue their supernatural aid, she reminds them of her witch's teat, "Where I was wont to feed you with my blood" (5.3.14).[29] At the same time, he discloses her dependence on an adult male devil, the "lordly monarch of the north" (6). Her familiars are his "substitutes" (5) or agents, called "Fiends" in the stage directions, not the small animals or childlike demonic imps of village witches. Joan's power comes not from an omnipotent "God's mother" after all, but from a superior male power; the maternal body signifies not male lack but female powerlessness. Even after she offers to "lop off a member" (in what on stage could be a covert reminder of the powers invested in male bodies) or to give her body to them in sexual embrace, her fiends abandon her, and she is forced to admit, "My ancient incantations are too weak, / And hell too strong for me to buckle with" (5.3.27–28).

As Joan is led away to execution, male characters use the maternal body to enact their revenge, as if punishing Joan for her fraudulent use of it—for presenting herself as a site of nurture when she was actually feeding a demonic rival. Joan's father curses her through the breast after she denies him as father: "I would the milk / Thy mother gave thee when thou suckedst her breast / Had been a little ratsbane for thy sake" (5.4.27–29). Her attempt to escape execution by an appeal to a (presumably feigned) pregnancy is a futile stratagem, displaying only the powerlessness of the maternal body. The empty womb of a lower-class

29. The one other clear reference in the play to village-level belief occurs when Talbot first encounters her: "Devil or devil's dam, I'll conjure thee. / Blood will I draw on thee— thou art a witch— / And straightway give thy soul to him thou serv'st" (1.5.5–7). Talbot appropriates the belief that scratching a witch will undo her power and gives it a military twist.

strumpet, disowned by her father and lacking even in the minimal value a peasant father's lineage might confer,[30] can prompt only ridicule. It is something that may be used, abused, and discarded without remorse or fear, wholly "other" to the dominant male order. Significantly, Joan receives her father's curse as patriarchal power triumphs.

The English and French make peace over Joan's executed body; ostensibly, the witch creates unity through her expulsion as rebel, class upstart, and betraying mother. Yet despite this seemingly unequivocal victory, Joan's death carries unsettling implications. This peace seems humiliating, "effeminizing" to the English. Moreover, it is not the hero Talbot who takes Joan prisoner but the machiavellian York. He gloats over his invulnerablity to her powers: "See how the ugly witch doth bend her brows / As if, with Circe, she would change my shape!" (5.3.34–35). Yet York is not a character the audience has been invited to trust. His feuding and his ambition for the crown have marked him as a primary agent of "faction." Indeed, he is Joan's mirror image; Joan takes on the persona of an aristocratic military hero much like York himself, driven by a desire for false honor, ambitious without restraint. York too is a base-born upstart, at least in Somerset's view, his aristocratic blood tainted by his father's traitor death. In his triumph over Joan, York reasserts the primacy of male over female; yet the male order York stands for is flawed in its internal relations. He embodies the "disorder" of clan-centered ambition within a state-centered body politic. Joan and York's confrontation ends, appropriately enough, in a standoff as they exchange curses, each correctly predicting the other's violent end (5.4.86–91).

Margaret

Most important, as Joan is led away, another Frenchwoman with a masculine spirit steps forward to fill the position she has vacated; the scenes of Joan's capture and execution are chiasmically interwoven with the scenes of Margaret's capture by—and of—Suffolk. Though not literally a witch, Margaret has witchlike effects on the Englishmen she encounters which parallel Joan's. She too is a masculine-feminine hybrid, a beautiful erotic object with masculine traits; though lacking Joan's supernaturally empowered physical prowess, Margaret is possessed of a

---

30. A lineage that is illegitimate in any case; Joan's father mentions in passing that she was born out of wedlock (5.4.13).

"valiant courage and undaunted spririt" that enable her to be an effective player in the male world of political power and eventually to become a general on the battlefield. This masculine spirit also gives a special potency to her maternal potential: she is all the more likely to be the bearer of heroic "issue" for Henry VI.

If the witch can be defeated, not so the witchlike powers invested in Margaret; her aristocratic lineage, temperament, and social position accord her a value males cannot easily dismiss. The play locates a more powerful witchcraft in Margaret's masculine "spirit"; far from being demonic illusion, this power comes from deep within patrilineality itself. Displayed as daughter of a kingly father—a father who is "a soldier . . . unapt to weep / Or to exclaim on fortune's fickleness" (5.3.133–34)—Margaret is heir to a "princely majesty" that is manifest both in her physical beauty and in her soldierly courage and self-assertiveness. Birth alone would give her a significant value within the patrilineal marketplace even if she were a purely passive creature, but her masculine spirit enhances her worth, for it increases the likelihood that she will produce heroic sons for her husband's patrilineage. Thus is it that after long debate over the relative advantages and disadvantages of a match between Margaret and Henry VI, Suffolk carries the day when he foregrounds Margaret's potential as a "masculine" mother:

> Her peerless feature, joined with her birth,
> Approves her fit for none but for a king.
> Her valiant courage and undaunted spirit,
> More than in women commonly is seen,
> Will answer our hope in issue of a king;
> For Henry, son unto a conqueror,
> Is likely to beget more conquerors,
> If with a lady of so high resolve
> As is fair Margaret he be linked in love. (*1H6*, 5.5.68–76)

The subtext of Suffolk's speech is, of course, that Henry himself, despite his heroic ancestry, is lacking in soldierly qualities. Margaret's possession of them can appeal to a national body politic anxious not only about succession but about the leadership abilities of a legitimate heir. At the same time, she offers to Henry a compensatory masculinity along with her feminine charms—the masculinity that York and others feel he lacks, given his "tender youth" (81) and religious inclinations.

Yet if in this particular context Margaret as masculine-feminine hybrid can carry positive implications, she also carries destabilizing ones: hence her "bewitching" effects. The feminine beauty/masculine spirit that does her kingly father proud and may benefit her future sons is a seductive danger to husbands and lovers in the present, for it can undermine male identity. "Wilt thou be daunted at a woman's sight?" Suffolk chides himself in his first encounter with Margaret, "disabled" by her beauty (5.3.69, 67); his tongue-tied disorientation recalls the effect of Joan's witchcraft on Talbot in their first encounter. As captive becomes captivator, Margaret arouses two competing urges in Suffolk. Shall he conquer or submit? Shall he free her or make her stay to endure his wooing? The conflict temporarily leaves him paralyzed, deprived of agency, muttering to himself: "I have no power to let her pass; / My hand would free her, but my heart says no" (60–61). "He talks at random. Sure the man is mad," Margaret comments a few lines later (85). As she mocks him and turns his words and actions to her advantage, imitating his "mad" behavior by giving him "quid for quo" (109), he arrives at a compromise between his two competing urges which suits them both: he will do her "princely majesty" homage by freeing her to marry his king; at the same time, he will woo her for himself while winning her for Henry.

Margaret's witchlike ability to disorient and compel submission from her superiors is also evident in her effect on the king, as Suffolk's words in describing her virtues seem to exert an almost magical power, compelling Henry to fall in love almost instantaneously: he is "driven by breath of her renown / Either to suffer shipwreck or arrive / Where I may have fruition of her love" (5.5.7–9). Suffolk reproduces in the young king the conflicting desires that he had felt himself, using Margaret's masculine and feminine virtues to arouse, on the one hand, a desire to submit to, to worship, to venerate Margaret for her perfect beauty and valiant spirit and, on the other, a desire to command, protect, and enrich her in her dowerlessness (5.5.10–78). Henry agrees to the marriage in order to bring to an end "such sharp dissension in my breast, / Such fierce alarums both of hope and fear" as make him sick with working of his thoughts (84–86). As Joan was Elizabeth I's opposite and her twin, now Henry is revealed as the "perverse" dauphin's double. The young king's easy surrender recalls Charles's submission to Joan. To others this submission reveals Henry's weakness and extends the "effeminate peace" he has already made with France. Not only does he break his oath to marry the Earl of Armagnac's daughter, he gives away the lands of Maine and Anjou, won through manly conquest by his forefathers; the compensatory masculinity Henry may gain through Margaret seems a sham by comparison.

Margaret's witchlike effects on Suffolk at first take a somewhat different form. His initial paralysis gives way to a will-to-power he hopes to gratify by means of her ability to "top" other males. In the lines that close Part 1, Suffolk projects his hopes into the future: "Margaret shall now be Queen and rule the King; / But I will rule both her, the King, and realm" (5.5.107–8). Suffolk hopes to end up "on top," to harness the gender inversion produced by Margaret's witchlike qualities, to make her the vehicle of his own individualist ambition. Like York's triumph over Joan, Suffolk's boast points toward a restoration of gender hierarchy which at the same time implies disorder within male-male relations; his hoped-for dominance over Margaret will implicate him in "faction," adultery, and the gender inversion of other males.[31]

But as his relationship with the queen develops, his hopes for dominance and control are not fulfilled; rather, he becomes the instrument of Margaret's intrigues, placed in a role that eventually proves deadly for him. When he first takes Margaret prisoner, he imagines himself as a mother protecting a child ("Thou art allotted to be ta'en by me; / So doth the swan her downy cygnets save / Keeping them prisoner underneath her wings"; [1H6 5.3.55–57]); as he faces death for carrying out her plot to kill Gloucester, their roles have fully reversed. Suffolk's speech as they part for the last time associates his adulterous love for her with a fantasy of returning to childhood and fusing with an all-providing mother:

> If I depart from thee, I cannot live,
> And in thy sight to die, what were it else
> But like a pleasant slumber in thy lap?
> Here could I breathe my soul into the air,
> As mild and gentle as the cradle-babe
> Dying with mother's dug between its lips—
> Where, from thy sight, I should be raging mad
> And cry out for thee to close up mine eyes,
> To have thee with thy lips to stop my mouth;
> So shouldst thou either turn my flying soul,
> Or I should breathe it so into thy body,
> And then it lived in sweet Elysium.

31. It is also a surprisingly discordant note upon which to end the play, though in keeping with Shakespeare's trajectory throughout the last act. The binarisms that earlier in the play aroused expectations of happy nationalist closure instead give way to tension and ambivalence: we are confronted with a French defeat that is in another sense a French victory, an Amazon witch's fall matched by the rise of a witchlike Amazon, and an English masculine identity imploding from within.

To die by thee were but to die in jest,
From thee to die were torture more than death. (2H6 3.2.388–401)

Suffolk locates in the maternal body the power to provide a paradisiacal immortality: the maternal gaze produces sleep, not death; the maternal breast soothes; the maternal lips grant access to a "sweet Elysium," as Suffolk's soul becomes fused with her body. Separation from that body, on the other hand, produces "raging madness" and "torture more than death." As Margaret's paramour he enjoyed a temporary ascendancy, but the magical protection Suffolk imagines to be within her power, the play emphasizes, is ultimately illusory. To give in to the desire for fusion with the "individualist" mother is to leave oneself vulnerable to attack as soon as one leaves the magic circle of her embrace. Separated from Margaret, Suffolk proves an easy target for mockery as well as murder, undoing his fantasy. Punning on his given name (William de la Pole, that is, "pool"), the murderers equate him with contaminated liquid, as if the milk Suffolk had drunk from Margaret's "mother's dug" had turned him into a "kennel, puddle, sink, whose filth and dirt / Troubles the silver spring where England drinks." They then condemn this "sink" as a "yawning mouth" that has swallowed up England's treasure. Margaret's immortalizing kiss returns as the threat of eternal punishment: "Thy lips that kiss'd the Queen shall sweep the ground . . . And wedded be thou to the hags of hell / For daring to affy a mighty lord / Unto the daughter of a worthless king." As this witchlike queen's consort in life, he deserves nothing less than bondage to a literal witch in death; his "devilish policy" in Margaret's service has been to cannibalize his true mother, England, becoming "like ambitious Sylla, overgorged / With gobbets" of her "bleeding heart" (2H6, 4.1.70–85).

Thus, Suffolk's murderers metaphorically castrate as well as kill him, reducing his male body to its "female" openings, converting his "pole" into a "pool," leaving him finally a trunkless "poll." As if to underscore the idea that a male's regressive desire for a return to fusion with the mother is both castrating and deadly, Margaret appears on stage after Suffolk's death in a wonderfully macabre scene, cradling Suffolk's head as if it were a child. "But who can cease to weep and look on this?" she asks. "Here may his head lie on my throbbing breast, / But where's the body that I should embrace?" (2H6 4.4.5–7). The scene confirms Suffolk's fear that separation from Margaret will be "torture more than death"; at the same time, this memento mori is also a memento matrem, an ironic commentary on his hopes for immortality from a phallic mother's body: while Margaret emblematically retains life/child/phallus, Suffolk is reduced to a trunkless, fetishized body part.

With Suffolk as her paramour/agent and a king as her husband, Margaret is doubly "on top"; as a result, she can survive the exposure of Gloucester's murder, whereas the more vulnerably positioned Suffolk cannot. Her skill at negotiating a shifting and unstable male cultural economy is further highlighted by her victory over Eleanor, Duchess of Gloucester, a rival with whom she has a great deal in common. Eleanor is another ambitious female with an "invincible spirit" who eludes an "unmanly" husband's control; she too gives voice to clan-centered values that prize individual advancement over a state-centered "common good" and family loyalty over submission to the rule of law. And Eleanor too is linked to witchcraft; she consults with a witch and a conjurer as part of her plot against Henry's life.

Margaret and Eleanor's rivalry evolves into an aristocratic version of a village-level witchcraft quarrel, which begins in a contest over social status and ends in a charge of consulting with witches. Shakespeare uses their (historically unfounded)[32] rivalry not only to underscore the vices of female ambition and gender transgression but also to bring out the similarities between their quarrel and the factional quarreling of aristocratic males.[33] Theirs is a female version of faction, in which a struggle for precedence focuses on clothing and courtly display: "She sweeps it through the court with troops of ladies, / More like an empress than Duke Humphrey's wife," complains Margaret to Suffolk, "Strangers in court do take her for the Queen" (2H6 1.3.77–79). Eleanor is in appearance a usurper of Margaret's position, "the very train of her worst wearing gown" worth more than all Margaret's father's lands (85–86). Her recourse to witchcraft displays her willingness to seek out knowledge about Henry's future by transgressive means, violating the sovereign's right to protection from his subjects' divinatory gaze. In scenes intertwined with those that focus on Eleanor, this use of an ungodly form of

---

32. The sources do not link the two women; historically the duchess's fall preceded Henry's marriage to Margaret by four years. See Peter Saccio, *Shakespeare's English Kings: History, Chronicle, and Drama* (London: Oxford University Press, 1977), p. 119.

33. It thus functions differently from, say, the fight between the widow and Kate in *Taming of the Shrew*, where men look on for sport; here the male subject is implicated too, the substance of the quarrel hardly more trivial than the argument between Somerset and York in the Temple Garden scene.

divination is contrasted with the king's own use of a "godly" technique—trial by combat—to discern the truth in a quarrel between his subjects.

Yet though the play privileges godly over ungodly knowledge, loyal submission over treasonable ambition, it also discloses the presence of the ungodly within the godly, the treasonable desires within the heart of order. For though Eleanor's turn toward witchcraft is represented as her own "free" choice, flowing naturally from her transgressive ambition and fully deserving punishment, the exposure of her involvement and the legal proceedings against her are themselves cynical acts of manipulation. Suffolk plots with other nobles to monitor and entrap the duchess in order to serve Margaret and bring about his own advancement; York carries out her arrest; all have individualist reasons to pursue the fall of Gloucester through the attainture of his wife. Order as well as disorder is subject to transgressive desire.

Given the extent of the similarities between Margaret and Eleanor, why does Margaret succeed where Eleanor fails? Why does witchlike Margaret prevail over a character with access to a literal witch's powers? A possible answer, I believe, lies in the relative absence of the maternal from Eleanor: the witchlike power of the maternal is in these plays more genuinely dangerous than real witchcraft. When Margaret insults Eleanor by boxing her ears as if she were a mere lady-in-waiting, Eleanor's comments bring out this aspect of Margaret's power. "She'll hamper thee and dandle thee like a baby," Eleanor says to Henry. "Though in this place most master wear no breeches, / She shall not strike Dame Eleanor unrevenged" (1.3.145–47). Eleanor is blind to the implications of her own remarks: Margaret's power lies in her linkage of the masculine with the maternal, her appeal to Henry precisely in her ability to make him her child. Eleanor does not fashion herself as a mother in relation to her husband or find a paramour hungry for such love. Rather, she relies on mere economic exchanges, paying Hume gold for his services; thus it is easy for her enemies to trap her by buying Hume off. Nor is Eleanor able to make use of the potential power of the mother within a patrilineal system. A "baseborn callet" (83) (Gloucester, the reverse of Henry, married a woman rich in wealth but poor in class standing), Eleanor lacks Margaret's highborn, soldierly father and has no heroic paternal inheritance to pass on to her sons; in fact, she has no children at all.

The maternal also seems absent from the witch and sorcerer she hires, surfacing only in a brief reference to "Mother" Jourdain (1.4.11). Margery Jourdain plays a largely passive role in relation to sorcerer Bolingbroke; she must lie "prostrate and grovel on the earth" (11–12) and speaks only one short command to the spirit he raises within the magic circle. Bolingbroke, assisted by two male "priests," performs a book-learned form of sorcery, reading spells in Latin. Jourdain's function seems to be much like that of the magic circle itself: she is the female O, the vessel through which the distinctly male power of magician and diabolic spirit may be "raised."[34] In this magic of a male elite, the woman's subjugated, "open" body replaces the relatively autonomous maternal agency of the village-level witch. Margery Jourdain, like the mistress she serves, does not know her own power.

Like Joan, Eleanor is undone by York, and the "witch-hunt" that follows is represented in even more suspect terms: it is the work of political intrigue, not "godly" order. York, Margaret, and Suffolk triumph over Eleanor, Margery Jourdain, and Bolingbroke because they serve a stronger devil. And as Eleanor falls, Margaret grows in power, more successful both as mother and as clan-centered aristocrat. As order itself is disclosed as disorder, Margaret usurps husband, king, and father's role, becoming general of the Lancastrian army in order to support her son Ned's claims; by Part 3 of *Henry VI*, her actions come to be represented as to an extent justifiable and even admirable. Margaret highlights Henry's failings as she moves to fill the space he vacates; she is more courageous on the battlefield (2H6 5.2.73–77; 3H6 1.1.243–45, 2.2.56–80), more active in defense of her son's patrilineal inheritance (1.1.216–56), more articulate as a critic of York's claims (1.4.66–108). As clan-centered aristocratic mother, unwilling to compromise family interest on behalf of national unity or abstract rules of succession, she adopts a logically inconsistent position that bespeaks the intensity of her bond to her son, in effect becoming her son's father because she is such a good

---

34. The association of the magic circle with female genitals, "raising a spirit" with male erection, is made explicit in *Romeo and Juliet* when Mercutio seeks to "conjure" Romeo by Rosaline's "bright eyes, / . . . quivering thigh, / And the desmesnes that there adjacent lie." To Benvolio's remark that this irreverent rhetorical use of his mistress will anger Romeo, Mercutio replies (even more irreverently):

> This cannot anger him. 'Twould anger him
> To raise a spirit in his mistress' circle
> Of some strange nature, letting it there stand
> Till she had laid it and conjur'd it down:
> That were some spite. My invocation
> Is fair and honest; in his mistress' name
> I conjure only but to raise up him. (2.1.23–29)

mother. "Would I had died a maid," she says to Henry after he agrees that the crown should pass to the York line upon his death,

> And never seen thee, never borne thee son,
> Seeing thou hast proved so unnatural a father!
> Hath he deserved to lose his birthright thus?
> Hadst thou but loved him half so well as I,
> Or felt that pain which I did for him once,
> Or nourished him as I did with my blood,
> Thou wouldst have left thy dearest heart-blood there,
> Rather than have made that savage duke thine heir
> And disinherited thine only son. (Part 3, 1.1.216–25)

Her willingness to ignore the Yorkist "birthright," the patrilineal inheritance due York, is inconsistent no doubt, but logical consistency is not especially a virtue within a clan-centered value system.[35] Margaret thus constructs Henry as an "unnatural father" for disinheriting his son (even though that inheritance may not be his to give); her own "natural" maternal tie leads her to take up a masculine military role: "Had I been there, which am a silly woman, / The soldiers should have tossed me on their pikes / Before I would have granted to that act" (243–45). Her most "masculine" achievements, as courageous general and defender of her son's patrilineal rights, flow directly from her passionate commitment to the role of mother.

But like the witch's nurturance of demonic imps to bring death to human children, Margaret's maternity has a dual aspect. In Part 3 she is an exemplary clan-centered mother, fighting valiantly for her son's rights, but she is also a monstrous *national* mother, malevolently turning on England's children. In the imagery of the dysfunctional family running throughout this play, fathers turn against sons, sons against fathers, brothers against brothers, and mothers murder, dismember, even cannibalize children and desecrate their remains. The murder of "young Rutland" in particular symbolizes the barbarism to which England has succumbed. This murder, although carried out by her supporter Clifford, clearly enacts Margaret's wishes; Clifford links himself to her through his reference to

---

35. That it is not is brought out especially when Clifford vows to support Henry "right or wrong": "King Henry, be thy title right or wrong, / Lord Clifford vows to fight in thy defense. / May that ground gape and swallow me alive / Where I shall kneel to him that slew my father!" (3H6 1.1.159–62). For the clan-centered aristocrat, the family project in the here and now always takes priority over any other value.

Medea, another witch figure: "Henceforth I will not have to do with pity. / Meet I an infant of the house of York, / Into as many gobbets will I cut it / As wild Medea young Absyrtus did" (2H6 5.2.56–59).[36] The image of Medea underscores the idea of the primacy of a "national" family; Medea's murder of her *own* children as well as her younger brother Absyrtus is used here to suggest the savagery of killing a child of another clan. The image also foreshadows Margaret's conduct in her final confrontation with York, during which she exults in the death of young Rutland and ridicules York's other son. Offering York a handkerchief dipped in Rutland's blood, she attempts to coerce tears from him to mock his manhood.[37] York defends himself by attacking Margaret's conduct in gendered terms, denouncing her especially for her animalistic lack of pity, that hallmark maternal trait:

> O tiger's heart wrapped in a woman's hide!
> How couldst thou drain the lifeblood of the child,
> To bid the father wipe his eyes withal,
> And yet be seen to bear a woman's face?
> Women are soft, mild, pitiful, and flexible;
> Thou stern, obdurate, flinty, rough, remorseless. (3H6, 1.4.137–42)

She is worse than savage "That face of his the hungry cannibals / Would not have touched, would not have stained with blood" (152–53). Later, upon the death of her own son, her words will comment ironically on her behavior in this scene: "Butchers and villains, bloody cannibals," she calls the three York sons who have just stabbed her son to death, "How sweet a plant you have untimely cropped! / You have no children, butchers; if you had, / The thought of them would have stirred up remorse" (5.5.61–64). Margaret is a mother with a child; yet motherhood has not stopped her from remorselessly celebrating the murder of young Rutland and using it to humiliate the grieving father.

Both Margaret and York code pity and grief as exclusively female, shameful for a man to display; in coercing tears from York, Margaret implicitly seeks to triumph over him by turning him into a crying child at the mercy of a masculine mother's castrating scorn. Only in Northumberland's

---

36. Clifford does the killing, but Margaret tends to be held responsible for it later in the sequence, most notably by Edward and Richard; some critics have complained about this assignment of blame; yet it is clear that Margaret wants credit for the murder.

37. Even earlier, York had constructed himself as a victim of another child-killing mother, Althea (2H6 1.1.230–33).

response do we glimpse an alternative form of masculine identity, one that allows an aristocratic warrior to feel pity and shed tears: "Had he been slaughterman to all my kin, / I should not for my life but weep with him, / To see how inly sorrow gripes his soul" (1.4.169–71). Though the audience is invited to sympathize with his response, Northumberland must nevertheless endure Margaret's ridicule for it: "What, weeping-ripe, my Lord Northumberland? / Think but upon the wrong he did us all, / And that will quickly dry thy melting tears" (172–74).

Margaret's response to Northumberland underscores the tetralogy's difficulty in imagining a "state-centered" version of male identity which can elude—or transvalue—a charge of effeminacy. Thus though nobles such as York are clearly objects of the plays' critique, the problem with them is not explicitly constructed in gendered terms. Rather, they have transgressed against key features of a state-centered honor code, and these transgressions seem to support a specifically masculine identity more than they undermine it. State-centered alternatives to clan-centered or individualist identities falter in these plays, it appears, because of this gender problematic. The attempt to form bonds with others which compete with loyalty to self, clan, and father's line, to construct a "national" manhood purportedly committed to a more inclusive notion of the "public good," almost inevitably leaves males vulnerable to a charge of effeminacy, to failing to live up to the "manly" image of an idealized warrior father and the honor of his name.

Margaret's "witchcraft" is a product of this unresolved problem; her masculine motherhood makes her simultaneously monstrous and heroic, and it is of a piece with the plays' larger ambivalence toward the late feudal honor culture. Margaret doubly embodies the feudal father as daughter of a soldierly aristocrat infused with his heroic spirit. But she also is an object of ambivalence specifically *as* a wife/mother—needed to mirror affirmatively the husband/son's male identity but also feared for making the price of deviation from the feudal father's role the loss of her love and respect. Her approval is both desired and resented, and whether it is achieved or not, the result is the same: Ned, who receives it, and Henry, who does not, end up equally dead. Sons in this play cannot fully free themselves from dependence on this mother's approval to construct a state-centered alternative for male identity. Such an alternative, it would seem, also requires an alternative mother, a female gaze that would help to authorize "softer" versions of male identity, would allow female pity and empathy into the male public sphere.

To be sure, Part 3 does grope toward a more positive evaluation of male effeminacy; Henry, the "gentlehearted king" is treated more sympathetically as he approaches death. His softer traits make him unfit for kingly office or other positions of authority in the world of secular power, but the play suggests there may be a world elsewhere. In act 2, scene 5, Henry seeks out the molehill that so humiliates York and imagines life in pastoral terms as a "homely swain" or shepherd. From this perspective he can see—but remains powerless to stop—the "trickle-down" effect of aristocratic honor, which leads fathers (unwittingly) to murder sons and sons fathers, among lower classes "pressed" into service.[38] Later, in act 4 scene 6, he consigns himself to a "private life" of religious devotion, becoming in effect the monk others thought he ought to be. Significantly, the only acceptable context for such traits is well outside the military and political spheres and involves the surrender of his class identity. Clan-centered or state-centered, warriorlike or effeminate, Yorkist or Lancastrian—all constructions of male identity remain deeply problematic in the civil war meltdown of *3 Henry VI*.

Richard's Mothers

In the middle of *Richard III*, as Richard is consolidating his power en route to his short-lived kingship, he makes a blatantly fraudulant charge of witchcraft against Queen Elizabeth and Jane Shore:

> Look how I am bewitched! Behold, mine arm
> Is like a blasted sapling withered up.
> And this is Edward's wife, that monstrous witch,
> Consorted with that harlot strumpet Shore,
> That by their witchcraft thus have marked me. (3.4.68–72)

What has been suggested in the tetralogy's two earlier examples of witchcraft prosecution is now taken one step farther. Richard initiates a "witch-hunt" in the modern sense; his charges against Elizabeth and Jane Shore are a piece of machiavellian theater, a politically expedient

---

38. The emblem of father-son murder is resonant in multiple ways in the *Henry VI* plays, recalling among other things the death of young Talbot in the act of attempting to live up to his father's warrior role. Talbot "murders" his father's line in his own death and is "murdered" by his father's heroism.

way of staging Hastings's arrest and impending execution. As Shakespeare also makes clear, this witchcraft charge is embedded in Richard's history of relations with women. Elizabeth (Edward's widow) and Jane Shore (Edward's mistress) make an unlikely team; yet for Richard it makes perfect sense to link them. Both have made his rival Edward, first son and true likeness of the father, the object of their love; their alleged act of witchcraft, moreover, recalls Richard's account of the deforming effects of his mother's womb, articulated first in his soliloquy in the middle of *3 Henry VI*

> Why, love forswore me in my mother's womb;
> And, for I should not deal in her soft laws,
> She did corrupt frail nature with some bribe
> To shrink mine arm up like a withered shrub;
> To make an envious mountain on my back,
> Where sits deformity to mock my body;
> To shape my legs of an unequal size;
> To disproportion me in every part,
> Like to a chaos, or an unlicked bear whelp
> That carries no impression like the dam.
> And am I then a man to be beloved? (3.2.153–63)

Richard's soliloquy has been lucidly analyzed by Janet Adelman as the fantasy of Shakespeare's "first fully developed male subject," who defines his masculinity in terms of violent escape from a malevolent maternal matrix.[39] Richard blames his deformity on his mother's womb and attendent female presences; to redefine himself, he must hack his way out of the suffocating "thorny wood" that he associates with them. In Adelman's reading, moreover, the speech "localizes a whole range of anxieties about masculinity and female power" in the tetralogy as a whole. And so it does. Yet Shakespeare, I believe, points to more than the maternal body through Richard's richly imagined fantasy. The mother's womb is inevitably also home to the father's generative seed; the "thorny wood" through which Richard must hack his way to gain the crown is also associated with the family tree of the father's patrilineage. Witnessing Edward's proposal of marriage to Elizabeth, Richard starts off by envisioning the future in these terms:

39. Adelman, *Suffocating Mothers*, pp. 2–3.

Would [Edward] were wasted, marrow, bones, and all,
That from his loins no hopeful branch may spring
To cross me from the golden time I look for!
And yet, between my soul's desire and me—
The lustful Edward's title buried—
Is Clarence, Henry, and his son young Edward,
And all the unlooked-for issue of their bodies,
To take their rooms ere I can place myself.
A cold meditation for my purpose! (125–33)

The father's first two sons, their sons, and their "unlooked-for issue" possess the womblike "room" of kingship now and into the future; the "hopeful branch" of this expanding family tree is the obstacle that returns to haunt Richard in the image of the "thorny wood" that separates him from the crown. By contrast with this flourishing forest of brothers' issue, Richard as "deformed" third son is but a "withered shrub," a "blasted sapling withered up," an unhealthy branch of the York patrilineage which deserves to be discarded and passed by.

Richard indeed directs his rage over these exclusions especially at the mother's womb and women who become associated with it. His deformity encodes the failure that supposedly causes it—the mother's failure to nurture her son properly. Love "foreswore" him; he is "like to a chaos, or an unlicked bear whelp / That carries no impression like the dam" (161–62), an "indigested lump" (2H6 5.1.157). But the plays place Richard's fantasies in a context that also brings out the father's role. Moreover, images of the mother's womb segue into images of the mother's voice—specifically the voice of the patrilineal mother, who articulates the values of the aristocratic honor culture. And having first rejected him in the womb, the mother and her proxies continue to reject him after birth. Richard's mother, we are later told, loved Edward and Clarence as "two mirrors" of her husband's "princely semblance," but she rejected Richard as a "false glass" (R3 2.2.51–54). Other female voices do likewise: "The midwife wondered and the women cried / 'O, Jesus bless us, he is born with teeth!' / And so I was, which plainly signified / That I should snarl and bite and play the dog" (3H6 5.6.74–77); Margaret calls him "a foul misshapen stigmatic / Marked by the destinies to be avoided, / As venom toads or lizards' dreadful stings" (3H6 2.2.136–38); Anne later calls him "devil," "dreadful minister of hell," "lump of foul deformity" (R3 1.2.45, 46, 57); the list could easily go on. Males, too, apply such language to Richard; yet it is clearly from women—and usually women positioned as mothers—from whom Richard has heard it first.

Mothers, nurses, and wives, themselves inscribed within patrilineal discourse, in turn inscribe Richard, denigrating him as devil, monster, "foul misshapen stigmatic." Women's voices encode hierarchies of difference sanctioned by the patrilineal order, privileging older sons over younger, "normal" bodies over deformed. It is a history shaped as much by Richard's fantasized constructions as by women's actual conduct; Richard scapegoats them for the oppressive, marginalizing effects of patrilineality and for a discourse about the abnormal body. Though the plays to an extent share in Richard's scapegoating they also expose its limits. Women are witches—and they are not; the plays invite sympathy with Richard's misogyny and also interrogate it.

Interestingly, and consistent with his treatment of women elsewhere, Richard does not pursue the witchcraft charges against Elizabeth and Jane Shore. Whereas he seeks to control, humiliate, and punish women, he seldom actually has them killed. His violence is directed instead at the male rivals they have preferred over him. The witchcraft charge makes Hastings (a supporter of the claims of Edward's young heir, son of Queen Elizabeth, grandson of Richard's own mother) another casualty of a fantasy of maternal betrayal in which mothers are punished through the murder of their sons and their sons' supporters; the mothers themselves must be alive to suffer the knowledge of those deaths. The first such murder is that of Margaret's son, young Ned, before his mother's eyes; in that scene, all three of the York sons join together to stab him in turn. It is made clear that in so doing they are symbolically killing the mother in the son. In contrast to Richard, who "carries no impression like the dam," Ned is the image of his mother in his valiant spirit and high-sounding words; Richard himself comments on those words in one of their early confrontations: "Whoever got thee, there thy mother stands; / For, well I wot, thou hast thy mother's tongue (3H6 2.2.133–34). And as the York brothers stab him in front of Margaret, Edward echoes Richard's sentiments, remarking with a rather childish nastiness, "Take that, thou likeness of this railer here" (5.5.38). Although Richard seems ready to kill Margaret at this point, he stops at the request of Edward (who "loves the breeder better than the male" [2.1.42]). In punishing the mother by means of the son, Richard also enacts the punishment of the mother *in* the son.

Richard's fantasy of a mother's deforming influence on sons is embedded in cultural beliefs that often did locate the cause of a child's deformity in the maternal body. As Janet Adelman notes, his fantasy "reiterates the belief that the mother could literally deform fetuses through her excessive imagination, her uncontrollable longings, her unnatural lusts."[40] Richard's mother voices a related belief when she says she "sees her shame" in Richard; a child's deformity could be the consequence of a parent's shameful, sinful act, especially a mother's. But "shame" here is a term that may tilt both ways: that is, it may imply that the mother *is shamed by* a deformity that comes from a different source. A few lines earlier in the same scene, his mother has said of Richard, "He is my son—ay, and therein my shame; / Yet from my dugs he drew not this deceit" (2.2.29–30). Here, she is shamed by her son's deceitful and vicious actions but denies responsibility for them; the cause does not lie in her milk. Others in the plays also locate the cause of Richard's deformity elsewhere. Thus Margaret, in calling Richard a "foul misshapen stigmatic," notes that he is not like either "sire or dam" and sees his deformity as "marked by the destinies to be avoided." An ambiguous supernatural power has caused Richard's deformity, not his parents. Later Henry expands upon this view, describing the seeming omens that surrounded his birth:

> The owl shrieked at thy birth—an evil sign;
> The night crow cried, aboding luckless time;
> Dogs howled, and hideous tempest shook down trees;
> The raven rooked her on the chimney's top,
> And chattering pies in dismal discords sung.
> Thy mother felt more than a mother's pain,
> And yet brought forth less than a mother's hope,
> To wit, an indigested and deformed lump,
> Not like the fruit of such a goodly tree.
> Teeth hadst thou in thy head when thou wast born,
> To signify thou cam'st to bite the world. (5.6.44–54)

Again both mother and father, the "goodly tree," are exonerated; the mother, in fact, is figured as a victim of this ominous supernatural event, confronted after an especially painful birth with a child who is "less than a mother's hope." Exactly what sort of supernatural power is inscribing Richard's deformity Henry does not make clear (Richard terms it "the heavens" shortly thereafter). By the end of *Richard III*, of course, this power is more clearly aligned with divine providence,

40. Ibid., p. 6.

Richard's deformity signifying that he is God's scourge. Ultimately, however, the plays leave the source of Richard's deformity—physical and mental—undecidable; multiple explanations are offered, but the question of origins is left tantalizingly unresolved. Mothers may—or may not—be to blame.

The plays more clearly endorse Richard's sense of rejection and locate its source in women's stigmatizing speech. Richard from the moment of his birth seems to have been surrounded by women telling him his deformity marks him as someone "less than a mother's hope"; mother, midwife, and female servants, moreover, are the first to articulate the various theories explaining Richard's deformity as ominous supernatural sign. Early modern mothers often interpreted abnormalities in their newborn infants in similar fashion—sometimes with dire consequences. Infanticide was one result of the belief that a deformed child was a changeling, a devil, a monstrous prodigy.[41] A deformed child allowed to survive might also be subjected to particularly abusive treatment by parents seeking to "beat the devil out of him."[42] Since mothers in a patrilineal culture were under pressure to produce male heirs, they had a special investment in their sons, and their own status and access to power would depend in particular on bearing a son who was the father's likeness and accepted as his heir. The mother who bore a deformed child was at the very least faced with "less than a mother's hope"; she was herself likely to be stigmatized in some way by husband and neighbors whether or not she was openly blamed for the child's deformity. Shakespeare situates the beginning of Richard's sociopathic career in this problematic relation between patrilineal mother and deformed child. And yet, while the plays arouse sympathy for Richard's sense of rejection, they also toy with the idea that "mother" may be right. Is Richard a "devil," possessed of an innate aggressiveness that causes his mother to reject him, a "grievous burden" to her at birth and "tetchy and wayward" in his infancy, as she herself later describes him? (4.4.168–69). Or is it her stigmatizing, marginalizing discourse and her rejecting behavior that help to nurture a retaliatory violence in Richard? The plays provide evidence for both views, inviting the

41. Just before she delivers her final curse to Richard, the Duchess of York recalls her lost opportunity of infanticide (abortion, actually), combining a murderous will with beliefs about the deforming power of the womb as she describes herself to her son as "she that might have intercepted thee, / By strangling thee in her accursed womb, / From all the slaughters, wretch, that thou hast done!" (4.4.137–39).

42. See Hoffer and Hull, *Murdering Mothers*, pp. 149–50.

audience to see that both mother and son are implicated in the son's construction of identity but allowing no fixed conclusion.

Richard appropriates the mother's discourse and attempts to turn it against her. If mothers insist that his deformity means that he will "snarl and bite and play the dog," he will do so but on his own terms, transforming their power relations. If he is a "devil," she will be a "witch"— a powerless one, subordinated to his will. Her words become mere words, with no power to injure, deform, or render impotent. Thus, Margaret the "railer," having lost crown, husband, son, and all the powers that went with them, returns in *Richard III* to be harassed by Richard as a "foul wrinkled witch" and "hateful withered hag" with only "frantic curses" for weapons (1.3.164, 215, 247). Richard literally turns the curse she utters about him back against her by interrupting her with her own name, making her assume the position of the "elvish-marked, abortive rooting hog," the "loathed issue," the "rag of honor" he is meant to be (228, 232, 233). "Thus have you breathed your curse against yourself," comments Elizabeth dryly to Margaret afterwards (240). And for much of the play, Richard's skill with words, theatrical dissembling, and spectacle allow him to overcome all his opponents; like Iago, he works "by wit, and not by witchcraft" to gain the upper hand. Margaret, Elizabeth, the Duchess of York, Lady Anne—we see them almost entirely as vulnerable, weak, and powerless, in transit to and from the Tower, bemoaning the loss of the husbands, brothers, and (especially) children they are utterly unable to protect. Neither "mother" nor "witch" can match this son's diabolic wit; both terms are evacuated of power.

Yet before the end of the play, the mother's discourse recovers some of its sting. After Margaret leaves the stage in act 1, scene 3, Buckingham admits, "My hair doth stand on end to hear her curses" (304). And as one by one the predictions her curses contain begin to come true, the witchlike attributes of Margaret and the other mothers in the play begin to acquire a new potency. If at first the play seems to substitute mother-hunting for witch-hunting, inviting the audience to take pleasure in Richard's triumphs over women while recognizing his misogyny, by the play's end not only do mothers reclaim some of their lost witchlike powers, but those powers also take on an oddly positive value. In act 4, scene 4, Margaret passes on her power to curse to her old enemies, Queen Elizabeth and the Duchess of York, and witch tropes underlie the scene in a variety of ways. Margaret begins by taking malevolent pleasure in the suffering of the female rivals who have injured her in the past and, like an aristocratic version of the typical village witch, utters a curse on a rival's child—the "hellhound" and "carnal cur" that has crept from the Duchess of York's womb (4.4.47–58). Again like the typical witch, she expresses her curse as a prayer to an "upright, just, and true-disposing God" (55). It is a curse that we know will very quickly be answered, will indeed "light" upon her enemy, as her earlier curses have already done.

Margaret is still very much her clan-centered, vengeful self, the "Amazonian trull" triumphing in her enemies' woes, articulating the revenge code of the feudal honor culture without modification. For her, divine justice does not temper or in any way transform revenge, it is identical with it. Yet because Richard (who "preys on the issue of his mother's body") has alienated his own mother (and sister-in-law), Margaret's curses also provide the possibility of a bond between these old clan enemies. "Sorrow admits society" as the women's reproaches of each other give way to shared grief and anger at Richard, and Elizabeth requests that Margaret teach her how to curse. It is the Duchess of York, however, who makes best use of Margaret's teaching, becoming another witchlike, child-killing mother in cursing her own son. "Go with me," she invites Elizabeth, "and in the breath of bitter words let's smother / My damned son that thy two sweet sons smothered" (132–34). Her curse will not only "light," its phrasing will also seem to conjure up the supernatural, ghost-filled dream that Richard has the night before his final battle:

> Therefore take with thee my most grievous curse,
> Which in the day of battle tire thee more
> Than all the complete armor that thou wear'st!
> My prayers on the adverse party fight,
> And there the little souls of Edward's children
> Whisper the spirits of thine enemies
> And promise them success and victory! (188–94)

Richard's dream contains exactly such a scene with the ghosts of Edward's children; subtly, his mother's witchlike curse recalls the powers attributed to the real witch Margery Jourdain, glimpsed in 2 *Henry VI* raising spirits to prophesy the future. Richard dies on the battlefield, undermined by the feelings aroused by that dream as much as overwhelmed by his enemies, "providentially" murdered not only by Henry of Richmond but also by his own mother's voice, unnerved not only by his prophetic dream of defeat but also by a sudden eruption of conscience which suggests his internalization of maternal rejection is finally complete. "There is no creature loves me, / And if I die no soul will pity me. / And wherefore should they, since that I myself / Find in myself no pity to myself?" (5.3.200–203). Maternal rejection has been, as it were, internalized by Richard; mother speaks in his rejection of himself.

There is room here to stage these scenes so that these women's words do seem to have a "real" magical power; in some productions, Margaret in particular has been presented in such a way as to suggest she has some genuinely witchy features. But Margaret has described herself as a "prophetess" (1.3.301); "witch" is Richard's term for her. And Elizabeth and the duchess construct their own curses as mere words, "windy" words, "Poor breathing orators of miseries." They nevertheless have value for the women: "Let them have scope! Though what they will impart / Help nothing else, yet do they ease the heart" (4.4.127–31). And as it turns out, even mere words have power—the power to injure Richard and to deceive him, among other things. Richard can hardly bear to hear these women's "bitter words"; like a child, he tries to drown out their voices with drumbeats: "Strike alarum, drums! / Let not the heavens hear these telltale women / Rail on the Lord's anointed. Strike, I say!" (149–51). It is his mother in particular he does not want to hear, agreeing finally to listen to her only after she promises never to speak to him again. Those words—the words of her curse—seem to have a power over his soul as deadly as any literal witch's curse.

Elizabeth, least witchy of the three women in that she has least "spirit to curse" (197), neverthless also has a witchlike ability to deceive and to manipulate the emotions. As Richard seeks to win her consent in arranging a marriage to her daughter (also named Elizabeth), attempting to repeat his victory over Anne at the beginning of the play in another conquest of a "shallow, changing woman" (4.4.431), he meets instead an adversary well able to match his wit and confound his meaning. At last, dissembling her submission, she wins time to arrange her daughter's marriage to his rival, Richmond. Before doing so, however, she forces him to acknowledge his impotence as a lover and his dependence on a mother's power: "Myself myself confound! . . . / Therefore, dear Mother—I must call you so— / Be the attorney of my love to her. / Plead what I will be, not what I have been" (399, 412–14). Desperate for this marriage to secure his title and power, he is again in a position where his need for a mother's favor makes him vulnerable to rejection.

Thus, mothers reclaim control of the discourse that Richard appropriated from them; they define him as "carnal cur," "devil," and "rag of honor" and call down a punishment that even he must concede is deserved. They do not speak or act alone, of course, but are part of a larger process in which witch's curse and godly prayer, conjuration and prophecy, revenge and divine justice (not to mention house of York and house of Lancaster) become inseparably intertwined in opposing Richard and bringing about his fall. Margaret's curse ends in a prayer for Richard's death: "Cancel his bond of life, dear God, I pray, / That I may live and say, 'The dog is dead!' " (77–78); Richard's mother's curse ends, "Bloody thou art, bloody will be thy end" (195). The language of both mothers is echoed in Richmond's declaration of victory: "The day is ours; the bloody dog is dead" (5.5.2). Through Richmond, maternal authority is reunited with patrilineal right, the mother's voice absorbed into the male warrior's reassertion of control.

To an extent, then, Shakespeare at the end of this sequence opens up a space for the mother as white witch, who heals with her destructive violence. In the interests of constructing a national family, even participating in the murder of one's own son can be a good thing. Margaret, Elizabeth and the Duchess of York—a coven of cursing mothers—in helping to destroy Richard, aid Richmond, a son whose own mother loves and blesses him (see 5.3.82–83), and though they still play a largely marginalized and subordinate role in the male-centered political and military world, they are allowed some scope for action within it. They survive in part because they are on the margins of that world, becoming witnesses of the costs when masculinist honor violence has crippled it. Of all the supernatural powers attributed to the witch, Shakespeare seems to take most seriously the witch's power as diviner or prophetess (especially in *Macbeth*). Mothers see what men in the thick of action choose to ignore; they have a prophetic insight that may depend in part on a perspective they can have only because they are liminally positioned on the margins. More broadly, Shakespeare relates the witch's power to the de facto power of aristocratic mothers at court, whose special perspective and positioning allows them to exert influence from behind the scenes, enacted through patronage, intrigue, or as matchmaking "attorneys." At best ambivalent about this power throughout most of the tetralogy, Shakespeare here at the end recuperates a witchlike maternal malevolence to a surprising degree:

Richard yields to the power of mothers as well as to Richmond's advancing army.[43]

Yet a number of things render this recuperation problematic, most of them related to the "problem" of the ending itself. As readers and audiences have often complained, Richmond is an unsatisfying hero, no match for the hero-villain Richard. The order he stands for is largely undefined. And though by now we are tired of Richard's act, though clearly his multiplying villainies have earned him his end, the vitality and interest of the play—indeed of the tetralogy as a whole—has been generated by its upstarts. Joan, York, Margaret, Suffolk, Cade, Richard—all suffer some form of exclusion. Though their resistance to exclusion is always represented as transgressive, their outraged dignity is allowed a voice, and the wounds to their self-esteem act as challenges, prompting them to dazzling displays of ingenuity, wit, and Machiavellian stratagems. In Richard's first soliloquy, his long meditation on the "torment" of his separation from the crown gives way to exuberant boasting: "I can add colors to the chameleon, / Change shapes with Proteus for advantages. / . . . Can I do this, and cannot get a crown? / Tut, were it farther off, I'll pluck it down" (3H6 3.3.191–92, 194–95). The individualist ambitions that drive Richard (and other upstarts) find expression through theater: the desire to achieve honor, glory, higher class standing, the "Elysium" of the crown is indistinguishable from the desire to be on center stage, as it were, to be recognized and admired by an audience. Audiences, actors, and playwrights necessarily have an investment in their enterprise by virtue of the theatrical medium itself. Shakespeare locates within the feudal culture a theatrical imperative. Joan's desire for glory, York's ambition to be king, and especially Richard's quest for the "Elysium" of the crown, all seem to reflect a yearning to be the object of a gaze that reproduces the mother's seemingly unconditional worship of "his majesty the baby," to recreate through the theatricality of power the illusion of being the mother's phallus. The inability of these upstarts to modify their aims, to take into account the needs of others or their own occasional empathic impulses,

---

43. Not all critics would agree. Janet Adelman, for one, sees a dramatic structure "that moves women from positions of power and authority to positions of utter powerlessness, and finally moves them off the stage altogether" (*Suffocating Mothers*, p. 9). Marilyn Williamson, for another, also sees the women as powerless, though an illusory power imputed to them functions to mask the historical process by which men produce civil war, as when Margaret's prophecies produce a false sense that she is responsible for their destinies. "When Men Are Rul'd by Women," pp. 56–57.

leads finally to the failure of their projects; their destructive trajectory ends also in self-destruction, and the audience is ultimately distanced from them.

Yet while displaying both the attractions and the limits of feudal individualism, the plays grope toward but fail to offer a satisfying alternative. Richmond is too much like the pious, one-dimensional king Richard pretends to be before the Commons in act 3, scene 4. His "God is on our side" rhetoric, moreover, has been emptied out and exposed as subject to manipulation. His new order is an order without theater or wit. Presenting him only on the battlefield, the play takes us back to the narrowly militarist world of Talbot. And Richard's mockery of him may raise doubts about his status even as a warrior. Richmond is "a paltry fellow, / Long kept in Brittany at our mother's cost . . . / A milksop, one that never in his life / Felt so much cold as over shoes in snow" (5.3.323–26). Shakespeare's historical "error" here seems entirely appropriate; of course Richard would imagine his own mother has been providing support for his rival.[44] Yet the play, in emphasizing Richmond as mother's darling—blessed by his own mother, aided by Queen Elizabeth in marrying her daughter, patronized by Richard's mother—may recall the specter of the mother-dominated male from earlier plays, as if the alternative to Richard could only be another Henry VI. Richmond is linked to the "effeminate" French, his army a "scum of Bretons," "overweening rags of France . . . whom our fathers / Have in their own land beaten, bobbed, and thumped" (317, 328, 333–34). As far as we see or hear, he has no father—only a host of mothers, who support him in an invasion of England from France.

Richmond's final speech is emblematic of the problem:

> England hath long been mad, and scarred herself;
> The brother blindly shed the brother's blood,
> The father rashly slaughtered his own son,
> The son, compelled, been butcher to the sire.
> All this divided York and Lancaster,
> Divided in their dire division.
> O, now let Richmond and Elizabeth,
> The true succeeders of each royal house,
> By God's fair ordinance conjoin together!

44. Actually, the error is Holinshed's; the second edition of his *Chronicles* contained a misprint, substituting "mother's" for "brother's"; Richmond had been supported by Richard's brother-in-law, the duke of Burgundy. See Bevington's footnote, Bantam edition.

And let their heirs, God, if thy will be so,
Enrich the time to come with smooth-faced peace,
With smiling plenty, and fair prosperous days!
Abate the edge of traitors, gracious Lord,
That would reduce these bloody days again
And make poor England weep in streams of blood!
Let them not live to taste this land's increase
That would with treason wound this fair land's peace!
Now civil wounds are stopped, peace lives again.
That she may long live here, God say amen! (5.5.23–41)

Here, Richmond's gender-coded imagery condenses a pattern that has become familiar: male treason originates in a self-destructive female matrix; brothers, fathers, and sons, divided against one another, enact the "mad" female will of an "England" who scars her own body—much like the mother's womb that produces a son who preys on its own issue. Similarly, mothers throughout the plays have supported and encouraged the factiousness of sons, lovers, and male kin; they have thus brought on, to an extent, their own suffering and wounds. This madness is brought to a conclusion by the marriage of Elizabeth and Richmond, "true succeeders of each royal house": a patrilineal "line" is securely reestablished with a new father at its head, enabled by the transmissibility of the royal succession through the female as well as the male; Elizabeth, daughter of a royal father and now sole heir, as mother will pass on the Yorkist paternal inheritance, as Richmond will the Lancastrian one: in a sense, only by feminizing one of the warring fathers—by reducing the York patrilineage to its female members—can homosocial peace be attained. The powers of aristocratic women as heirs and as mothers proves necessary to this restored male order, and the return of a nurturant, "good" mother to England—"smooth-faced peace," who will bring "smiling plenty, and fair prosperous days"—is made possible only by acknowledging a limited agency for women within that order.[45]

The problem here—and elsewhere in this ending—is that this construction of "England" excises the role of the father and of a patriarchal symbolic in the production of civil war disorder: the father exists only as another son, another extension of a "mad" maternal body. In ascribing a

45. An agency for mothers, but perhaps not for daughters; Elizabeth seems to protect her daughter's right to reject an unwelcome suitor, as Richard is likely to be; yet the audience never sees her daughter give that consent. The daughter has no voice of her own and is treated as an extension of the mother whose name she shares.

primarily female origin to male treason, the play leaves the door open not only to idealizing the mother (in the form of white witches, supportive mothers, or peace's smiling plenitude) but also to scapegoating the mother-as-witch, toward which the tetralogy has tended in its earlier scenes; it replays maternal complicity in a patriarchal order as matriarchy. Mothers in these plays are indeed complicit in the male order, but they are not its main authors; scapegoating the mother becomes a refuge from the anxieties aroused by more directly confronting the father's excesses and vulnerabilities and by facing the weaknesses in a sociopolitical order organized around patrilineality, patriarchy, and primogeniture. In blaming his mother's womb and speech for his deformity and his exclusion from patrilineal power, Richard need not face the fact that his mother's preferences also enact his (loved) father's will. In affirming mothers and accepting their help, Richmond no less than Richard avoids confronting problems in his paternal inheritance. The potential for disorder within order, foregrounded in the *Henry VI* plays, remains: patrilineality may still bring to the throne a geek, a monster, a tyrant, a "weak king"; its ambiguities may still produce crises of legitimacy; its exclusionary hierarchies may still breed envy, faction, and individualist ambition.

An alternative male subjectivity is only gestured toward, not reached. Richmond embodies a hope more than an actual reconfiguration of identity. It is through the mothers themselves rather than "son" Richmond that Shakespeare comes closest to imagining a positive alternative to Richard—an alternative that draws upon Richard's strengths as well as punishes his villainies, that uses those strengths in the service of new affiliative bonds. The women appropriate his dissembling, his wit, his skill with words, and turn it against him, matching him pun for pun, confounding his meaning as he has confounded theirs, duping him with seeming submission to his construction of them as fickle and changeable. Insofar as we glimpse an alternative to the individualist and clan-centered ties that have driven honor violence throughout the plays, it is in the precarious bond established between old enemies—in Lancastrian Margaret teaching Yorkist mothers how to curse. In the end, of course, this bond does little more than enable the reinstatement of the rule of another patrilineal·father, the hegemony of a new Tudor clan. The plays do not subvert patriarchy or abandon their androcentric focus; yet as sons attempt to differentiate themselves from as well as sustain a connection to a problematic inheritance from the father, the plays do, I believe, open up a larger space within patriarchy for acknowledging an inheritance from the mother and for valorizing female solidarity and self-assertion, even when these take violent form.

The trope of witch as malevolent mother, for Shakespeare, marks the problem of maternal power within patriarchy and also the problem that *is* patriarchy. Maternal authority, predating the encounter with the father, reasserts itself as an ambivalently desired, subversive alternative when the father, subject to death, limits, vulnerabilities, shows himself to be inadequate to the son's idealizing yearnings. But rather than fully break with this ideal (and thus with the hope of inheriting the father's greater authority), sons choose to blame only the mother for the deforming effects of patrilineality and other problematic aspects of the father's order. In the end, chastened mothers may recuperate some of their power, becoming "white" witches, but only, it would seem, by consenting to make the son into an idealized father, first in a new patrilineal "line" that disavows any frailties.

At the same time, Shakespeare decenters the persecutory impulse his culture directed against both witches and mothers. The witch trope marks the problematic intersection of the "real" and the "imaginary"; it doubly calls attention to the mother as a locus of threat and to a potential in the male for persecutory fantasy. In these plays, a literal witchcraft is exposed as part deception and theater, then superseded by the figurative witchcraft of mothers. As witch-hunting segues into mother-hunting, the persecutory impulse becomes subject to a more skeptical critique. The audience is invited to take pleasure in Richard's denigrations of women and his punishment of them, yet also to see there is something excessive about his persecutory aim. The tetralogy, while never quite freeing itself from Richard's core fantasy, does not fully endorse it either. For Shakespeare, witchcraft accusation points "in" to the self as well as "out" to an other, making the woman accused an unstable locus where it is never clear who really is to blame.

CHAPTER SIX
STRANGE BREW

S hakespeare's *Macbeth* offers a multilayered representation of witchcraft which draws on literary and intellectual traditions as well as contemporary beliefs, both from the village level and from the elites. The Weird Sisters have familiars and practice maleficium, and the play's imagery links them to the village-level witch's malevolent maternity. They become perverse mothers of the traitor Macbeth: like the familiar who enacts the witch's malevolent will in exchange for her care, Macbeth enacts his/their malice against the established order in exchange for their nourishment of his hopes for "greatness." Yet images linking demonic agency with an all-female realm of sovereignty coexist with images of females who transgressively choose to serve an "other" master: the three witches are also represented in elite terms as servants of diabolic masters, their powers dependent on, even subsumed by, a "higher" satanic power gendered male. Such slippages between popular and elite discourses help to structure the witches' riddling, equivocal relation to Macbeth as well as the play's shifts of perspective.

Macbeth himself recalls aristocratic "traitors" such as the earls of Bothwell and Gowrie—men who "consulted with witches" and were accused of attempts on their king's life. The pamphlet *Newes from Scotland*, with its allusions to Bothwell's links to the North Berwick witches, has been cited as a possible source for *Macbeth*.[1] Perhaps more immediately pertinent to the play's early performances was the Gowrie plot

1. See the Introduction to *Macbeth*, ed. Nicholas Brooke (Oxford: Oxford University Press, 1990), pp. 78–79.

against James in 1600, also the subject of a pamphlet that circulated in England as well as of a "lost" play by Shakespeare's company.[2] Both men looked to the magic arts for "security" through divining future events, and Bothwell was notably aided by women, including his wife and the "ghost" of Mary Queen of Scots as well as the North Berwick witches. Both men questioned the king's prerogative in the light of ancient rights of the nobility. Their violent resistance enacted an ideology of male identity rooted in these traditions: what from the king's "state-centered" view was godly obedience could easily have looked to these men like degrading "effeminate" submission.[3] The king's slights to their honor required being "more the man" in response.

Was *Macbeth* a "royal" play designed to flatter James, now king of England as well as Scotland? Was it flattery that misfired or was mistimed? Was it subtle criticism of James's views? Arguments have been advanced supporting all these positions, and it is clear that the play's engagement with Scottish history, kingship, and witchcraft gives it relevance to many of James's concerns.[4] The play's sharp contrasts would

2. The pamphlet is *Gowries Conspiracie: A Discourse of the unnaturall and vyle Conspiracie, attempted against the Kings Maiesties Person at Sanct-Ionstown* (1600), reprinted in *A Selection from the Harleian Miscellany* (London: C. and G. Kearsley, 1798), pp. 190–98. On the "lost" Gowrie play and the relevance of the conspiracy to *Macbeth*, see Stanley J. Kozikowski, "The Gowrie Conspiracy against James VI: A New Source for Shakespeare's *Macbeth*," *Shakespeare Studies* 13 (1980): 197–212. Steven Mullaney also takes the Gowrie conspiracy as the starting point for his essay on *Macbeth* in *The Place of the Stage: License, Play, and Power in Renaissance England* (Chicago: University of Chicago Press, 1988), pp. 116–34.

The play's debt to another famous conspiracy—the Gunpowder Plot—has been acknowledged by scholars since the eighteenth century (Brooke, *Macbeth*, pp. 59–60). In *Witches and Jesuits: Shakespeare's Macbeth* (New York: The New York Public Library and Oxford University Press, 1995), Garry Wills advances a reading of the play in which this Catholic plot against James and his Parliament assumes central importance. Yet though it is true that Protestant polemicists frequently vilified Catholic practices by likening them to magical rites, the Gunpowder plotters were not formally accused of consulting with witches or sorcerers.

3. As it did to one contemporary commentator on the present "emasculated" state of the Scottish aristocracy (quoted in David Norbrook, "*Macbeth* and the Politics of Historiography," in *The Politics of Discourse: The Literature and History of Seventeenth-Century England*, ed. Kevin Sharpe and Steven Zwicker [Berkeley: University of California, 1987], pp. 78–116).

4. For discussions of *Macbeth*'s relation to James's political concerns, see especially Herbert N. Paul, *The Royal Play of "Macbeth"* (Cambridge: Harvard University Press, 1950); Kozikowski, "The Gowrie Conspiracy"; Norbrook, "*Macbeth* and the Politics of Historiography"; and Michael Hawkins, "History, Politics, and *Macbeth*," in *Focus on "Macbeth,"* ed. John Russell Brown (London: Routledge and Kegan Paul, 1982), pp. 155–88.

seem at first glance to make it likely to appeal to James politically, even if, as some have suggested, he no longer had a pressing interest in witchcraft. Macbeth's crime of regicide is presented as unjustified and profoundly "unnatural." It violates not only political and kinship ties but the cosmos itself, producing signs, omens, and ghosts along with human avengers. Family order and political order are shown to be interlocking, as James liked to suggest: when rebellion breaks out in one sphere it spreads to others it resembles. Old women and wives who step out of submissive roles are demonized. The ideology of "manhood" voiced by Lady Macbeth, with its echoes of machiavellian *virtù* and aristocratic defiance, is exposed as suspect. A manhood more suitably state-centered replaces it, with a place for the "milk" of human kindness and pity to check violence against the political "family" headed by the king; submission to the king as sole source of honors can thus be regarded not as effeminizing but as that which "becomes a man." When Macbeth is finally defeated at the end of the play, the "time is free"; Malcolm and Macduff have purged the kingdom of the witch-inspired traitor by means of their healing violence, restoring an order that looks toward James's own reign as heir of Banquo's line.

Yet since 1975 many critics have produced quite different readings of the play's political implications. Some have found ways to link the play with the views of Buchanan (James's old tutor) on elective monarchy and the right to rebel against tyranny—views against which James reacted in advancing his own absolutist theories. Other critics have offered subtle accounts that complicate any effort to align the play one-dimensionally with either James's or Buchanan's positions.[5] Simi-

5. Alan Sinfield has advanced a lively but (in my view) ultimately unconvincing Buchanan-centered reading in his essay "*Macbeth*: History, Ideology, and Intellectuals," now included in *Faultlines: Cultural Materialism and the Politics of Dissident Reading* (Berkeley: University of California Press, 1992), pp. 95–108. In "*Macbeth* and the Politics of Historiography," a subtle, detailed study of the play's political implications, David Norbrook suggests that the play implies criticism of both James's and Buchanan's views, and relates Shakespeare's position to that of Montaigne (pp. 98–99). Michael Hawkins, in "History, Politics, and *Macbeth*," relates the play less to specific positions than to "day-to-day political practice" as a playwright "enmeshed in the patronage network" might have perceived it, that is, to what might be thought of as the social dimension of political relationships; he stresses the play's complex, ambiguous relation to the Jacobean "political jungle" (pp. 158, 179).

All three of these authors are specifically writing against the James-centered view of the play advanced by Herbert Paul in *The Royal Play of "Macbeth"*. This is also the view implied in many pre-1975 interpretations of the play which do not address topical matters. As Norbrook puts it, "Such critics as L. C. Knights, Maynard Mack, and Wilbur Sanders . . .

larly, studies of witchcraft have unsettled the idea that the three witches are a primary source of "evil" or of political disorder in the play.[6] Despite the problematic features of some of these arguments, a narrowly James-centered reading of *Macbeth* is hard to sustain. The witches do not neatly correspond to James's views in *Daemonologie*, nor are they punished or brought under control by the play's end. Above all, Shakespeare's choice of tragic protagonist calls into question the notion of the play's appeal to James. Perhaps I underestimate the reach of James's imaginative sympathies, but it is difficult to envision him taking pleasure or intellectual satisfaction in a play that puts a Bothwell- or Gowrie-like traitor in this central role, inviting admiration and pity for him as well as censure.

Though it is tantalizing to speculate, I do not pursue a primarily topical reading here. Rather I rehearse these topical questions to call attention to the play's tendency (like that of so many other Shakespeare plays) to evoke divergent, even diametrically opposed readings. My own reading seeks not to link the play to specific positions of Shakespeare's contemporaries but to make sense of its multiplying ambivalences and ambiguities in the light of a broad range of cultural beliefs about gender, politics, and witch-hunting. Whereas the play indeed associates demonic agency with unruly women and constructs the murder of a father-king as a profoundly "unnatural" act, it also arouses considerable anxiety about the "godly" social/political order headed by Duncan and then Malcolm. The interplay between the witches and Macbeth highlights a problematic associated not so much with women as with fathers and kings; a tragic

---

present a view of the play that, perhaps unconsciously, echoes the most determined of absolutist theorists. They see the play as presenting an absolute choice between natural, harmonious, monarchical order and an amoral energy that, though exercising an imaginative appeal, ultimately descends to barbarism and savagery" (p. 93). The limitations of such interpretations, which usually emphasize the play's movement toward *restoration*, have been decisively demonstrated by Harry Berger in "The Early Scenes of *Macbeth*: Preface to a New Interpretation," *ELH* 47 (1980): 1–31.

6. Terry Eagleton has provocatively claimed the witches to be the "heroines" of *Macbeth* in *William Shakespeare* (Oxford: Basil Blackwell, 1986), pp. 1–8. Stephen Greenblatt expresses a more representative view: "Within *Macbeth*'s representation of the witches, there is profound ambiguity about the actual significance and power of their malevolent intervention. If the strange prophecies of the Weird Sisters had been ignored, the play seems to imply, the same set of events might have occurred anyway" ("Shakespeare Bewitched," in *New Historical Literary Study: Essays on Reproducing Texts, Representing History*, ed. Jeffrey N. Cox and Larry J. Reynolds [Princeton: Princeton University Press, 1993], pp. 108–35).

mechanism inheres in godly patriarchal rule, seemingly dooming it to produce traitors out of loyal subjects. That mechanism has much to do with the conflicting emotions aroused by the experience of displacement by a rival. Closely associated with the perverse maternity of witches and wives, that experience is ultimately referred to the world of the fathers: the oracular, ironic "truth" the witches have to impart is the truth of royal patronage and patrilineality.

Thus, my argument departs from Janet Adelman's important study of witchcraft and gender in *Macbeth*, especially with regard to the play's ending.[7] Adelman's essay brilliantly analyzes the ambivalent male fantasies about maternal power encoded in the plays, fantasies that account not only for the malevolent maternity located in the witches and Lady Macbeth but also for the play's equivocal attitude toward masculinity. Yet the play's movement toward an all-male ending does not finally suggest to me the gratification of a fantasy of escape from the female, as Adelman goes on to argue. Rather, the scenes stress the collapse of that fantasy: they direct us instead to a recognition that the play's all-male restoration of order nevertheless depends on the violent exclusion of other males. It is ultimately from within this patrilineal matrix, the play suggests, that the witches draw their power. Concealing, then revealing, the inevitable effects of the displacements which structure patrilineal social relations, the witches (along with their male master, the Fiend) are tacitly present during the final battle. Malcolm's order remains haunted by what it excludes, vulnerable to the "coalition politics" of displaced men and marginalized women.

Weird Sisters

As a number of critics have noted, in act 1, scene 3, the first witch describes what is recognizable as a typical village-level witchcraft quarrel, which begins in an encounter between two women and expands outward to include the accuser's larger domestic unit:

> A sailor's wife had chestnuts in her lap,
> And mounch'd, and mounch'd, and mounch'd: "Give me," quoth I:—
> "Aroynt thee, witch!" the rump-fed ronyon cries.
> Her husband's to Aleppo gone, master o'th'Tiger:
> But in a sieve I'll thither sail,

7. Janet Adelman, " 'Born of Woman' "; and *Suffocating Mothers*, pp. 130–47.

And like a rat without a tail;
I'll do, I'll do, and I'll do. (1.3.4–10)[8]

The first witch dwells on what appears to be the complacent oral greed of the "rump-fed" sailor's wife, who "mounch'd, and mounch'd, and mounch'd" her chestnuts and probably has a generally comfortable, well-nourished life. All it takes is a bare-bones, imperative command—"Give me"—to elicit the sailor's wife's denigrating dismissal: "Aroynt thee, witch." The scene of feeding becomes the site of a contest over status and social identity. As in village witchcraft quarrels, a refusal of food is also an act of social exclusion, a personal slight. This story's association of food and social recognition will resonate throughout the play: honor in the feudal military world is a surrogate food, celebrated through feasts and banquets; to be deprived of food or to have one's feeding interrupted is also to have one's social identity challenged or denied.

Out of such deprivations of food/social identity comes the desire for revenge: the scene also prefigures later developments in its emphasis on an excessive retaliatory violence. The witch's response to the refusal of her request at first glance seems to balance the injury sustained; for every "mounch," she'll "do." Yet these nameless deeds have an unsettling open-endedness, ominously leaving room for an excessive response. And so it turns out: the witch will use her magic to "drain" the woman's sailor husband "dry as hay," vex him with sleeplessness and disease, starve him and toss him at sea for weeks on end—all for his wife's single act of refusing chestnuts:

> Weary sev'n-nights nine times nine
> Shall he dwindle, peak, and pine:
> Though his bark cannot be lost,
> Yet shall it be tempest-tost. (1.3.22–25)[9]

To be sure, the witches' powers have limits here; they can torment the sailor but not cause his death—just as the pamphlet *Newes from Scotland*

8. All citations are to the Arden edition of *Macbeth*, ed. Kenneth Muir (London: Methuen, 1977).
9. Some, reading the scene in the light of continental demonology, find in the witch's threats a more sexual meaning; to Dennis Biggins, for example, the line "I'll drain him dry as hay" refers to the witch's intention of "draining the unfortunate man of his semen" while in the form of a succubus. Biggins, "Sexuality, Witchcraft, and Violence in *Macbeth*," *Shakespeare Studies* 8 (1975): 257.

had suggested about the witches who tried to drown James, a "godly king" under divine protection. Yet the lingering torments they devise seem harrowing enough to establish vividly the malevolent, retaliatory nature of their magic. As if the witches' spell were able to affect the whole of Scotland, these torments are echoed frequently later in the play—in the sleeplessness that plagues the Macbeths, in the "wild and violent sea" of men's fears after Duncan's murder (4.2.21), in the language of disease, infection, and "perturbation in nature" (5.1.9) which recurs almost everywhere. More immediately, as the scene moves toward the witches' first meeting with Macbeth, ("A drum! a drum! / Macbeth doth come"), sailor and thane become linguistically confused, each potentially the object of the charm the witches "wind up." As Macbeth enters, echoing the "fair and foul" of the witches' earlier incantations, we know him for their new prey.

Or do we? In the larger context of the play, the witches' motives and the extent of their powers remain maddeningly opaque. "Paltering" with Macbeth "in a double sense," they also invite, yet frustrate an audience's attempt to hold them responsible for Macbeth's crimes or for other events in the play (5.8.20). Their very identity is a matter of debate.[10] If in this scene they appear to be village witches practicing maleficium, elsewhere they appear as diviners or prophetesses, even, in some interpretations, "goddesses of destinie."[11] Banquo assumes a satanic source for their

---

10. As Stephen Booth has said, "What matters here is not hunting down an answer to the question 'What are the witches?' All the critical and theatrical efforts to answer that question demonstrate that the question cannot be answered. What those frantic answers also demonstrate—and what matters—is the fact of the question. The play does not require that it be answered. Thinking about the play's action does. As we watch the play, the witches have definition, but we cannot afterward say what that definition is" (*"King Lear," "Macbeth," Indefinition, and Tragedy* [New Haven: Yale University Press, 1983], p. 102). The hybridity of the witches has been accepted for perhaps longer than Booth's remarks imply, though there is a tendency for older criticism to stress their classical or continental features and for newer criticism to stress their affinities with the lower-class witches who were Shakespeare's contemporaries. Studies of witchcraft in *Macbeth* include (along with the essays by Adelman, Eagleton, and Greenblatt mentioned earlier) Ian Robinson, "The Witches and Macbeth," *Critical Review* 11 (1968): 101–5; Biggins, "Sexuality, Witchcraft, and Violence"; Stallybrass, "*Macbeth* and Witchcraft"; Harris, *Night's Black Agents*, pp. 33–63; Newman, *Fashioning Femininity*, pp. 51–70; Beckwith, "The Power of Devils," pp. 143–61; Lorraine Helms, "The Weyward Sisters: Towards a Feminist Staging of *Macbeth*," *New Theatrical Quarterly* 8 (May 1992): 167–177.

11. The phrase is from Holinshed. Shakespeare's ambiguous representation of the witches has precedent in his account of the Weird Sisters. When Banquo and Macbeth first meet the witches, they are described as "three women in strange and wild apparell, resembling creatures of elder world." After the encounter, "the foresaid women vanished imme-

prophecies ("What! can the Devil speak true? [1.3.107]), much as George Gifford or other Protestant critics of such practices would. But their powers of divinition can also be interpreted as a form of "white" magic. Macbeth responds as some of Gifford's characters in his *Dialogue* might, describing them in more liminal terms (their "supernatural soliciting / Cannot be ill; cannot be good"; they have "more in them than mortal knowledge" [1.3.130–31, 1.5.2–3]). Lady Macbeth refers to them even more positively, as "fate and metaphysical aid" (29).

Later in the play, they take on still other identities. Their role in Macbeth's crime is similarly ambiguous. The play repeatedly compels us to see that persecutory malice and murderous desire are shared constructions; they have no single origin.[12] Yet the witches' ambiguity also becomes the vehicle by which others construct Macbeth's murderous motive. After his first encounter with the witches, Macbeth writes to his wife: "When I burned in desire to question them further, they made themselves air, into which they vanish'd" (1.5.3–5). They leave gaps for others to fill. Into those gaps both Macbeth and Lady Macbeth insert their own meanings: there are few stable boundaries between the witches and the interpretations other characters make of them. The witches' ambiguous utterances enable them to function as artful manipulators of unconscious process, speaking just enough to make Macbeth "burn in desire" and leaving the rest to his own transferential projections—his dull brain "wrought / With things forgotten"—as well as to the constructions of those around him. They do not create that desire; we know from his starts and his asides that murdering Duncan has probably already occurred to him and is not the necessary consequence of their predictions ("If Chance will have me King, why Chance may Crown me, /

---

diatlie out of their sight. This was reputed at the first but some vaine fantasticall illusion by Mackbeth and Banquho. . . . But afterwards the common opinion was, that these women were either the weird sisters, that is (as ye would say) the goddesses of destinie, or else some nymphs or feiries, indued with knowledge of prophesie by their necromanticall science, bicause everie thing came to passe as they had spoken." Quoted in the Arden edition of *Macbeth*, pp. 171–72.

12. Cf. Carol Thomas Neely's cogent remarks in her study of madness in *Macbeth*: the play presents "a continuum of alienation and malevolence . . . which blurs the boundaries between natural and supernatural agency, among witchraft of English or Continental sorts, antisocial behavior, and madness. This continuum has made it tempting to ask of the play just as the period (through witchcraft prosecutions and through reading madness) was asking: who is to blame? Who or what is the source of harm and evil? The questions produce conflicting and incompatible answers, as they did in the period" (" 'Documents in Madness,' " pp. 315–38).

Without my stir" [1.3.143–44]). But they create the terms within which that desire surfaces and takes shape.

By positioning the witches at the beginning of the play, by making their words seem to exert a controlling power over the speech of others and representing their utterances as "solicitors" of Macbeth's desire, the play constructs a female origin for male desire. As Janet Adelman has said, "Whether or not he is rapt by the witches' prophecies because the horrid image of Duncan's murder has already occurred to him, their role as gleeful prophets constructs Macbeth's actions in part as the enactments of their will."[13] The play, she goes on to suggest, in effect recapitulates the intersubjective process by which the son's sense of identity emerges in relation to the mother. We see the witches first, and the play's early scenes show Macbeth moving between worlds sharply divided by gender. The maternal is evoked both by the witches and Lady Macbeth.

Yet it may be useful to distinguish between "mothers" here: whereas Lady Macbeth, as I will later discuss, embodies aspects of the aristocratic mother, the witches more closely parallel the lower-class wet nurse. The play emphasizes their class difference in these scenes: they occupy the margins, haunting the borders of an all-male military world from which they are excluded, largely distanced from its concerns.[14] Nonpartisan spectators, they will meet again "when the battle's lost *and* won" (1.1.4); from their outsider's perspective they can observe what happens to both sides. In contrast to the highly hierarchized, conflict-ridden world of the upper-class thanes, theirs is egalitarian and cooperative: the other two aid the first witch in her maleficium against the sailor's wife, giving her winds to help her create a storm. "Th'art kind," the first witch responds (1.3.12). Among themselves they are supportive and helpful, "sisters" who can share, but when they abruptly greet Macbeth and Banquo with their all-hails, they appear as beings wholly "other," possessed of special powers and a seemingly superior "strange intelligence." They enact the uncanny return of a women's world once familiar, now "made strange" through a process of enculturation which takes elite sons from nurses and mothers and puts them into the hands of tutors, fathers, and patrons. The witches recall in dis-

13. Adelman, " 'Born of Woman,' " p. 93.

14. For Terry Eagleton, the witches "inhabit an anarchic, richly ambiguous zone both in and out of official society. . . . They are poets, prophetesses and devotees of female cult, radical separatists who scorn male power and lay bare the hollow sound and fury at its heart." Though his claim that the witches are "the heroines of the piece" strains credulity, his account has much charm. See *William Shakespeare*, pp. 1–3.

guised, twisted form the world of infancy and childhood, in which normative gender roles were inverted, in which males were ruled by women and vulnerable to their special powers. Or perhaps more accurately, they recall the anxious childhood fantasies that world could generate.

It is Banquo who constructs the witches as beings who, like mothers, may have a special knowledge about the growth cycle, about the passage from infancy to maturity, about which "seed" will prosper and which will not: "If you can look into the seeds of time, / And say which grain will grow, and which will not, / Speak then to me," he asks (1.3.58–60).[15] But it is Macbeth who is especially affected by their preternatural insight. What they promise to him follows a rising curve that sounds at first unequivocally gratifying: he will be not only Thane of Glamis but also Thane of Cawdor and "King hereafter" (50). Their predictions about Banquo's future, however, make clear that sons grow into a world where success is unevenly distributed: not only do some seeds grow and some not, but those that do grow enter a society ordered by "less" and "more." What they promise Banquo destabilizes the happy vision of Macbeth's future: Banquo will be "lesser" than Macbeth but also "greater," "not so happy" yet "much happier"; his children will be kings though he himself be none (65–67). Macbeth's success, in other words, will be qualified by Banquo's succession, his position "on top" reinscribed within a hierarchy that will again subordinate him.

The witches' predictions thus hint at a pattern that underlies much else in the play, as they nurse hopes that are then disappointed or destroyed— hopes tied to achieving dominance within an all-male hierarchy, then deflated by the unanticipated ascendancy of a rival. Macbeth's destruction is enacted through encounters with a series of such rivals, which have devastating consequences because he has first been encouraged to believe in his own absolute centrality. The witches single Macbeth out with their predictions, and promise what sounds like absolute success and preeminence. They speak to Banquo only after he asks them to; in so doing, they reveal a future that includes Macbeth's displacement from power, embodying a truth that Macbeth knows, partly denies, and then comes to feel persecuted by; witch-hunting becomes for him a quest for further knowledge which is also a resistance to it. It is not until he has murdered Duncan that he fully faces the implications of being "lesser" than Banquo

15. This special knowledge at the same time hints at magical control; Banquo's words also arouse the possibility that in "saying" which grain will grow the witches may also be "doing"—choosing which son to favor.

as well as "greater"; "under" Banquo, Macbeth's "genius is rebuk'd" (3.1.55). Before that realization takes place, however, other characters take on aspects of the witches' role, similarly arousing, then partially deflating Macbeth's hopes for a dominant and central position: Duncan tells Macbeth he deserves "more than all" for his loyal service, yet turns around and makes Malcolm Prince of Cumberland; Lady Macbeth greets him with her version of the witches' "all-hails" to his "greatness," yet fashions herself as a rival who threatens to outdo him in masculinity and even annihilate him unless he murders Duncan.

Viewed as embodiments of persecutory fantasy, the witches may be conjured into being by rage against the nurse/mother and her decentering gaze, but the play also defers that rage. Macbeth's vulnerability to the witches is in part a consequence of his problematic interactions with the father-king, Duncan, and the all-male honor community that he heads— interactions that similarly arouse and deflate Macbeth's hopes, provoking ambivalence and rage as well as promise of reward. The witches' prophecies point him first toward this father, away from their own uncanny reinscription of the mother's realm; their "strange intelligence" is in fact knowledge about how the father-king and other males will evaluate Macbeth. The success they promise can be realized—or thwarted—only within the male military-political world the father rules.

Duncan

Duncan has often been read as a father—*the* father—in both psychoanalytic and nonpsychoanalytic treatments of the play. It may be useful, however, to recall some of the differences between the roles of "father" and "king" that such readings elide. In the feudal world the play imagines, family loyalty did not always neatly line up with duty to the king. Even if a thane's actual father was dead ("By Sinel's death I am thane of Cawdor," as Macbeth says), the father's patrilineage was not, and a thane might himself be a father to sons who would carry that line into the future. The play brings out tensions in the two types of fatherhood in several ways. His murder of the father/king theoretically benefits Macbeth as future father of sons, and his concern with Banquo's line is an extension of his attempt to possess both types of fatherhood in one person. Later in the play Macduff's loyalty to the father/king makes him a "traitor" to his own family.

Moreover, as figurative "sons," thanes also might come into conflict with the king's actual children. The king ruled a restless, highly competitive brood, each of them used to being first sons within their own patrilineages. Except in the rarest of circumstances, none of these sons could ever hope to be a first son in relation to the king; they all had to settle, to some degree or another, for less-favored status. They were preeminent within their own households and regions, and arrogance was structured into their roles—hence the highly charged position of the king's "favorite," target of envy and resentment, who in effect attained "first son" status; hence the complex ambivalence a thane might feel in carrying out his subordinate role; and hence the quasi-fratricidal feuding and factionalism that often characterized relations within the nobility in James's Scotland as well as Shakespeare's.

In *Macbeth* the political equivalent of sibling rivalry is exacerbated by the mixed signals Duncan seems to give Macbeth when they first meet, which Macbeth interprets in the light of expectations the witches have aroused.[16] Duncan praises Macbeth as one who has done "more than all," "everything," flattering him as the be-all and end-all of the king's desire. Macbeth's exalted position seems further underscored by the odd way the king almost ignores Banquo, who has "no less deserv'd" but is given no new title nor honored with so much praise (1.4.30). In turn, Macbeth flatters the king by equating himself with the king's "children and servants," who "do but what they should, by doing everything / Safe toward your love and honour" (26–27). Does Macbeth's language also hint at a wish to be literally the king's child—his first child and potential heir, singled out by the father as the most valued extension of his own identity? If so, Duncan's next move will be an even sharper shock, for Duncan chooses almost this moment to name his actual son Malcolm Prince of Cumberland, and thus his most likely successor.

In blurring the line between a hereditary and an elective monarchy here, Shakespeare again underscores the theme of hopes aroused and deflated: since the king must actually name his heir, it is realistic for Macbeth to hope to be in that position. And Duncan's timing is not the only thing that seems arbitrary. Malcolm, as far as the audience knows, has performed no feats on the battlefield; he is honored for no apparent reason, other than that he is Duncan's first son. Like the witches' words to Banquo, this new pronouncement dethrones Macbeth and repositions him lower down within a hierarchy, his value to the king no longer absolute but relative. Duncan's imagery, in fact, casts him in the role of gardener in a way that

16. On the tensions in this scene, see especially Berger, "Early Scenes," pp. 20–24.

recalls the powers over "seeds of time" that Banquo attributes to the witches: "I have begun to plant thee," he says to Macbeth after his speech of praise, "and will labour ⁄ to make thee full of growing" (1.4.28–29). The witches have seen and described a future that is in fact constructed by the father-king: as the source of all noble honors, titles, and offices, Duncan is a gardener who can "say" which seed will grow and which will not; merely by "naming" Malcolm Prince of Cumberland, he establishes a limit to Macbeth's growth and extends Malcolm's—and he does so just after suggesting Macbeth is limitlessly deserving. The limit to Macbeth's "greatness" prophesied by the witches is located in a far-distant future that Macbeth, for the moment, can comfortably ignore; Duncan, on the other hand, infuriatingly imposes a limit in the here-and-now.

It is no wonder, then, that Duncan's decision inflames Macbeth's "black and deep desires":

> The Prince of Cumberland!—That is a step
> On which I must fall down, or else o'erleap,
> For in my way it lies. Stars, hide your fires!
> Let not light see my black and deep desires;
> The eye wink at the hand; yet let that be,
> Which the eye fears, when it is done, to see. (1.4.48–53)

The murderous impulse that Macbeth put on hold at the end of scene 3 returns here greatly intensified. Along with the anger of frustration, Macbeth may feel personally injured by the father-king's rejection of him as "first son"—a rejection that makes him all the more vulnerable to Lady Macbeth's mothering in the following scenes.

Lady Macbeth

Many critics have viewed Lady Macbeth as almost continuous with the witches, another embodiment of their persecutory malice, possibly even becoming one of them after her invocation of the "Spirits / That tend on mortal thoughts" (1.5.40–41).[17] Although I too will develop this linkage,

17. See, for example, Stephen Greenblatt's remarks: "Shakespeare achieves the remarkable effect of a nebulous infection, a bleeding of the demonic into the secular and the secular into the demonic. The most famous instance of this effect is Lady Macbeth's great invocation" ("Shakespeare Bewitched," p. 124). Other linkages of the witches and Lady Macbeth are made by Stallybrass, "*Macbeth* and witchcraft"; and Adelman, *Suffocating Mothers*. See Adelman's excellent footnotes for further references.

I also want to stress some differences. If gender links Lady Macbeth with the witches, class divides them; as a member of the aristocracy she is in a sense their enemy. If, like them, she is a perverse mother to Macbeth, she is a distinctly aristocratic mother, who expresses some class-specific concerns. It is tempting to imagine that offstage, before the play begins, she, like the sailor's wife, has somehow slighted the witches, that their seemingly motiveless malice toward Macbeth has roots in a quarrel with his wife. By the end of the play, at any rate, she has become one of their victims. Intentionally or not, the witches dupe her and destroy her just as effectively as they do Macbeth.[18]

When we first encounter her, however, she seems very much an extension of the witches, a voice that picks up where they left off. When Macbeth writes to his wife of the witches and "what greatness is promis'd thee," she sees the gap they have left, supplying her own answers to the questions Macbeth might have asked them had they not "made themselves into air." But whereas the witches have uncanny magical powers—powers that link them to the preoedipal fantasies of the very young child—Lady Macbeth, even after her conjuration speech, seems decidedly down to earth. They foretell the future; Lady Macbeth's vision has a shorter range. Their ambiguous language infects the play as a whole and is open-ended enough to sustain multiple interpretations; Lady Macbeth limits and localizes their meanings. She "knows" their prophecies must mean murdering Duncan. She "knows" also that to accomplish the murder requires further conjuration.

Her project takes shape as a quest for class-based "greatness" that can be achieved only by means of her husband. Macbeth must be "more the man" in order to help Lady Macbeth enact her own "vaulting ambition"; class identity, for aristocratic women, could provide a way out of the sense of "lack" associated with being female. In order to effect the masculinization of a husband she constructs as a son, she wills her own "unsexing" to counteract it, becoming a gender hybrid with both male and female features, much like the aristocratic mothers of the first tetralogy. She remakes herself in the image of the armored male body and of the

---

18. Carol Neely makes a similar point: "The witches are . . . ambiguously asociated with and dissociated from Lady Macbeth." In a footnote she adds, "I do not see their relationship as an 'alliance.' . . . In fact the witches wish Macbeth to fail while Lady Macbeth wishes him to succeed, and their relation to the supernatural is quite different from hers" (" 'Documents in Madness,' " p. 328). I would add only that the witches may even be actively hostile to Lady Macbeth: wittingly or unwittingly, they help to destroy her as well as her husband.

witch-mother whose powers of nurture bring death, trading her "milk" for "gall," closing off the vulnerable female openings associated with pity and remorse, and wielding a "keen knife." As in the first tetralogy, individualist ambition for class advancement is linked to gender inversion and to witchcraft, and Shakespeare draws on patriarchal beliefs that valorize the "masculine mother" as a producer of sons; Macbeth will explicitly laud his wife as such by praising her "undaunted mettle" that should "compose" nothing but males.[19]

But if she is masculine mother, she is also adoring wife, empowering herself through a language of deference. "Great Glamis! worthy Cawdor! / Greater than both, by the all-hail hereafter!" (1.5.54–55): thus she welcomes her husband home, echoing the witches' three greetings. In displaying herself as a subordinate and worshipful audience, she enables Macbeth to experience himself in the position of greatness to which he aspires—to feel "the future in the instant" that has already transported her (58) and to compensate, perhaps, for the wound Duncan has delivered by failing to recognize Macbeth as his "first" son. Shortly thereafter, she begins to assert her own leadership, as it becomes evident that Macbeth is again wavering: "you shall put / This night's great business into my dispatch; / Which shall to all our nights and days to come / Give solely sovereign sway and masterdom" (67–70); when Macbeth offers less than enthusiastic endorsement, she tells him, "Only look up clear; / To alter favour ever is to fear. / Leave all the rest to me" (71–73). Mother knows best; by the end of this scene she has reversed the position she assumed upon his entrance: now he must look "up" to her. Both roles—the servant/wife and the dominant, managerial mother—are necessary to her project of making him "more the man." Self-abasement allows him to experience the pleasure that would come with his success; authority invites him to give up his power and place himself in her hands, to take refuge, trustingly, in her care, becoming in effect a dependent child again. Having done so, he can be remade in her own image, the man-child of a mother of "undaunted mettle."

But as Janet Adelman has expressed with particular eloquence, Lady Macbeth's deployment of the role of mother takes on more ominous and terrifying implications as her project unfolds; it succeeds in part because, having made Macbeth psychically into her child again, she exploits his vulnerability to her with ruthless abandon. As Adelman puts it,

19. As Suffolk praises Margaret to Henry VI in *1 Henry VI* 5.5.70–76.

In the figure of Lady Macbeth, that is, Shakespeare rephrases the power of the witches as the wife/mother's power to poison human relatedness at its source; in her, their power of cosmic coercion is rewritten as the power of the mother to misshape or destroy the child. . . . As she progresses from questioning Macbeth's masculinity to imagining herself dashing out the brains of her infant son, she articulates a fantasy in which to be less than a man is to become interchangeably a woman or a baby, terribly subject to the wife/mother's rage.[20]

The textual locus, of course, is the following passage:

> I have given suck, and know
> How tender 'tis to love the babe that milks me:
> I would, while it was smiling in my face,
> Have pluck'd my nipple from his boneless gums,
> And dash'd the brains out, had I so sworn
> As you have done to this. (1.7.54–59)

Lady Macbeth's imagery here is a logical extension of her conjuration speech: having closed herself off from the "compunctious visitings of Nature," having poisoned her nurturant milk, she can now imagine her maternity in even more perverse terms. The theme of hopes aroused and disappointed recurs here as an abrupt and violent weaning. The mother becomes a witch to her own child.

What Adelman does not bring out, however, is that Lady Macbeth presents herself in class-specific terms: she recreates herself as a mother of the honor culture, for whom keeping an oath to "do" assumes more importance than attachment to her child. "Honor" drives her perverse maternity and inscribes her as a witch. Depriving the child of milk, she keeps the food of honor to herself. As in the first tetralogy, Shakespeare associates personal honor and narrow clan loyalties with "unnatural" female desire: pressure to be "more the man" comes from a suspect source. The mother herself becomes in a sense the son's rival, displacing him from a central, protected position. Lady Macbeth contests Macbeth's honor by offering her own as superior, reminding him of the class "greatness" as well as the exalted masculine identity that awaits him if he goes through with the plan. If he does not, he is in danger of her annihilating rage. The threat to Macbeth is clear; he will in effect be this infant if he fails her.

20. Adelman, *Suffocating Mothers*, pp. 137–38.

The image of the infant at risk recurs, of course, throughout the play, hinted at first in Macbeth's representation of Pity as a "naked newborn babe," protesting the deep damnation of Duncan's taking-off. Lady Macbeth further develops the association of the sleeping, "unguarded" Duncan with an infant (as Adelman points out, she makes it possible for Macbeth to share in her "fantasy of omnipotent malevolence" by locating in Duncan the vulnerability she has just invoked in the image of the feeding infant). And Banquo, too, immediately before the murder, describes the king "a-bed" and in "unusual pleasure," "shut up in measureless content" (2.1.12–13, 16–17). After the murder, Duncan's vulnerability is passed on to others, as Banquo speaks of "our naked frailties . . . / That suffer in exposure," as children's murders are attempted and accomplished, as "new widows howl, new orphans cry," as Malcolm fears that Macduff will think it wisdom to "offer up a weak, poor, innocent lamb, / T'appease an angry god" (2.3.124–25, 4.3.5, 16–17). Banquo's own murder may be thought of as a disruption of feeding; greeted by the Macbeths as "chief guest" at the "great feast" they will hold in the evening, he is then murdered en route (3.1.11–12).[21] Trust is dangerous in this world, as it is to make the risky crossing from day to night, waking to sleep; Macbeth's invocation of Night as he looks forward to the murder of Banquo and Fleance is only one of many such moments that convey this danger: "Come, seeling Night, / Scarf up the tender eye of pitiful Day; . . . / Good things of Day begin to droop and drowse, / Whiles Night's black agents to their preys do rouse" (3.2.46–47, 52–53). In the scene with Lady Macduff and her son we hear the counterpart to Lady

21. At the beginning of the banquet, the Macbeths further construct themselves as generous feeders, embodiments of the "good breast":

> Lady M. My royal Lord,
> You do not give the cheer: the feast is sold,
> That is not often vouch'd, while 'tis a-making,
> 'Tis given with welcome: to feed were best at home;
> From thence, the sauce to meat is ceremony;
> Meeting were bare without it.
> Macb. Sweet remembrancer!—
> Now, good digestion wait on appetite,
> And health on both! (3.4.31–38)

The audience is well aware that ceremony here is *mere* ceremony: Macbeth has been kept from "giving the cheer" because of his meeting with the murderers hired to kill Banquo. Lady Macbeth's distinction between food that is commodified and food that is "given with welcome" proves to be another invitation to a betrayal of trust.

Macbeth's image of maternal destructiveness, yet it offers little consolation: "The poor wren, / The most diminutive of birds, will fight, / Her young ones in her nest, against the owl" (4.2.9–11). Even with the mother's protection the "young one" will be devoured, as quickly becomes evident in the murder of her own son, "poor bird," in front of her (34).

The vulnerability of the infant to malevolent or unreliable parenting, recalled in moments of violated trust or betrayed bonds in adult experience, becomes in *Macbeth* both cause and effect of the feudal order's problematic construction of masculinity. To escape that vulnerability, Macbeth takes on the characteristics of the mother who has threatened him, like her, expelling "compunctious visitings" of nature and "pity," giving up attachment to her for identification with her. The malevolent, masculine mother is absorbed into the tyrant and child killer Macbeth subsequently becomes. Against this model of manhood, the play offers another, which requires retaining the capacity for pity and attachment the Macbeths have cast out, a capacity associated with mother's milk: "th'milk of human kindness," the "sweet milk of human concord" (1.5.17, 4.3.98). If Macbeth identifies with a malevolent mother, the alternative is to identify with a nurturing one: a "humane" male identity involves absorbing aspects of the "good" mother, not the bad. Yet at the same time, the play represents this version of manhood as a continuing locus of anxiety and conflict. For to retain elements of the nurturing mother is to find oneself again at risk—in effect, back in the vulnerable and threatened position of the infant. This fear is literalized in the person of Lady Macduff, who, like the "poor wren," stays with her young ones in the nest and is slaughtered. Attachment and pity—"feeling it as a man"—put Malcolm and Macduff at risk as well. What is threatening about these "maternal" traits, I think, does not primarily come from the pressures they put on male identity, although the fears they arouse are often defended against in gendered terms. Rather, threat lies in the experience of attachment itself, which in this play leads regularly to death and loss as well as to wounded self-esteem. Malcolm and Macduff struggle for an alternative to Macbeth's mode of response, but a tragic mechanism at work in the patriarchal world thwarts their attempts: the father's world, as well as the mother's, proves to be the site of malevolent nurture, regularly returning males to the vulnerable position of the infant.

The Problem of Mourning

Grief seems to be offered up by the play as the exemplary instance of "feeling it like a man," the alternative, articulated by Macduff, which contrasts most clearly with Lady Macbeth's emphasis on being "more the man." Yet it is also presented as a matter of uneasiness and debate several times in the last acts. This uneasiness, I believe, begins with the inability of Duncan's survivors to mourn him. When his murder is first discovered, the language Macduff uses turns Duncan into a sacred icon: "Most sacrilegious Murther hath broke ope / The Lord's anointed Temple, and stole thence / The life o'th building!" (2.3.66–68). Duncan is constructed as a virtual inanimate object even before his death, albeit a sanctified one. "Approach the chamber, and destroy your sight / With a new Gorgon," Macduff continues (70–71); Duncan's murdered body evokes horror and turns men to stone, not to grief. Throughout the scene, the thanes and other onlookers, fearful and under stress, cannot remember Duncan as a man, a respected king, a human father, but only as a concept, an allegory, an abstraction—"death itself," "the great doom's image" (76, 77).[22] Macbeth is the only one who speaks of "love" for the king, and he, of course, is using it merely as an excuse to explain his murder of the men of his chamber: "Who could refrain / That had a heart to love, and in that heart / Courage, to make's love known?" (114–16). His words' surface meaning sets the pattern for later responses to loss: grief is something that must immediately be turned into violent revenge.

Or so it is argued in the debates staged in response to later instances of loss. The first such debate takes place between Malcolm and Macduff—or perhaps more accurately, between Malcolm and Malcolm. When Rosse first announces the death of Macduff's family, Malcolm at first tells Macduff to "Give sorrow words; the grief, that does not speak, / Whispers the o'er-fraught heart, and bids it break" (4.3.209–10). But once Macduff does begin expressing his woe, Malcolm is quick to try to cut it off: "Be comforted: / Let's make us med'cines of our great revenge, / To cure this deadly grief" (213–15). It is as if an actual display of grief makes him uncomfortable, too uncomfortable to stand it for long; a few lines later he is gruffly telling Macduff to "Dispute it like a man," whereupon Macduff protests:

---

22. Harry Berger makes a parallel point in "Early Scenes," p. 16.

> I shall do so;
> But I must also feel it as a man:
> I cannot but remember such things were,
> That were most precious to me. (4.3.220–23)

Even then Malcolm cannot shut up, and again he urges Macduff to "let grief / Convert to anger; blunt not the heart, enrage it" (229). Finally, Macduff comes round: "O! I could play the woman with mine eyes, / And braggart with my tongue. —But, gentle Heavens, / Cut short all intermission" (230–32). He now becomes the "manly" revenger that Malcolm wants him to be.

The death of young Siward at the very end of the play becomes another occasion for a debate over grief and "being a man." Young Siward, whose "hurts" are on the front of his body, must therefore have died "like a man," and his father asserts he has no reason to mourn, for "God's soldier he be" (5.9.12, 9, 13). Here Malcolm, surprisingly, articulates the counterposition: "He's worth more sorrow, / And that I'll spend for him" (16–17). For this remark his father reproves him: "He's worth no more; / They say he parted well and paid his score: / And so, God be with him!" (17–19). This emphasis on Young Siward's manhood also makes reparation for Macbeth's scornful slight upon killing him: "Thou wast born of woman:— / But swords I smile at, weapons laugh to scorn, / Brandish'd by man that's of a woman born" (5.7.11–13).

What are we to make of this ambivalence about mourning? Clearly, there is anxiety about male identity here: grief, at least too much of it, is feminizing and threatens a man with loss of gender difference. Converting grief to revenge allows one to reestablish one's masculine identity; dying bravely—"unshrinkingly"—turns one's potentially feminizing wounds into the marks of a manly soldier. But the need to adopt a manly hardness is compelled by more than these men's need to reassert gender difference, to "excise the female," as Adelman puts it. The appeal of an armored masculinity arises from a larger crisis of trust which pervades the play at many levels. The preoccupation with "being a man" becomes the life raft the males cling to in the face of deeper fears—fears that arise from their encounters with loss and the vulnerabilities to which loss exposes them, in a world where a basic sense of trust in external bonds has already been called into question. For the "loyal" son who survives Duncan's death, for example, mourning him as a father or human king may mean confronting a powerful sense of abandonment. Duncan's death

leaves Malcolm exposed to the "daggers in men's smiles," radically unprotected in a realm where flight seems the only alternative (2.4.138).
Though Malcolm in no way directly expresses a sense of paternal abandonment (we never hear him acknowledge his loss at all, not even in the
abstract, sacralizing mode of Macduff), the play becomes preoccupied
with it in some of its later scenes. Lady Macduff uses the "wren" image
to criticize her husband for abandoning his family and goes on in frantic,
passionate terms to suggest he has been a coward and a traitor to them,
that he "loves us not" and "wants the natural touch" (4.2.8–9). Her
poignant, repeated question to her son echoes throughout the scene:
"How wilt thou do for a father?" (38). While the son insists touchingly
on his ability to survive "as birds do" with what he finds on his own, her
question is cruelly answered with the entrance of the murderers Macbeth
has sent. In the following scene Malcolm questions Macduff for his flight:
"Why in that rawness left you wife and child / (Those precious motives,
those strong knots of love), / Without leave-taking?" (4.3.26–28). Malcolm, testing Macduff to see if he is in league with Macbeth, rather oddly
takes Macduff's sudden flight as added evidence against him; one might
expect it to show Macduff's loyal willingness to put country above the
needs of his own family. In an oblique way, perhaps Malcolm is expressing feelings about his own father, who abandoned him to a similar "rawness," unprotected as a "weak, poor, innocent lamb." He may fear that
Macduff, as a new father-protector, may repeat not only Macbeth's tyrannical crimes but also his own father's disappearance in the middle of the
night, similarly "without leave-taking." To reproach his father directly
would mean acknowledging an anger that could poison the memory of
the loved parent, provoke guilt, or in other ways render the experience of
loss more painful. It is safer to direct the charge against Macduff.

Grief leads to a sense of abandonment; it may also lead to anger and
guilt. Macduff, in temporarily resisting Malcolm's injunction to dispute his
grief "like a man," also discloses some of the painful consequences of
"feeling it like a man." Of all the characters in the play, Macduff goes far-
thest in expressing the wrenching effects of losing persons "most precious"
to him; his expression, however, leads him first to question a heavenly father's negligence ("Did Heaven look on / And would not take their
part?" [4.3.223–24]), then to accuse himself ("Sinful Macduff! / They
were all struck for thee. Naught that I am, / Not for their own demerits,
but for mine, / Fell slaughter on their souls: Heaven rest them now!"
[224–27]). The price of his attachment to them is a terrible sense of being

at fault. It is after this outburst that Macduff acquiesces to Malcolm's injunction, stops "playing the woman," and converts his grief into retaliatory anger at Macbeth. Malcolm, looking on, may find Macduff's grief difficult for several reasons. Reminded by Macduff's loss of the loss of his own father, he may also fear losing this new father to his old attachments; a Macduff incapacitated by grief is a Macduff incapable of offering Malcolm the protection he needs. Moreover, Macduff's remorse-filled remarks call attention to God's seeming negligence and to paternal abandonment, again perhaps tapping into a reservoir of anger in Malcolm. Yet because Macduff's remarks are self-accusations, they may also make Malcolm consider the possibility of his own negligence: perhaps at some level, he feels responsible himself for failing to protect his murdered father, just as Macduff feels he has failed to protect his family.[23]

Old Siward's response to his son's death seems the coldest: his son's value to him is reduced to the single act of bravely dying in defense of patrilineal rule, making him "God's soldier." This father circumvents loss altogether by replacing it with pride in his son's manly death. It is—fleetingly—comforting to hear Malcolm say, "he's worth more sorrow," the line that bespeaks Malcolm's ambivalence. We glimpse the possibility of a continuance of the "work" of mourning beyond the end of the play. But this line occurs before the father's reproof—"he's worth no more"—to which Malcolm offers no further argument. For the most part, we are left at the end in a tensed, guarded world, where Malcolm and his followers seem unprepared to face the fact that, in triumphing over Macbeth, they will lose their main defense against the chaos of feelings their grief arouses.

Thus, an untrustworthy external world, where social bonds cannot be trusted, where loyal men cannot be distinguished from traitors, where murderers do not hesitate to kill the unprotected—also produces an untrustworthy inner one, where to feel grief is to become vulnerable to a different set of fears, to become aware that all attachments carry with them the risk of loss or abandonment. In the play as a whole, violations of trust

23. It should be pointed out that Macduff does not quite say that he has failed to protect his family; he accuses himself only in a very general sense, for undefined "demerits"—not quite confronting his strange act of abandonment. Arguably, he—and perhaps the play as well—does not quite face the fact that he has in some sense failed his family by choosing to help Malcolm. The price of saving the state comes at the expense of his family; he protects a "national" son but abandons his own. Macbeth allows him to localize blame. The anger Macduff might direct toward God or against himself is instead diverted to one who truly but not exclusively deserves it.

and the vulnerabilities they produce are linked to fathers as well as mothers, though less damningly. If Macbeth is destroyed by his submission to the (malevolent) mother in the wife and witch, Malcolm and his followers are impaired by ambivalence toward a (negligent) father they can avenge but not mourn, impoverished by their mistrust of strong attachments either to women or to one another. Macduff's association of a "new Gorgon" with Duncan's dead body brings the two ideas together. The image recalls the roles of Lady Macbeth and the witches in the regicide and recalls that their malevolent female power now threatens Duncan's surviving thanes/sons; yet Macduff's language so completely equates the two that it is as if in dying the father has actually taken on the malevolent mother's characteristics; paternal abandonment amounts to another act of abrupt and violent weaning, leaving sons vulnerable.

Juggling Fiends

If in the last two acts of the play, Malcolm and Macduff direct us to the problem of paternal abandonment, Macbeth directs us again to problems associated with patriarchal rule. Seeking to know the "worst" that the future can hold for him, Macbeth returns to the Weird Sisters: "More shall they speak" (3.4.131). Their cryptic predictions allow him the illusion of magical security even while reminding him that his success will give way to Banquo's succession, that the Banquo who is "lesser" than Macbeth is about to become "greater." As the locus of an "other" knowledge about the future, the witches are now openly operating as perverse mothers, whose divinatory techniques have some necromantic features but especially associate them with women's domestic labor, as they "boil and bake" their diabolic "gruel" (4.1.13, 32). Their cauldron has affinities with the elite magician's magic circle, within which spirits are conjured to appear (as in 2 Henry VI), and the ritualized combining of the gruel's ingredients draws upon necromancy (dismembered animals, parts of dead bodies) and the herbal lore of cunning folk (root of hemlock, slips of yew); it has both local (toad, newt, dog) and exotic features (nose of Turk, Tartar's lips, baboon's blood). Some of its most memorable ingredients reiterate the village witch's associations with child killing: "finger of birth-strangled babe, / Ditch-delivered by a drab" and blood from a sow "that hath eaten / Her nine farrow" (30–31, 64–65). The witches' brew also recalls Lady Macbeth's poisonous mother's milk; it too is a poisoned meal.

Presented to us at first as cannibalistic cooks and murderous mothers, the witches acquire another meaning once Macbeth arrives to make his demands. Their cauldron becomes the locus of birth as well as death and dismemberment, suggestive of vagina and womb as well as cooking vessel. The apparitions to which their cauldron gives uncanny birth are products of a "deed without a name" (49); two of the three take the form of children (the bloody child who encodes Macduff's Caesarean birth, the child crowned with a tree in his hand who encodes Malcolm's taking of Dunsinane Hill). They leave in their wake the "issue" of Banquo. The cauldron becomes a womb in which dead body parts are incorporated and recombined to create new, rival "issue" that is poisonous and castratingly phallic to Macbeth. What goes into the mother's body (mouth/womb/cauldron) comes out as food (gruel), excrement (entrails/hell-broth), but especially babies.

What we see is very much presided over by women, seemingly under their control. Yet for the first time we hear a brief reference to the witches' "masters," presumably male—confirming Banquo's remark at the beginning of the play that the devil speaks in them. Moreover, the future they reveal to Macbeth is ultimately the work of patriarchy, which they only simulate in the form of "shows." Their diabolic art converges with providential history, as Macbeth beholds the "horrible sight" of his rival's phallic plenitude. Banquo's all-male patrilineage stretches out "to th'crack of doom," and some of his royal descendants even carry "twofold balls and treble sceptres" (117, 121). Banquo even rubs it in by gloating in triumph: "Now, I see, tis true; / For the blood-bolter'd Banquo smiles upon me, / And points at [the apparitions] for his" (122–23). The witches' earlier prophecies return here to haunt Macbeth in persecutory fashion, a "horrible sight" that he has already known but disavowed.

Angry at these mothers for, as it were, giving birth to a rival, Macbeth scapegoats the witches for the work of patriarchy. The scene ends with the play's major instance of witchcraft accusation. For showing Macbeth what he wants/does not want to know, they are "filthy hags" (115); in addition, he calls down on them a curse that ironically implicates himself: "Infected be the air whereon they ride; / And damned all those that trust them" (138–39). Macbeth experiences their apparitions as another betrayal of trust, another instance of displacement. However much he wishes to blame only the mothers, it is clear that his displacement is the product of both the mother's and the father's world.

This convergence of the witches' malevolent nurture with the father's providential order continues in the final scenes: Macbeth's defeat is their triumph as much as it is Macduff's. Many productions have given extratextual expression to the lingering influence of the witches that can be felt in these scenes.[24] Nor can they be easily disentangled from the other cosmic forces implicitly present. Macbeth's despairing cry about the "juggling fiends" he can no more believe seems to equate the witches with their demonic male "masters," bringing male and female together (as Lady Macbeth is later called a "fiend-like" queen). Macduff's response to Macbeth's claim to have a charmed life seemingly conflates heaven and hell:

> Despair thy charm;
> And let the Angel, whom thou still hast serv'd,
> Tell thee, Macduff was from his mother's womb
> Untimely ripped. (5.8.13–16)

Macduff's use of "Angel" to refer to Satan here makes it curiously difficult to differentiate between God's providential order and the diabolic one. Moreover, Macduff's Caesarean birth, while effectively undermining Macbeth's last shred of "security," relocates anxiety about uncanny events in Macduff himself: such births might herald a hero—or a monster.[25] It is of a piece with other liminal happenings that follow Duncan's murder; though they comment on the horror of Macbeth's murderous act, such events are not unambiguously legible as signs of a righteous God's wrath. They equally suggest the unleashing of ungovernable powers of darkness, as likely to strike the innocent as the guilty. As Banquo says, "There's husbandry in heaven; / Their candles are all out." (2.1.4–5). And Lennox reports:

> The night has been unruly: where we lay,
> Our chimneys were blown down; and as they say,

24. One example occurs at the end of Roman Polanski's film version of *Macbeth*, where Donalbain is shown sneaking off to meet the witches after Malcolm's victory speech. For others, see Marvin Rosenberg, *The Masks of Macbeth* (Berkeley: University of California Press, 1978), pp. 654–55. "These uncanny figures who appear at the moment of a man's triumph, are never far away in this world," he remarks.

25. The duality of Caesarean birth is brought out in Renate Blumenfeld-Kosinski, *Not of Woman Born: Representations of Caesarean Birth in Medieval and Renaissance Culture* (Ithaca: Cornell University Press, 1990), although she focuses mainly on continental sources. Among other "satanic" examples, the Antichrist was widely represented as born via Caesarean section starting in the mid-fifteenth century (pp. 125–42).

> Lamentings heard i'th'air; strange screams of death,
> And, prophesying with accents terrible
> Of dire combustion, and confus'd events,
> New hatch'd to th' woeful time, the obscure bird
> Clamour'd the livelong night: some say, the earth
> Was feverous, and did shake. (2.3.53–60)

Nature, too, is not clearly divided from the unnatural but itself the site of an evil nature. "Merciful Powers," Banquo prays, "Restrain in me the cursed thoughts that nature / Gives way to in repose!" (2.1.7–9). And Macbeth associates his murderous plans with nature's twilight spaces:

> Ere the bat hath flown
> His cloister'd flight; ere to black Hecate's summons
> The shard-born beetle, with his drowsy hums,
> Hath rung Night's yawning peal, there shall be done
> A deed of dreadful note.
> . . . . .
> Light thickens; and the crow
> Makes wing to th'rooky wood;
> Good things of Day begin to droop and drowse
> Whiles Night's black agents to their preys do rouse. (3.2.40–44, 49–52)

Here, murderous impulses and acts, "Hecate's summons," and diabolic "black agents" are inscribed within the natural world; rather than an unnatural interruption, they are part of the cyclic movement of day and night, and night is regularly the site of violent death and injury. Even the divine justice seemingly implied by the idea that "blood will have blood" is complicated by the statement's unsavory associations with the practices of augurers, who operated outside the law to bring to light the "secret'st man of blood" (3.4.121–25). To be sure, other moments in the play do call up a more reassuring notion of a "just" providence at work: the owl that shrieks at the time of Duncan's murder, the voices Macbeth hears as he commits the murder, the Porter scene, the conversation between Rosse and the Old Man in act 2, scene 4, when Rosse comments that the "hours dreadful, and things strange" (3) reported by the Old Man show just that: "Ha, good Father, / Thou seest the heavens, as troubled with man's act, / Threatens his bloody stage" (4–6). The falcon killed by a mousing owl and the horses that eat each other, unsettling as these images are, can thus be read within the frame Rosse provides. The Old Man, for his part, reads them as unambiguously "unnatural." But these moments coexist with, rather than supersede, the others I have mentioned, inviting a providential reading that is then destabilized. And arguably, Rosse himself contributes to this destabilizing tendency, turning his confident assertion that such "unnatural" events may be read as signs of God's displeasure into a question:

> by the clock 'Tis day,
> And yet dark night strangles the travelling lamp.
> Is't night's predominance, or the day's shame,
> That darkness does the face of earth entomb,
> When living light should kiss it? (6–10)

Providential order is recast as a struggle between day and night, good and evil, which seems too evenly balanced, in which it seems impossible to say with any certainty which side will win. This world seems governed by a deity whose actions disturbingly resemble the play's other negligent and abandoning fathers, who, like them, leaves his earthly children all too vulnerable.

Janet Adelman has argued that the end of the play enacts what amounts to a fantasy of male parthenogenesis, in which all trace of the female is excised from the male "family" Malcolm reintroduces to Scotland. We are also, she implies, invited to accept this excision as a "restoration" of natural order.[26] As I have tried to show, however, in some ways "male" and "female," "fair" and "foul," remain interconnected to the end. Moreover, in moving toward its all-male conclusion the play moves away from its emphasis on a female origin for evil. What is most problematic now lies in the father's world, the world the witches' have shown to us in their apparitions. The play's tragic force lies precisely in the precariousness of Malcolm's order; a play with a "healthy" Macduff, a more idealized Malcolm would be a less subtle—and less honest—construction of feudal patriarchal rule. Certainly, the play invites us to choose Malcolm and Macduff over Macbeth, the father's son over the mother's, the defense of patrilineal rule over its violation, but it also makes it painfully clear that a truly restorative alternative for Scotland is

---

26. Adelman, *Suffocating Mothers*, pp. 139–46. Although Adelman's essay for the most part stresses the play's ambivalences and ambiguities, her treatment of the ending assumes a "restoration" model of the play which harks back to pre-1975 readings—albeit from a critical rather than a celebratory standpoint. (The same might be said of Peter Stallybrass "*Macbeth* and Witchcraft.")

not forthcoming. Malcolm's "healing" takes a purely military form, and the magical healing touch possessed by the king of England exists only in an offstage world remote from Scotland. In this guarded, mistrustful, all-male military world allies have difficulty feeling bonded even to each other. On stage especially we are likely to be aware of Malcolm as a young king, largely untested, as dependent on his warriors as his father was before him, "planting" his thanes without enough to give them in return, his promise to make them all earls an empty, inflationary move. The problem of loyalty remains. The play registers an ambivalence about Malcolm's order which is generated by its own inner tensions, through an honor-driven patronage system controlled by the king and through the vicissitudes of patrilineality. Such an order encourages the "vaulting ambition" it must also contain and regularly slights those whom it rewards. The collaboration of witches and traitors is one of its predictable by-products.

I locate my sense of the play's countermovement not only in the ambivalence both Macduff and Malcolm express toward their own grief and toward the "female" within them but more particularly in the way that the demise of the Macbeths generates the sense of "waste" A. C. Bradley found so characteristic of Shakespearean tragedy. Through them we feel the painful, isolating consequences of the loss of the "female" capacity for attachment, a capacity they have willfully sealed off in themselves and yet are haunted by. The play's last act makes us acutely aware of their solitude, their separation not only from each other but also from the rest of the world, the "wine of life drawn," only "the lees" remaining (2.3.93). In her sleepwalking scene, Lady Macbeth recalls Duncan's death, the knowledge she brushed aside—that this king reminded her of her father—returning in her frightened question: "Who would have thought the old man to have so much blood in him?" (5.1.37–38). She recalls also that "the Thane of Fife had a wife; where is she now?" (40). This unexpected hint of an identification with Lady Macduff is the only instance in which Lady Macbeth shows any sign of feeling for another woman. Finally, as she goes "to bed, to bed" she remarks "Come, come, come, come, give me your hand" (62, 63) reaching out for a partnership with her husband which no longer exists; having helped to produce a manliness defined by violent separation from the female, she has lost the only connection that sustained her.

Macbeth's own isolation is also clear, his "way of life" fallen "into the sere, the yellow leaf"; he as well as his enemies knows that

that which should accompany old age,
As honour, love, obedience, troops of friends,
I must not look to have; but in their stead,
Curses, not loud, but deep, mouth-honour, breath,
Which the poor would fain deny, and dare not. (5.3.22–28)[27]

Without such things, life becomes "a walking shadow" deprived of all meaning and purpose, "signifying nothing"—all these the powerfully evoked costs of denying a "female" milk of human kindness, attachment, and pity. In Malcolm's victory these things are not fully recovered, nor are we likely to feel much consolation in his boastful denunciation of "this dead butcher and his fiend-like Queen." The play does not, finally, allow us to align ourselves wholly with Malcolm's order or to turn grief into masculininizing revenge: we are also asked to mourn for what the Macbeths have lost.

27. Cf. Malcolm, 5.4.10–14.

NOTORIOUS DEFAMATIONS

One day when this book was in its early stages, I took a BART train to San Francisco. A young woman with the distracted look of the mad, poorly dressed, mumbling to herself, came and sat in the row of seats directly behind me. I had already begun to consider moving to a different seat when I heard her start to repeat, over and over as if it were a mantra, "What are you doing with that nose, bitch? What are you doing with that big fat nose?" I became more uncomfortable: was she addressing me? My nose is in fact rather large. Had she noticed this as she walked down the aisle? I eyed her reflection in the glass of the window beside me. She seemed to be looking off into space as distractedly as before, addressing an invisible adversary. I remained in my place—body tensed, unable to concentrate on the book I'd been reading—until it was time to transfer to a different train a few stops later.

Around this time I was living in Berkeley, where street people of many varieties often ask for spare change. One man in particular caught my attention: thin and wiry, he had a habit of stopping suddenly in the middle of a block to perform a series of karate thrusts and kicks, his face grimacing in seeming rage. Then he would walk on nonchalantly. Another man, similar in appearance, asked me for spare change one day while I was eating a piece of pizza in Berkeley's "gourmet ghetto." I gave him a dime, as, like the sailor's wife in *Macbeth*, I mounch'd and mounch'd and mounch'd. A dime was not enough: loudly and furiously the man denounced me for my unsatisfactory contribution. Recalling his lookalike's pantomime of violence, I attempted to disappear into a crowd of passersby.

Such encounters aroused in me milder versions of feelings that I came to associate with those experienced by accusers in the early modern English witch-hunts: guilt for a failure to be sufficiently "giving," accompanied by resentment and a vague dread of imminent attack.[1] As I continued my research and this book evolved, so did my interest in the implications of the accuser's point of view. It came to seem impossible to ignore women's complicity in the hunts, as many feminists had done, especially those writing in the 1970s when the witch was first appropriated as an emblem of women's oppression by men or by a patriarchal Sado-State.[2] At the same time, I wanted to "humanize" the accusers, whether female or male—that is, to render them intelligible to a more sympathetic understanding. It seemed to me it was much too easy for feminists to distance themselves from the experiences of accusers by constructing a male "other" who became the sole bearer of unwanted aspects of a (female) self, an "other" born of a disavowal of cruel or aggressive impulses. This "other" was also devoid of vulnerability. The accuser's persecutory impulses toward the witch seemed to emerge out of nowhere, or if "fear of woman" was cited as an underlying factor, it was used primarily to belittle or even render contemptible the subject who possessed such fears, and the aggressive impulses that might arise in response to them were condemned as if they were wholly volitional.

Hence I tried to think about the witch-hunts not only from the point of view of the witch but also from that of her accusers, with an emphasis on the latter. This was far from a painless effort, nor was it always successful. I found it easiest to find some basis for identification with the village-level female accusers of the witch and, in Shakespeare's plays, with Richard III and Macbeth; less so with George Gifford and James I; hardest of all with William Perkins. Some feminists may continue to think of such an effort as at best misguided. In an article in the *Women's Review of Books*, for

1. That this rather typical "guilty liberal" response is not everyone's was recently brought home to me during a visit to Santa Monica. While watching a group of street musicians, I began to dig out some money to contribute. As I did so a grizzled, probably alcoholic, old man passed by, extending a styrofoam cup to me; half-confusing him with someone associated with the musicians I dropped my money into his cup. A well-dressed woman beside me started to lecture me for encouraging "them," thus contributing to the decline and fall of the once-fair city of Santa Monica. In her view I had given too much, rather than too little. I offer this incident as a reminder that witchcraft accusation is the activity of a minority; only certain people have the sort of conflictual response to a poor neighbor's request that results in persecutory anxiety.

2. Mary Daly's phrase in her chapter on European witch burning in *Gyn/Ecology*, pp. 178–222.

example, the author of a book on war and war crimes was chided by the reviewer for failing to hold her subjects (male war criminals) sufficiently accountable as well as for failing to express enough outrage against them. "I lack the patience to embrace this tireless, undiscriminating will to understand," the reviewer went on to say. "I cannot accept the painstaking effort to read buried rage and grief into the minds and bodies of criminals and rapists."[3] While hardly tireless in my will to understand, neither have I been undiscriminating in my embrace of the effort to read buried rage and grief in the histories of the witch's accusers: rather, it has seemed to me imperative to do so if we are to invent new ways to intervene in the cultural practices that help to produce modern versions of witch-hunting or other forms of persecutory violence. I do not deny the need to hold criminals and rapists accountable for their actions. But calls to accountability take place only after the fact, after violence has already been done; they do little to prevent that violence or to forestall the development of a new generation of criminals. And effective prevention, it seems to me, requires at least some attempt to understand how criminals have themselves been victims.

As I have pointed out, some feminists have given more attention to the role of the female accuser in the English witch-hunts, Christina Larner and Catherine Belsey in particular. In their accounts, however, the female accuser tends to emerge as one-dimensionally complicit with early modern patriarchy, an enforcer of a normalizing code of woman's "proper"

---

3. Lise Weil, review of Susan Griffin, *A Chorus of Stones: The Private Life of War*, in *Women's Review of Books* 10 (December 1992): 12. (See also the February 1993 issue for a letter by Alix Kates Shulman expressing objections similar to mine [p. 4].) Weil's sentiments here continue in the tradition of the Daly-Dworkin-Morgan view of the witch-hunts. Here, for example, is Daly's comment on the historian Julio Caro Baroja, who concluded his book on witchcraft by acknowledging his "pity" not only for the persecuted "who wanted to do evil yet could not do it" but also for the "persecutors who were brutal because they believed that numberless dangers surrounded them." Daly retorts, "This pitiful analysis reveals the pitfalls of 'pity.' Since there is no reason to think that good witches [and in Daly's analysis there are only good witches] 'wanted to do evil,' this 'pity' is perverted and deceptive. Hags may well feel grief and anger for our tortured foresisters, but pity for their/our persecutors is not the appropriate response. Righteous anger is more in accord with the reality and can generate creative energy." Baroja can be faulted for a generalization that implies that *all* the persecuted intentionally practiced maleficium, when the historical record suggests a more mixed and ambiguous profile. Daly, however, goes to the opposite extreme in assuming that woman is never the locus of "evil."

Ironically, Susan Griffin, author of the book under attack by Weil, was in her earlier work (particularly *Women and Nature: The Roaring inside Her*) associated with the Daly-Dworkin-Morgan position on the witch-hunts.

behavior, at bottom little more than a patriarchal male in drag. What I found, on the contrary, was that when one woman accused another of witchcraft, she was very often responding to a personal attack; the other woman had lashed out at her for her unneighborly failure to be a "proper" female nurturer. The woman accused as a witch was often economically or socially of at least somewhat lower status and usually a member of an older generation, associated with mothers and village elders in a culture that put a very strong emphasis on obedience; children were expected to submit to the will of their parents and other authorities in almost all things. The witch chastised her often younger female neighbor, disparaging her for a failure to be giving enough, nurturing enough; she spoke assertively, strong-mindedly, invasively; she seized the moral high ground as the "wronged" party, who thus had a right to "get even" and invoke supernatural aid on her behalf. In the witch's curses a Christian discourse about almsgiving fused with a discourse of gender; one's neighbor should give you the shirt off her back as well as provide nurturance upon demand. Thus, curiously, in this instance it was the witch who was enforcing both a patriarchal and a religious norm.

At the same time the typical accused woman often did violate codes designed to curb women's angry speech and self-assertive behavior. She did indeed possess an unruly tongue. Yet she was not quite the "independent" woman celebrated and mourned in much feminist polemic of the last twenty years.[4] The most likely target of early modern English witchcraft accusations was an older woman with a strong sense of entitlement who was becoming increasingly dependent on her neighbors and whose needs they increasingly resented. She gave voice to her hunger and in so doing refused to be a nurturer of other women herself. The neighbor she implicitly attacked as a deficient nurturer fought back; curse was answered by "notorious defamation," and accusers constructed the witch as a malevolent mother who possessed an unnatural third nipple and nurtured childlike demonic imps. For magically causing sickness and death to her neighbor's household, she herself deserved death. Thus both the witch and her accuser enforced as well as transgressed patriarchal codes.

The discourse of male religious and secular authorities registered different, though at times overlapping, anxieties about the maternal power

4. As in Daly's work when she quotes admiringly the statements of late 1960s covens inspired by the women's movement: "You are a Witch by saying aloud, 'I am a Witch,' three times, and *thinking about that*. You are a Witch by being female, untamed, angry, joyous, and immortal" (*Gyn/Ecology*, p. 221).

figured in village-level constructions of the witch. These authors rewrote such constructions, turning the witch from a malevolent mother into a "drudge" of Satan with little or no agency of her own. Her crime became one of betrayal—compliance with a male rival (an adult male devil)—rather than her own act of harmful magic. She became an enemy of God, a rebel against the state. The malevolent mother did not fully disappear from many of these accounts; rather her reinscription within the frame of a traditional gender hierarchy had to be rehearsed: she had to be displayed being stripped of her powers. Yet even in her newly subordinated role she still had power to threaten. In submitting to a potent demonic rival, she injured the godly father and the son constructing himself in his likeness, exposing their relative inadequacy. Such a betrayal required a further rehearsal of "legitimate" patriarchal power. The godly father (not to mention God the Father) could recover his dominance and defeat his invisible adversary through the prosecution and punishment of the witch.

Competing definitions of the witch's crime in the early modern period, then, were also gendered definitions; maleficium tends to be part of "woman's story" about the witch, whereas male authors of religious and secular elites were more likely to embrace continental theories about the demonic pact. Other factors were of course involved, class, education, and religious alignments among them. Moreover, it is possible that in other texts than the ones I have discussed we might glimpse ways in which demonic theory could find an audience among women—perhaps especially among those emergent puritan groups in which women were "silent but for the Word." The boundary between maleficium and demonic theory is in any case permeable. The malevolent mother does not wholly disappear from elite male accounts of the witch, nor is the demonic rival wholly absent from village-level accounts.

The Shakespeare plays discussed in this book contain strong elements of both ways of constructing the witch. In them we also glimpse the "buried rage and grief" that may at times have impelled males to reassert patriarchy by a displacement of anger at the mother onto the witch. Richard III's literal and figurative witchcraft accusations against Elizabeth, Jane Shore, and Margaret are embedded in a history that begins in his experience of the deforming power of the mother's womb, voice, and gaze, which cannot find in his misshapen body the father's true likeness. Macbeth's accusations of the "juggling fiends" who eventually betray him begin in the "soliciting" of his hopes and the manipulation of his deepest fears by witches and wives fashioned and self-fashioned in the likeness of the maternal. Both plays locate the origins of the persecutory impulse in the relation between sons and mothers who make those sons the vehicle of their patriarchally informed desires (a relation that may be replayed in that of husbands and wives). But the persecutory impulse is spurred, the plays also suggest, by disrupted relations between sons and fathers and, more broadly, by the complex cultural matrices within which families are constructed and intersubjective histories unfold.

If I am right that witch-hunting in early modern England has a connection to historically specific anxieties about maternal power (and related aspects of women's roles), it is also clear that much more was involved. Changing beliefs about the boundaries between nature and supernature; anxieties about aging, social mobility, and "reputation"; religious controversies; conflicts among elites and at the village level—these and other factors interacted with early modern constructions of gender, and all played a part in shaping the hunts. Still other questions might be asked. What, for example, is the relation of the English malevolent mother to the European witch, who flies and meets with other witches to engage in orgies and cannibalistic rites? And what of the similarities between witch-hunting and other forms of persecution? Persecutory practices are not confined to England or the early modern period, nor do they always take women as their object. What then is the relation of witch-hunting to persecutions of other marginalized groups—lepers, Jews, heretics, sodomites?[5] In these persecutions, gender is not overtly an organizing trope, nor is the role of mother ostensibly a factor. Yet the scapegoat mechanism involved clearly resembles that of the witch-hunts. What accounts for this resemblance?

It is worth recalling, moreover, that not all victims of persecutory violence are drawn from lower social levels. Indeed in some of the most virulent of the twentieth-century "witch-hunts" violence has been directed against symbolic "fathers" or other figures of authority, in countries where newly emergent but precarious ruling elites needed "others" to blame for the serious economic or other problems they faced.[6] Thus dur-

---

5. Some explorations of connections between different forms of persecutions occur in Ginzburg, *Ecstasies*, pp. 33–88; Levack, *The Witch-Hunt in Early Modern Europe*, pp. 25–92; R. I. Moore, *The Formation of a Persecuting Society: Power and Deviance in Western Europe, 950–1250* (Oxford: Basil Blackwell, 1987).

6. Here there are some interesting parallels with the situation of early modern nation-states at the time of the witch-hunts, as described by Christina Larner. She maintains that the crises of legitimacy experienced by relatively weak central governments in an age of religious controversy were major factors in engendering the hunts. See *Enemies of God*.

ing the 1930s and 1940s in Stalin's Soviet Union, leadership fractured at all levels, not only within Stalin's "inner circle" but also within local and regional party machines (paralleling in some ways the neighborly quarrels and religious controversies that divided early modern communities).[7] As power oscillated between different factions, purges were carried out in the name of Stalin, "Father of the Country," "the Great and Wise Teacher," "the Friend of Mankind," against the antifathers and betraying sons who had perverted the socialist program, the "enemies with party cards." Underlying the psychology of the purges may have been, among other things, the magical beliefs of the Russian peasantry, still lively in the late nineteenth and early twentieth centuries, translated after the Revolution into the language of "scientific socialism."[8] Rather than the female witch, however, it was the male possessed by evil spirits who anticipated the typical target of persecutory violence—the "evil spirits" of foreign, class-alien, or counterrevolutionary ideas. Demystified, secularized, stripped of his supernatural power, the great demonic adversary no longer needed to seduce a weaker vessel but could walk among the elect as one of their own.

7. I am indebted to J. Arch Getty for this account of the Soviet purges (although my sketchy summary here does little justice to his arguments, in which the purges are the work of a complex interplay of factors both "from above" and "from below"). See "The Politics of Stalinism," in *Stalinist Terror: New Perspectives*, ed. J. Arch Getty and Roberta T. Manning (Cambridge: Cambridge University Press, 1993).

8. See Getty, "Politics," pp. 122–23 for some tantalizing remarks on the influence of magical beliefs and other aspects of peasant culture upon the purges, including forms of "peasant informal justice" which were often extremely violent—among them "tarring, whipping, fatal mob beatings and stabbings, stakes driven through offenders' bodies," as well as the killing of witches.

WORKS CITED

Witchcraft—Primary Sources

Ancient Criminal Trials in Scotland, part III. Ed. Robert Pitcairn. Edinburgh: Maitland Club, 1829–33.

The Apprehension and confession of three notorious Witches, Arreigned and by Justice condemned and executed at Chelms-forde. London, 1589.

Bodin, Jean. *De la Demonomanie des Sorciers*. Paris, 1580.

Bower, Edmond. *Dr. Lamb Revived; or, Witchcraft Condemn'd in Anne Bodenham a Servant of His*. London, 1653.

Calendar of Scottish Papers. Vol 5. 6, 10 (1589–93). Ed. William K. Boyd and Henry W. Meikle. Edinburgh, 1936.

Dasent, John R., ed. *Acts of the Privy Council*. New series. 25 vols. London: Eyre and Spottiswoode, 1897.

A detection of damnable drifts, practized by three Witches arraigned at Chelmisforde in Essex. London, 1579.

The examination and confession of certaine Wytches at Chensforde in the Countie of Essex. London, 1566.

The examination of John Walsh . . . upon certayne Interrogatories touchyng Wytchcrafte and Sorcerye. London, 1566.

Gifford, George. *A Dialogue concerning Witches and Witchcraftes*. 1593. Ed. Beatrice White. London: Oxford University Press, 1931.

——. *A Discourse of the subtill Practises of Devilles by Witches and Sorcerers*. 1587.

—— *Foure Sermons*. London, 1598.

Goodcole, Henry. *The wonderfull discoverie of Elizabeth Sawyer, a Witch, late of Edmonton*. London, 1621.

Gowries Conspiracie: A Discourse of the unnaturall and vyle Conspiracie, attempted against the Kings Maiesties Person at Sanct-Ionstown. 1600. Rpt. in

A Selection from the Harleian Miscellany, 190–98. London: C. and G. Kearsley, 1798.

Guazzo, Francesco. *Compendium Maleficarum*. Milan, 1608.

James I. *Daemonologie*. London, 1597. Rpt. in *Elizabethan and Jacobean Quartos*, ed. G. B. Harrison. New York: Barnes and Noble, 1966.

Knox, John. *The First Blast of the Trumpet against the Monstrous Regiment of Women*. Rpt. in *The Political Writings of John Knox*. Ed. Marvin A. Breslow. Washington, D. C.: Folger Books, 1985.

Kramer, Heinrich, and Jacob Sprenger. *Malleus Maleficarum*. Cologne, 1486.

Marston, John. *The Wonder of Women, or The Tragedy of Sophonisba*. In *Three Jacobean Witchcraft Plays*, ed. Peter Corbin and Douglas Sedge. Manchester: Manchester University Press, 1986.

Middleton, Thomas. *The Witch*. In *Three Jacobean Witchcraft Plays*, ed. Peter Corbin and Douglas Sedge. Manchester: Manchester University Press, 1986.

The most strange and admirable discoverie of the three Witches of Warboys, arraigned, convicted, and executed at the last Assizes at Huntington, for the bewitching of the five daughters of Robert Throckmorton Esquire, and divers other persons. London, 1593.

Newes from Scotland. London, 1591. Rpt. in *Elizabethan and Jacobean Quartos*, ed. G. B. Harrison. New York: Barnes and Noble, 1966.

Perkins, William. *A Discourse of the Damned Art of Witchcraft*. Cambridge, 1608.

A Rehearsall both straung and true, of hainous and horrible actes committed by Elizabeth Stile, Alias Rockingham, Mother Dutten, Mother Devell, Mother Margaret, Fower notorious Witches, apprehended at winsore in the Countie of Barks. London, 1579.

Rowley, William, Thomas Dekker, and John Ford. *The Witch of Edmonton*. 1621. In *Three Jacobean Witchcraft Plays*, ed. Peter Corbin and Douglas Sedge. Manchester: Manchester University Press, 1986.

Scot, Reginald. *The Discoverie of Witchcraft*. 1584. Ed. Hugh Ross Williamson. Carbondale: Southern Illinois University Press, 1964.

Strype, John. *The Life of Sir Thomas Smith*. Oxford: Clarendon Press, 1820.

W. W. *A true and iust Recorde, of the Information, Examination and Confession of all the Witches, taken at S. Oses in the countie of Essex: whereof some were executed, and other some entreated according to the determination of Lawe*. 1582. Facsimile. Ed. Anthony Harris. Delmar, N.Y.: Scholars' Facsimiles and Reprints, 1981.

The Witches of Northamptonshire . . . Who were all executed at Northampton. London, 1612.

The Wonderful Discoverie of the Witchcrafts of Margaret and Phillip Flower. London, 1619.

Witchcraft—Secondary Sources

Anderson, Alan, and Raymond Gordon. "The Uniqueness of English Witchcraft: A Matter of Numbers?" *British Journal of Sociology* 30 (September 1979): 359–61.

———. "Witchcraft and the Status of Women—the Case of England." *British Journal of Sociology* 29 (June 1978): 171–84.

Anglo, Sydney, ed. *The Damned Art: Essays in the Literature of Witchcraft.* London: Routledge and Kegan Paul, 1977.

Balfe, Judith H. "Comments on Garrett's 'Women and Witches.'" *Signs* 4 (Autumn 1978): 201–2.

Barstow, Anne Llewellyn. "On Studying Witchcraft as Women's History: A Historiography of the European Witch Persecutions." *Journal of Feminist Studies in Religion* 4 (1988): 17–18.

Beckwith, Sarah. "The Power of Devils and the Hearts of Men: Notes towards a Drama of Witchcraft." In *Shakespeare in the Changing Curriculum*, ed. Lesley Aers and Nigel Wheale, 143–61. London: Routledge, 1991.

Biggins, Dennis. "Sexuality, Witchcraft, and Violence in *Macbeth.*" *Shakespeare Studies* 8 (1975): 255–77.

Bovenschen, Silvia. "The Contemporary Witch, the Historical Witch, and the Witch Myth: The Witch, Subject of the Appropriation of Nature and Object of the Domination of Nature." *New German Critique* 15 (Fall 1978): 83–119.

Clark, Stuart. "Inversion, Misrule, and the Meaning of Witchcraft." *Past and Present* 87 (May 1980): 98–127.

———. "King James's *Daemonologie*: Witchcraft and Kingship." In *The Damned Art: Essays in the Literature of Witchcraft*, ed. Sydney Anglo, 156–81. London: Routledge and Kegan Paul, 1977.

Cohn, Norman. *Europe's Inner Demons: An Enquiry Inspired by the Great Witch-hunt.* New York: Basic Books, 1975.

Daly, Mary. *Gyn/Ecology: The Meta-ethics of Radical Feminism.* Boston: Beacon Press, 1978. Pp. 178–222.

Demos, John. *Entertaining Satan: Witchcraft and the Culture of Early New England.* Oxford: Oxford University Press, 1983.

Dolan, Frances E. *Dangerous Familiars: Representations of Domestic Crime in England, 1550–1700.* Ithaca: Cornell University Press, 1994.

Dworkin, Andrea. *Woman Hating.* New York: E. P. Dutton, 1974.

Ehrenreich, Barbara, and Deirdre English. *Witches, Midwives, and Nurses: A History of Women Healers.* New York: Feminist Press, 1973.

Estes, Leland. "The Medical Origins of the European Witch Craze: A Hypothesis." *Journal of Social History* (Winter 1983): 271–84.

Ewen, C. L'Estrange. *Witchcraft and Demonianism: A Concise Account Derived from Sworn Depositions and Confessions Obtained in the Courts of England and Wales.* London: Heath Cranton, 1933.

———. *Witch Hunting and Witch Trials.* London: Kegan Paul, Trench, Trubner, 1929.

Forbes, Thomas R. "Midwifery and Witchcraft." *Journal of the History of Medicine* 17 (1962): 264–83.

———. *The Midwife and the Witch.* New Haven: Yale University Press, 1966.

Garrett, Clarke. "Women and Witches: Patterns of Analysis." *Signs* 3 (Winter 1977): 461–70.

Geertz, Hildred. "An Anthropology of Religion and Magic I." *Journal of Interdisciplinary History* (Summer 1975): 71–89.

Ginzburg, Carlo. *Ecstasies: Deciphering the Witches' Sabbath.* New York: Pantheon, 1991.

Godbeer, Richard. *The Devil's Dominion: Magic and Religion in Early New England.* Cambridge: Cambridge University Press, 1992.

Gregory, Annabel. "Witchcraft, Politics, and 'Good Neighborhood' in Early Seventeenth-Century Rye." *Past and Present* 133 (November 1991): 31–66.

Greenblatt, Stephen. "Shakespeare Bewitched." In *New Historical Literary Study: Essays on Reproducing Texts, Representing History,* ed. Jeffrey N. Cox and Larry J. Reynolds, 108–35. Princeton: Princeton University Press, 1993.

Harley, David. "Historians as Demonologists: The Myth of the Midwife-Witch." *Social History of Medicine* 3 (1990): 1–26.

Harris, Anthony. *Night's Black Agents: Witchcraft and Magic in Seventeenth-Century English Drama.* Manchester: Manchester University Press, 1980.

Hart, W. H. "Observations on Some Documents relating to Magic in the Reign of Queen Elizabeth." *Archaeologia; or, Miscellaneous Tracts Relating to Antiquity* 40 (1866): 389–97.

Helms, Lorraine. "The Weyward Sisters: Towards a Feminist Staging of *Macbeth.*" *New Theatrical Quarterly* 8 (May 1992): 167–77.

Hester, Marianne. *Lewd Women and Wicked Witches: A Study of the Dynamics of Male Domination.* London: Routledge, 1992.

Hitchcock, James. "George Gifford and Puritan Witch Beliefs." *Archiv fur Reformationsgeschichte* 58 (1967): 90–99.

Holmes, Clive. "Popular Culture? Witches, Magistrates, and Divines in Early Modern England." In *Understanding Popular Culture: Europe from the Middle Ages to the 19th Century,* ed. Steven L. Kaplan, 86–111. Berlin: Mouton, 1984.

———. "Women: Witnesses and Witches." *Past and Present* 140 (August 1993): 45–78.

Honegger, Claudia, Nelly Moia, and Clarke Garrett, "Comments on Garrett's 'Women and Witches.'" *Signs* 4 (1979): 792–804.

Jones, William R. "Political Uses of Sorcery in Medieval Europe." *The Historian* 34 (1972): 670–87.

Karlsen, Carol F. *The Devil in the Shape of a Woman: Witchcraft in Colonial New England.* New York: Norton, 1987.

Kelly, H. A. "English Kings and the Fear of Sorcery." *Mediaeval Studies* 39 (1977): 206–38.

Kieckhefer, Richard. *European Witch Trials: Their Foundation in Popular and Learned Culture.* Berkeley: University of California Press, 1976.

——. *Magic in the Middle Ages.* Cambridge: Cambridge University Press, 1990.

Kittredge, George Lyman. *Witchcraft in Old and New England.* Cambridge: Harvard University Press, 1929.

Kors, Alan C., and Edward Peters, eds. *Witchcraft in Europe: A Documentary History.* Philadelphia: University of Pennsylvania, 1972.

Larner, Christina. *Enemies of God: The Witch-Hunt in Scotland.* London: Chatto and Windus, 1981.

——. *Witchcraft and Religion: The Politics of Popular Belief.* Oxford: Basil Blackwell, 1984.

Levack, Brian P. *The Witch-Hunt in Early Modern Europe.* London: Longman, 1987.

LeVine, Robert A. *Culture, Behavior, and Personality.* Chicago: Aldine, 1973.

Macfarlane, Alan. "A Tudor Anthropologist: George Gifford's *Discourse* and *Dialogue.*" In *The Damned Art: Essays in the Literature of Witchcraft,* ed. Sydney Anglo, 140–55. London: Routledge and Kegan Paul, 1977.

——. *Witchcraft in Tudor and Stuart England: A Regional and Comparative Study.* New York: Harper and Row, 1970.

Morgan, Robin. "The Network of the Imaginary Mother." *Lady of the Beasts: Poems.* New York: Random House, 1970.

Notestein, Wallace. *A History of Witchcraft in England from 1558 to 1718.* 1911. Reprint. New York: Russell and Russell, 1965.

Quaife, G. R. *Godly Zeal and Furious Rage: The Witch in Early Modern Europe.* London: Croom Helm, 1987.

Robbins, R. H. *The Encyclopedia of Witchcraft and Demonology.* New York: Crown, 1959.

Robinson, Ian. "The Witches and Macbeth." *Critical Review* 11 (1968): 101–5.

Rosen, Barbara, ed. *Witchcraft in England, 1558–1618.* Amherst: University of Massachusetts Press, 1991.

Rushton, Peter. "Women, Witchcraft, and Slander in Early Modern England: Cases from the Church Courts of Durham, 1560–1675." *Northern History* 18 (1982): 116–32.

Sawyer, Ronald C. " 'Strangely Handled in All Her Lyms': Witchcraft and Healing in Jacobean England." *Journal of Social History* 22 (Spring 1989): 461–85.

Scarre, Geoffrey. *Witchcraft and Magic in 16th and 17th Century Europe.* Atlantic Highlands, N.J.: Humanities Press International, 1987.

Sharpe, J. A. "Witchcraft and Women in Seventeenth-Century England: Some Northern Evidence." *Continuity and Change* 6 (1991): 179–99.

——. *Witchcraft in Seventeenth-Century Yorkshire: Accusations and Counter-Measures.* Borthwick Paper No. 81. York: University of York, 1992.

Stafford, Helen. "Notes on Scottish Witchcraft Cases, 1590–91." In *Essays in Honour of Conyers Read*, ed. Norton Downs, 96–118. Chicago: University of Chicago Press, 1953.

Stallybrass, Peter. "*Macbeth* and Witchcraft." In *Focus on "Macbeth,"* ed. John Russell Brown, 189–209. London: Routledge and Kegan Paul, 1982.

Swales, J. K., and Hugh V. McClachlan. "Witchcraft and the Status of Women: A Comment." *British Journal of Sociology* 30 (September 1979): 349–57.

Thomas, Keith. "An Anthropology of Religion and Magic II." *Journal of Interdisciplinary History* 6 (Summer 1975): 91–109.

———. *Religion and the Decline of Magic*. New York: Scribner's, 1971.

Trevor-Roper, H. R. *The European Witch-Craze of the Sixteenth and Seventeenth Centuries*. New York: Harper, 1969.

General Studies

Adelman, Janet. " 'Born of Woman': Fantasies of Maternal Power in Macbeth." In *Cannibals, Witches, and Divorce: Estranging the Renaissance*, ed. Marjorie Garber, 90–121. Baltimore: Johns Hopkins University Press, 1987.

———. *Suffocating Mothers: Fantasies of Maternal Origin in Shakespeare's Plays, "Hamlet" to "The Tempest."* New York: Routledge, 1992.

Alford, C. Fred. *Melanie Klein and Critical Social Theory*. New Haven: Yale University Press, 1989.

Amussen, Susan Dwyer. *An Ordered Society: Gender and Class in Early Modern England*. Oxford: Basil Blackwell, 1988.

Barber, C. L., and Richard P. Wheeler. *The Whole Journey: Shakespeare's Power of Development*. Berkeley: University of California Press, 1986.

Beier, Lucinda McCray. *Sufferers and Healers: The Experience of Illness in Seventeenth-Century England*. London: Routledge and Kegan Paul, 1987.

Beilin, Elaine V. *Redeeming Eve: Women Writers of the English Renaissance*. Princeton: Princeton University Press, 1987.

Belsey, Catherine. *The Subject of Tragedy: Identity and Difference in Renaissance Drama*. London: Methuen, 1985.

Benson, Pamela. *The Invention of the Renaissance Woman: The Challenge of Female Independence in the Literature and Thought of Italy and England*. University Park: Pennsylvania State University Press, 1992.

Bentley, Gerald. *The Profession of Dramatist in Shakespeare's Time*. Princeton: Princeton University Press, 1971.

Berger, Harry. "The Early Scenes of *Macbeth*: Preface to a New Interpretation." *ELH* 47 (1980): 1–31.

Bergeron, David. *Royal Family, Royal Lovers: King James of England and Scotland*. Columbia: University of Missouri Press, 1991.

Berry, Edward. *Patterns of Decay: Shakespeare's Early Histories*. Charlottesville: University Press of Virginia, 1975.

Bevington, David. "The Domineering Female in *1 Henry VI*." *Shakespeare Studies* 2 (1966): 51–58.

Bingham, Caroline. *James VI of Scotland*. London: Weidenfeld and Nicolson, 1979.

Blumenfeld-Kosinski, Renate. *Not of Woman Born: Representations of Caesarean Birth in Medieval and Renaissance Culture*. Ithaca: Cornell University Press, 1990.

Boose, Lynda E. "Scolding Brides and Bridling Scolds: Taming the Woman's Unruly Member." *Shakespeare Quarterly* 42 (Summer 1991): 179–213.

Booth, Stephen. *"King Lear," "Macbeth," Indefinition, and Tragedy*. New Haven: Yale University Press, 1983.

Brown, John Russell, ed. *Focus on "Macbeth."* London: Routledge and Kegan Paul, 1982.

Butler, Martin. *Theater and Crisis, 1632–1642*. Cambridge: Cambridge University Press, 1984.

Bynum, Carolyn Walker. *Jesus as Mother: Studies in the Spirituality of the High Middle Ages*. Berkeley: University of California Press, 1982.

Cahn, Susan. *Industry of Devotion: The Transformation of Women's Work in England, 1500–1660*. New York: Columbia University Press, 1987.

Chodorow, Nancy. *Feminism and Psychoanalytic Theory*. New Haven: Yale University Press, 1989.

——. *The Reproduction of Mothering: Psychoanalysis and the Sociology of Gender*. Berkeley: University of California Press, 1978.

Cioni, Mary L. *Women and Law in Elizabethan England with Particular Reference to the Court of Chancery*. New York: Garland, 1985.

Collier, Susanne. "Recent Studies in James VI and I." *English Literary Renaissance* 23 (Autumn 1993): 509–19.

Collins, Stephen L. "Where's the History in the New Literary Historicism? The Case of the English Renaissance." *Annals of Scholarship* 6 (1989): 231–47.

Collinson, Patrick. *The Religion of Protestants: The Church in English Society, 1559–1625*. Oxford: Clarendon Press, 1982.

Cook, Ann Jennalie. *The Privileged Playgoers of Shakespeare's London, 1576–1642*. Princeton: Princeton University Press, 1981.

Cowan, Edward J. "The Darker Vision of the Scottish Renaissance: The Devil and Francis Stewart." In *The Renaissance and Reformation in Scotland*, ed. Ian B. Cowan and Duncan Shaw, 125–40. Edinburgh: Scottish Academic Press, 1983.

Crawford, Patricia. "The Construction and Experience of Maternity in Seventeenth-Century England." In *Women as Mothers in Pre-industrial England: Essays in Memory of Dorothy McLaren*, ed. Valerie Fildes, 3–38. London: Routledge, 1990.

——. " 'The Sucking Child': Adult Attitudes toward Childcare in the First Year of Life in Seventeenth-Century England." *Continuity and Change* 1 (1986): 23–54.

Cressy, David. "Foucault, Stone, Shakespeare, and Social History." *English Literary Review* 21 (Spring 1991): 121–33.

Dash, Irene. *Wooing, Wedding, and Power: Women in Shakespeare's Plays*. New York: Columbia University Press, 1981.

Davis, Natalie. "Woman on Top." In Davis, *Society and Culture in Early Modern France*, 124–51. Stanford: Stanford University Press, 1975.

Dinnerstein, Dorothy. *The Mermaid and the Minotaur*. New York: Harper and Row, 1976.

Doane, Janice, and Devon Hodges. *From Klein to Kristeva: Psychoanalytic Feminism and the Search for the "Good Enough" Mother*. Ann Arbor: University of Michigan Press, 1992.

Dolan, Frances E. "The Subordinate('s) Plot: Petty Treason and the Forms of Domestic Rebellion." *Shakespeare Quarterly* 43 (Fall 1992): 317–40.

Eagleton, Terry. *William Shakespeare*. Oxford: Basil Blackwell, 1986.

Eccles, Audrey. *Obstetrics and Gynaecology in Tudor and Stuart England*. London: Croom Helm, 1982.

Erickson, Carolly. *The First Elizabeth*. New York: Macmillan, 1983.

Ezell, Margaret J. M. *The Patriarch's Wife: Literary Evidence and the History of the Family*. Chapel Hill: University of North Carolina Press, 1987.

Fast, Irene. *Gender Identity: A Differentiation Model*. Hillsdale, N.J.: Analytic Press, 1984.

Ferguson, Margaret W., et al., eds. *Rewriting the Renaissance: The Discourses of Sexual Difference in Early Modern Europe*. Chicago: University of Chicago Press, 1986.

Fildes, Valerie. "The English Wet-Nurse and Her Role in Infant Care, 1538–1800." *Medical History* 32 (1988): 142–73.

Fine, Sidney, and Esther Fine. "Four Psychoanalytic Perspectives: A Study of Differences in Interpretive Interventions." *Journal of the American Psychoanalytic Association* 38 (1990): 1017–41.

Fletcher, Anthony J. "Honour, Reputation, and Local Officeholding in Elizabethan and Stuart England." In *Order and Disorder in Early Modern England*, ed. Anthony J. Fletcher and John Stevenson, 92–115. Cambridge: Cambridge University Press, 1985.

Fletcher, Anthony J., and John Stevenson, eds. *Order and Disorder in Early Modern England*. Cambridge: Cambridge University Press, 1985.

Fraser, Antonia. *Mary Queen of Scots*. New York: Delacorte Press, 1969.

Frye, Susan. *Elizabeth I: The Competition for Representation*. Oxford: Oxford University Press, 1993.

Getty, J. Arch. "The Politics of Stalinism." In *Stalinist Terror: New Perspectives*, ed. J. Arch Getty and Roberta T. Manning. Cambridge: Cambridge University Press, 1993.

Goldberg, Jonathan. *James I and the Politics of Literature: Jonson, Shakespeare, Donne, and Their Contemporaries*. Baltimore: Johns Hopkins University Press, 1983.

Gowing, Laura. "Gender and the Language of Insult in Early Modern London." *History Workshop* 35 (Spring 1993): 1–21.

Greenblatt, Stephen. "The Cultivation of Anxiety: King Lear and His Heirs." *Raritan* 2 (Summer 1982): 92–114.

———. "Psychoanalysis and Renaissance Culture." In *Literary Theory/Renaissance Texts*, ed. Patricia Parker and David Quint, 210–224. Baltimore: Johns Hopkins University Press, 1986.

———. "Resonance and Wonder." In *Literary Theory Today*, ed. Peter Collier and Helga Geyer-Ryan, 74–90. Ithaca: Cornell University Press, 1990.

———. "Towards a Poetics of Culture." In *The New Historicism*, ed. H. Aram Veeser. New York: Routledge, 1989.

Grosskurth, Phyllis. *Melanie Klein: Her World and Her Work*. New York: Knopf, 1986.

Gurr, Andrew. *Playgoing in Shakespeare's London, 1576–1642*. Cambridge: Cambridge University Press, 1987.

Gutierrez, Nancy A. "Gender and Value in 1 *Henry VI*: The Role of Joan de Pucelle." *Theatre Journal* 42 (May 1990): 183–93.

Haigh, Christopher. *Elizabeth I*. London: Longman, 1988.

Harris, Barbara J. "Property, Power, and Personal Relations: Elite Mothers and Sons in Yorkist and Early Tudor England." *Signs* 15 (Spring 1990): 606–32.

———. "Women and Politics in Early Tudor England." *Historical Journal* 33 (1990): 259–81.

Hawkins, Michael. "History, Politics, and *Macbeth*." In *Focus on "Macbeth*," ed. John Russell Brown, 155–88. London: Routledge and Kegan Paul, 1982.

Henderson, Katherine Usher, and Barbara F. McManus. *Half Humankind: Contexts and Texts of the Controversy about Women in England, 1540–1640*. Urbana: University of Illinois Press, 1985.

Herrup, Cynthia B. *The Common Peace: Participation and the Criminal Law in Seventeenth-Century England*. Cambridge: Cambridge University Press, 1987.

Hinshelwood, R. D. *A Dictionary of Kleinian Thought*. London: Free Association Books, 1991.

Hoffer, Peter C., and N. E. H. Hull. *Murdering Mothers: Infanticide in England and New England, 1558–1803*. New York: New York University Press, 1981.

Hull, Suzanne W. *Chaste, Silent, and Obedient: English Books for Women, 1475–1640*. San Marino: Huntington Library, 1982.

Ingram, Martin. *Church Courts, Sex, and Marriage in England, 1570–1640*. Cambridge: Cambridge University Press, 1987.

Jackson, Gabriele Bernhard. "Topical Ideology: Witches, Amazons, and Shakespeare's Joan of Arc." *English Literary Renaissance* 18 (1988): 40–65.

James, Mervyn. *Society, Politics, and Culture: Studies in Early Modern England*. Cambridge: Cambridge University Press, 1986.

Jordan, Constance. *Renaisssance Feminism: Literary Texts and Political Models*. Ithaca: Cornell University Press, 1990.

Kahane, Claire. "Questioning the Maternal Voice." *Genders* 3 (Fall 1988): 82–91.

Kahn, Coppelia. "The Absent Mother in *King Lear*." In *Rewriting the Renaissance: The Discourses of Sexual Difference in Early Modern Europe*, ed. Margaret W. Ferguson et al., 33–49. Chicago: University of Chicago Press, 1986.

——. *Man's Estate: Masculine Identity in Shakespeare*. Berkeley: University of California Press, 1981.

Kelso, Ruth. *The Doctrine of the English Gentleman in the Sixteenth Century*. Gloucester, Mass.: Peter Smith, 1964.

Klein, Melanie. *The Selected Melanie Klein*. Ed. Juliet Mitchell. New York: Free Press, 1987.

——. *The Writings of Melanie Klein*. 4 vols. Ed. Roger Money-Kyrle et al. London: Hogarth Press, 1975.

Kohut, Thomas A. "Psychohistory as History." *American Historical Review* 91 (1986): 336–54.

Kozikowski, Stanley J. "The Gowrie Conspiracy against James VI: A New Source for Shakespeare's *Macbeth*." *Shakespeare Studies* 13 (1980): 197–212.

Laqueur, Thomas. *Making Sex: Body and Gender from the Greeks to Freud*. Cambridge: Harvard University Press, 1990.

Lee, Maurice, Jr. *Great Britain's Solomon: James VI and I in His Three Kingdoms*. Urbana: University of Illinois Press, 1990.

——. "James and the Historians: Not a Bad King after All?" *Albion* 16 (Summer 1984): 151–63.

Lee, Patricia-Ann. "Reflections of Power: Margaret of Anjou and the Dark Side of Queenship." *Renaissance Quarterly* 34 (1986): 183–217.

Letters of Mary Stuart, Queen of Scotland, Selected from the "Recueil des Lettres de Marie Stuart." Ed. William Turnbull. London: Charles Dolman, 1845.

Letters of Queen Elizabeth and King James VI of Scotland. Ed. John Bruce. [London?]: Camden Society, 1849.

Levine, Howard B. "Freudian and Kleinian Theory: A Dialogue of Comparative Perspectives." *Journal of the American Psychoanalytic Association* 40 (1992): 801–26.

Levine, Mortimer. "The Place of Women in Tudor Government." In *Tudor Rule and Revolution: Essays for G. R. Elton from His American Friends*, ed. Delloyd J. Guth and John McKenna, 109–23. Cambridge: Cambridge University Press, 1982.

Macdonald, Michael. *Mystical Bedlam: Madness, Anxiety, and Healing in Seventeenth-Century England*. Cambridge: Cambridge University Press, 1981.

Macfarlane, Alan. *The Justice and the Mare's Ale: Law and Disorder in Seventeenth-Century England*. London: Oxford, 1981.

Marcus, Leah S. *Puzzling Shakespeare: Local Reading and Its Discontents*. Berkeley: University of California Press, 1988.

Maus, Katharine Eisaman. "Proof and Consequences: Inwardness and Its Exposure in the English Renaissance." *Representations* 34 (Spring 1991): 29–52.

McLuskie, Kathleen. *Renaissance Dramatists*. Atlantic Highlands, N.J.: Humanities Press International, 1989.

Montrose, Louis Adrian. "*A Midsummer Night's Dream* and the Shaping Fantasies of Elizabethan Culture: Gender, Power, Form." In *Rewriting the Renaissance: The Discourses of Sexual Difference in Early Modern Europe*, ed. Margaret W. Ferguson et al., 65–87. Chicago: University of Chicago Press, 1986.

Moore, R. I. *The Formation of a Persecuting Society: Power and Deviance in Western Europe, 950–1250*. Oxford: Basil Blackwell, 1987.

Mullaney, Steven. *The Place of the Stage: License, Play, and Power in Renaissance England*. Chicago: University of Chicago Press, 1988.

Neale, J. E. *Queen Elizabeth I: A Biography*. 1934. Reprint. Garden City, N.Y.: Doubleday, 1957.

Neely, Carol Thomas. "Constructing the Subject: Feminist Practice and the New Renaissance Discourses." *English Literary Renaissance* 18 (Winter 1988): 5–18.

———. " 'Documents in Madness': Reading Madness and Gender in Shakespeare's Tragedies and Early Modern Culture." *Shakespeare Quarterly* 42 (Fall 1991): 315–38.

Newman, Judith. "History as Usual? Feminism and the 'New Historicism.' " *Cultural Critique* 9 (Spring 1988): 87–121.

Newman, Karen. *Fashioning Femininity and English Renaissance Drama*. Chicago: University of Chicago Press, 1991.

Norbrook, David. "*Macbeth* and the Politics of Historiography." In *The Politics of Discourse: The Literature and History of Seventeenth-Century England*, ed. Kevin Sharpe and Steven Zwicker, 78–116. Berkeley: University of California Press, 1987.

Orgel, Steven. "Nobody's Perfect; or, Why Did the English Stage Take Boys for Women?" *South Atlantic Quarterly* 88 (Winter 1989): 7–29.

Papers relative to the Marriage of King James the Sixth of Scotland. Edinburgh: Bannatyne Club, 1828.

Paster, Gail Kern. *The Body Embarrassed: Drama and the Disciplines of Shame in Early Modern England*. Ithaca: Cornell University Press, 1993.

Paul, Herbert N. *The Royal Play of "Macbeth."* Cambridge: Harvard University Press, 1950.

Perkins, William. *The Work of William Perkins*. Ed. Ian Breward. Appleford, England: Sutton Courtney Press, 1970.

Perry, Maria. *The Word of a Prince: A Life of Elizabeth I from Contemporary Documents*. Woodbridge: Boydell Press, 1990.

Plowdon, Alison. *Two Queens in One Isle: The Deadly Relationship of Elizabeth I and Mary Queen of Scots*. Sussex: Harvester Press, 1984.

Pollock, Linda. " 'Teach Her to Live under Obedience': The Making of Women in the Upper Ranks of Early Modern England." *Continuity and Change* 4 (1989): 231–58.

Porter, Carolyn. "Are We Being Historical Yet?" *South Atlantic Quarterly* 87 (Fall 1988): 743–86.

Rackin, Phyllis. "Anti-Historians: Women's Roles in Shakespeare's Histories." *Theatre Journal* 37 (October 1985): 329–44.

——. *Stages of History*. Ithaca: Cornell University Press, 1990.

Riggs, David. *Ben Jonson: A Life*. Cambridge: Harvard University Press, 1989.

Riviere, Joan. "Womanliness as a Masquerade." In *Formations of Fantasy*, ed. Victor Burgin et al., 35–61. London: Methuen, 1986.

Rose, Mary Beth. "Where Are the Mothers in Shakespeare? Options for Gender Representation in the English Renaissance." *Shakespeare Quarterly* 42 (Fall 1991): 291–314.

Rosenberg, Marvin. *The Masks of Macbeth*. Berkeley: University of California Press, 1978.

Saccio, Peter. *Shakespeare's English Kings: History, Chronicle, and Drama*. London: Oxford University Press, 1977.

Sandler, Joseph. "On Internal Object Relations." *Journal of the American Psychoanalytic Association* 39 (1991): 859–79.

Schiesari, Juliana. *The Gendering of Melancholia: Feminism, Psychoanalysis, and the Symbolics of Loss in Renaissance Literature*. Ithaca: Cornell University Press, 1992.

Schoenbaum, Samuel. *William Shakespeare: A Compact Documentary Life*. Oxford: Oxford University Press, 1977.

Scott, Ann. "Melanie Klein and the Questions of Feminism." *Woman: A Cultural Review* 1 (November 1990): 127–34.

Segal, Hanna. *Introduction to the Work of Melanie Klein*. London: Hogarth Press, 1973.

Shakespeare, William. *Henry VI, Parts One, Two, and Three*. Ed. David Bevington. Toronto: Bantam, 1988.

——. *Macbeth*. Ed. Nicholas Brooke. Oxford: Oxford University Press, 1990.

——. *Macbeth*. Ed. Kenneth Muir. Arden Edition; London: Methuen, 1977.

——. *Othello*. Ed. David Bevington. Toronto: Bantam, 1988.

——. *Richard III*. Ed. David Bevington. Toronto: Bantam, 1988.

——. *The Winter's Tale*. Ed. J. H. P. Pafford. Arden Edition; London: Methuen, 1973.

Sharpe, J. A. "Debate: The History of Violence in England: Some Observations." *Past and Present* 108 (August 1985): 206–15.

——. *Defamation and Sexual Slander in Early Modern England: The Church Courts at York*. Borthwick Papers No. 58. York: University of York, 1980.

Sinfield, Alan. "*Macbeth*: History, Ideology, and Intellectuals." In *Faultlines: Cultural Materialism and the Politics of Dissident Reading*, 95–108. Berkeley: University of California Press, 1992.

Sprengnether, Madelon [Gohlke]. "'I Wooed Thee with My Sword': Shakespeare's Tragic Paradigms." In *Representing Shakespeare: New Psychoanalytic Essays*, ed. Murray M. Schwartz and Coppelia Kahn, 170–87. Baltimore: Johns Hopkins University Press, 1980.

——. "Reading Lady Macbeth." In *Women's Revisions of Shakespeare*, ed. Marianne Novy, 227–41. Urbana: University of Illinois Press, 1990.

Stafford, Helen. *James VI of Scotland and the Throne of England*. New York: Appleton-Century, 1940.

Stallybrass, Peter. "Transvestism and the 'Body Beneath': Speculating on the Boy Actor." In *Erotic Politics: Desire on the Renaissance Stage*, ed. Susan Zimmerman, 64–83. New York: Routledge, 1992.

Stone, Lawrence. *Crisis of the Aristocracy, 1558–1641*. Abridged. London: Oxford University Press, 1965.

——. *The Family, Sex, and Marriage in England, 1500–1800*. Abridged. New York: Harper and Row, 1979.

——. "Interpersonal Violence in English Society, 1300–1980." *Past and Present* 101 (November 1983): 22–33.

——. "A Rejoinder." *Past and Present* 108 (August 1985): 215–24.

Suleiman, Susan Rubin. "On Maternal Splitting: A Propos of Mary Gordon's *Men and Angels*." *Signs* 14 (Autumn 1988): 25–42.

Tennenhouse, Leonard. *Power on Display: The Politics of Shakespeare's Genres*. New York: Methuen, 1986.

Thomas, Brook. *The New Historicism and Other Old-Fashioned Topics*. Princeton: Princeton University Press, 1991.

Towler, Jean, and Joan Bramell. *Midwives in History and Society*. London: Croom Helm, 1986.

Traub, Valerie. *Desire and Anxiety: Circulations of Sexuality in Shakespearean Drama*. London: Routledge, 1992.

——. "Prince Hal's Flagstaff: Positioning Psychoanalysis and the Female Reproductive Body." *Shakespeare Quarterly* 40 (1989): 456–74.

Travitsky, Betty S. "The New Mother of the English Renaissance: Her Writings on Motherhood." In *The Lost Tradition: Mothers and Daughters in Literature*, ed. Cathy N. Davidson and E. M. Broner, 33–43. New York: Frederick Ungar, 1980.

Tyson, Phyllis, and Robert L. Tyson. *Psychoanalytic Theories of Development: An Integration*. New Haven: Yale University Press, 1990.

Underdown, D. E. "The Taming of the Scold: the Enforcement of Patriarchal Authority in Early Modern England." In *Order and Disorder in Early Modern England*, ed. A. J. Fletcher and J. Stevenson, 116–36. Cambridge: Cambridge University Press, 1985.

Veeser, H. Aram, ed. *The New Historicism*. New York: Routledge, 1989.

Wayne, Valerie, ed. *The Matter of Difference: Materialist Feminist Criticism of Shakespeare*. Ithaca: Cornell University Press, 1991.

Webster, John. *The Devil's Law-Case.* In *Three Plays*, ed. D.C. Gunby. London: Penguin, 1986.

Weil, Lise. Review of Susan Griffin, *A Chorus of Stones: The Private Life of War. Women's Review of Books* 10 (December 1992): 12.

Wiesner, Merry E. *Women and Gender in Early Modern Europe.* Cambridge: Cambridge University Press, 1993.

Williamson, Arthur H. "The Failure of Antichrist and the Emergence of Satan." In *Scottish National Consciousness in the Age of James VI: The Apocalypse, the Union, and the Shaping of Scotland's Public Culture*, ed. Williamson, 48–63. Edinburgh: John Donald, 1979.

Williamson, Marilyn L. " 'When Men Are Rul'd by Women': Shakespeare's First Tetralogy." *Shakespeare Studies* (1986): 41–59.

Willson, David Harris. *King James VI and I.* New York: Oxford University Press, 1956.

Woodbridge, Linda. *Women and the English Renaissance: Literature and the Nature of Womankind, 1540–1620.* Urbana: University of Illinois Press, 1986.

Wormald, Jenny. *Court, Kirk, and Community.* Toronto: Toronto University Press, 1981.

———. "James VI and I: Two Kings or One?" *History* 68 (1983): 187–209.

Wrightson, Keith. *English Society, 1580–1680.* New Brunswick, N.J.: Rutgers University Press, 1982.

———. "Two Concepts of Order: Justices, Constables, and Jurymen in Seventeenth-Century England." In *An Ungovernable People: The English and Their Law in the Seventeenth and Eighteenth Centuries*, ed. John Brewer and John Styles. London: Hutchinson, 1980.

Youings, Joyce. *Sixteenth-Century England.* Harmondsworth: Penguin, 1984.

INDEX